yǒu zhì zhě   shì jìng chéng

		有	志	者	,	事	竟	成	！			

Nothing is impossible to a willing heart !

This Chinese workbook belongs to:

的

中文练习本

qiān   lǐ   zhī   xíng   shǐ   yú   zú   xià

千	里	之	行	，	始	于	足	下	。

A journey of a thousand miles begins with a single step.

有志者，事竟成！

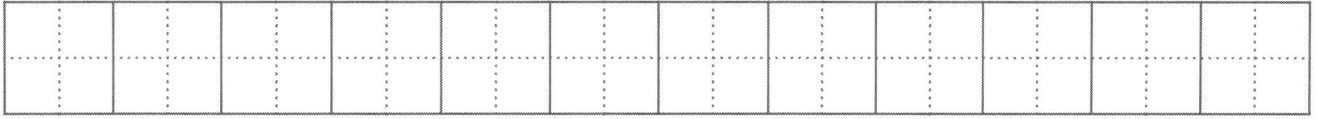

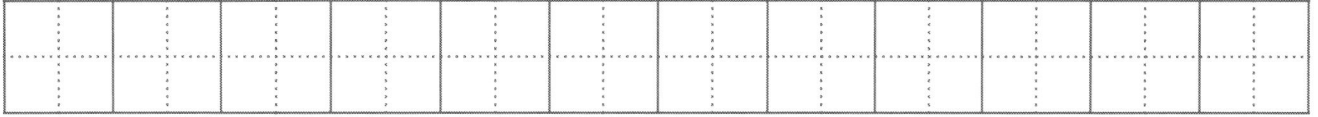

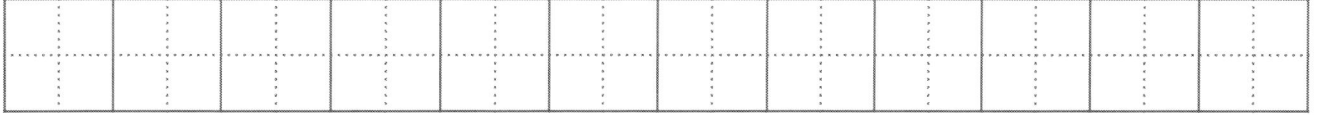

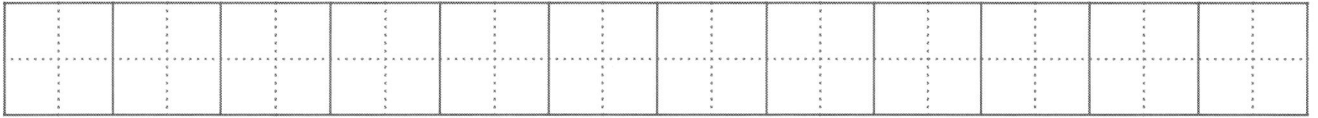

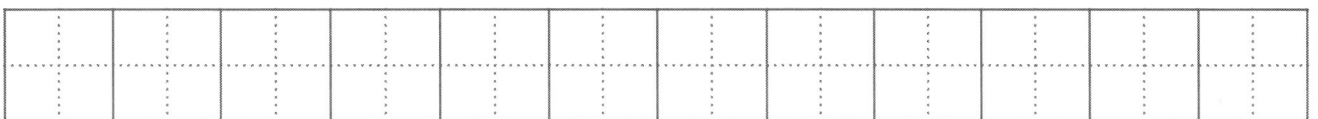

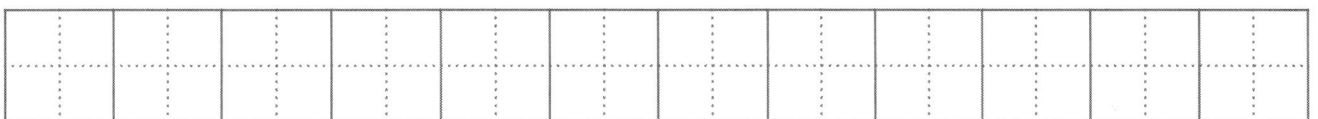

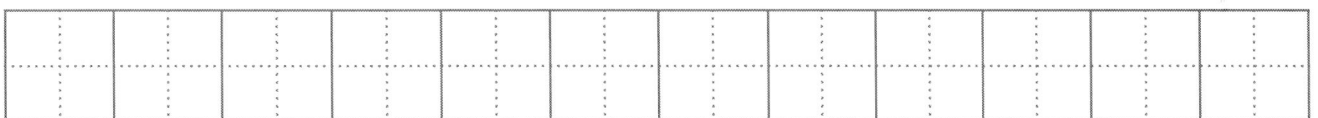

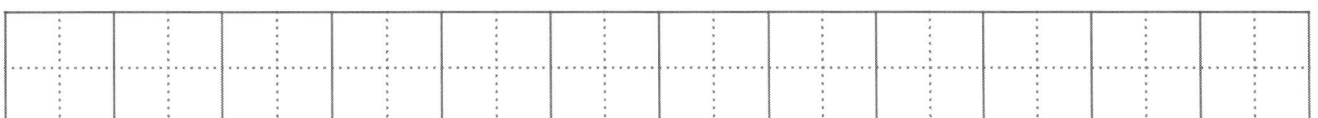

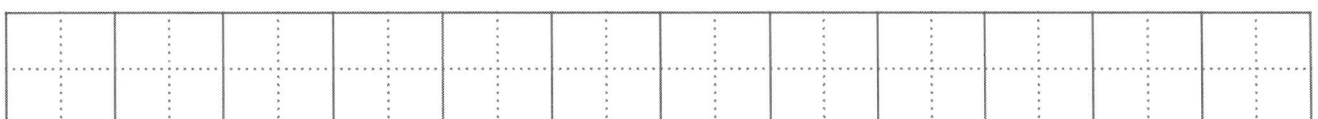

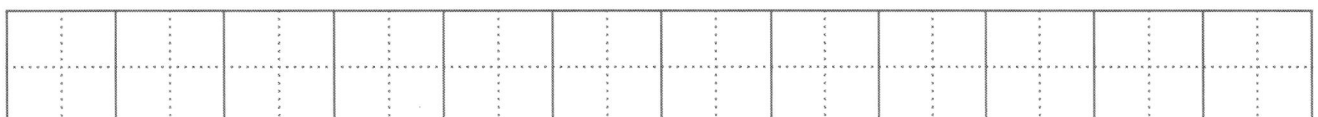

有志者，事竟成！

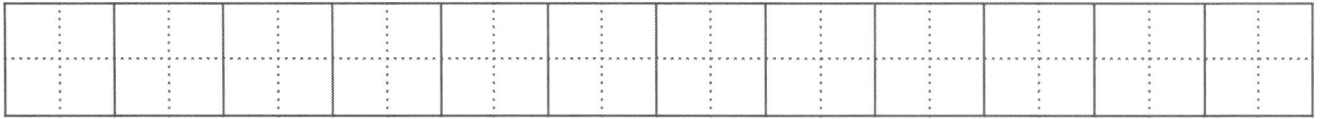

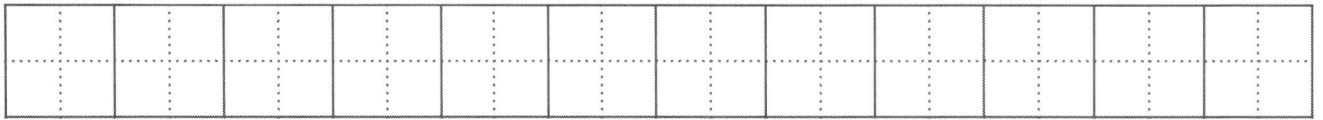

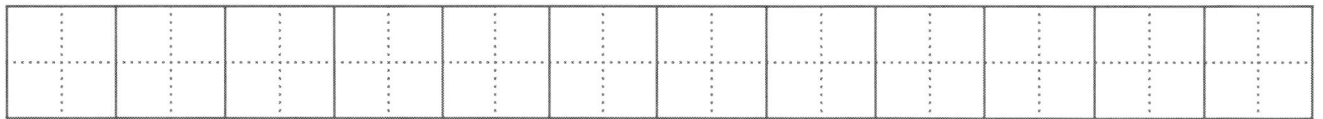

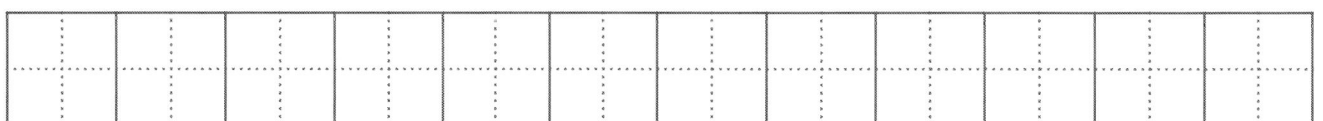

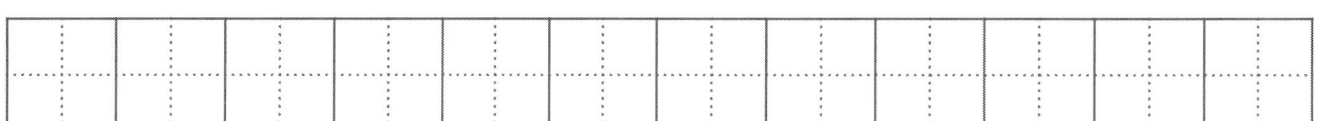

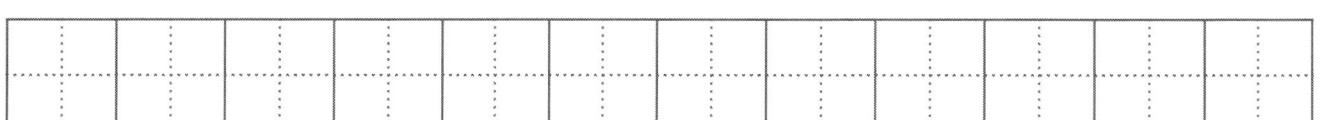

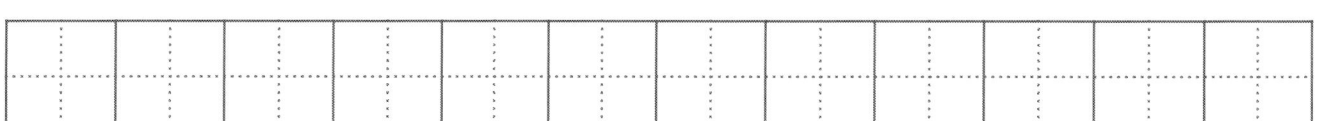

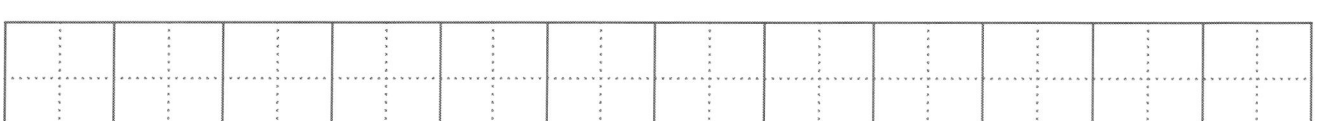

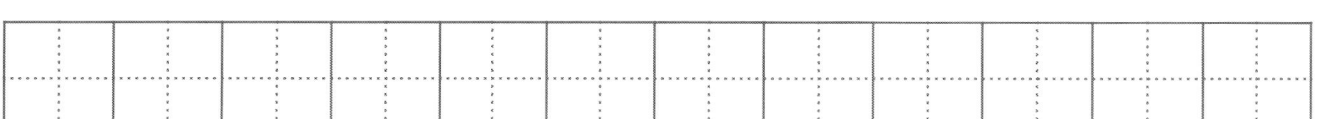

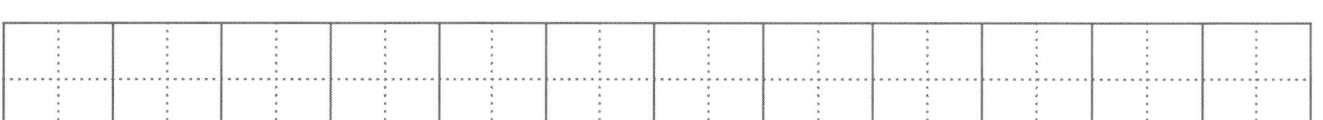

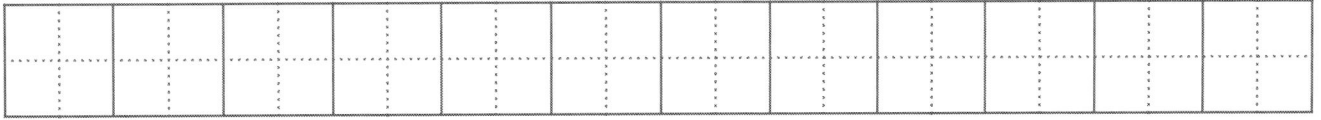

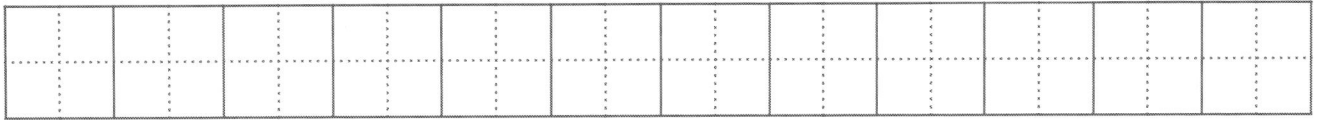

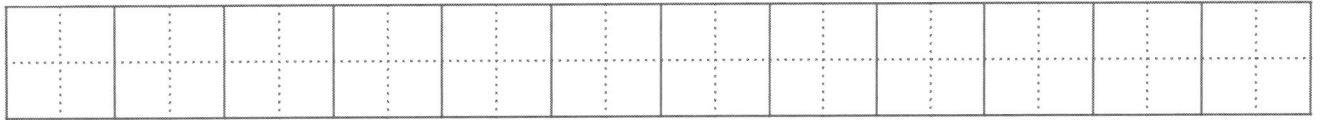

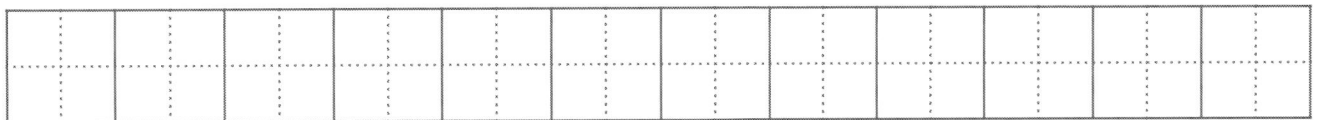

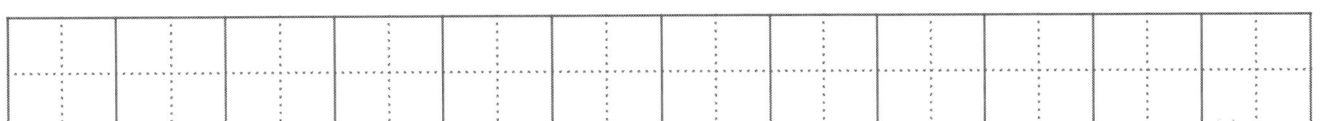

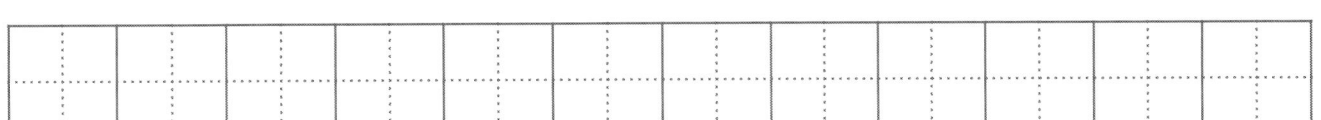

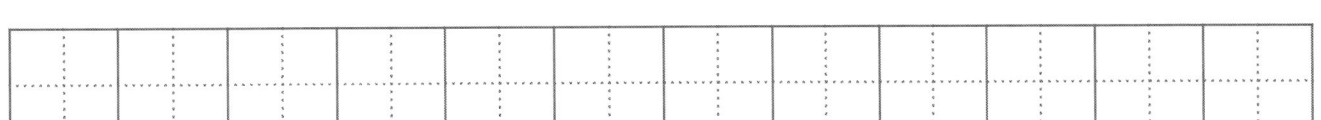

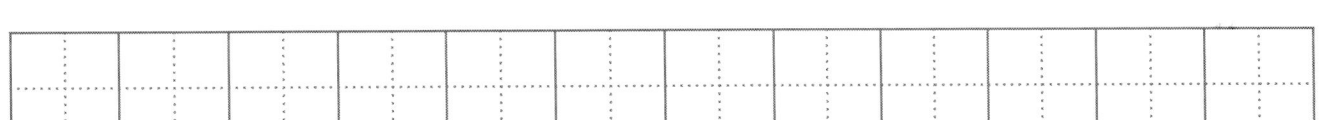

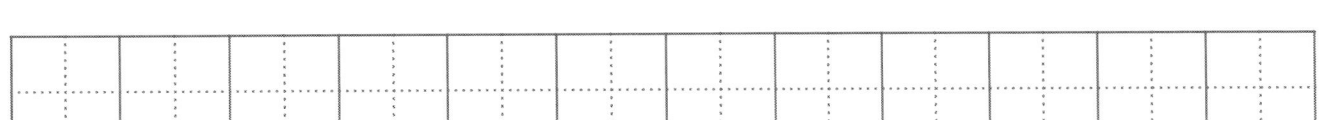

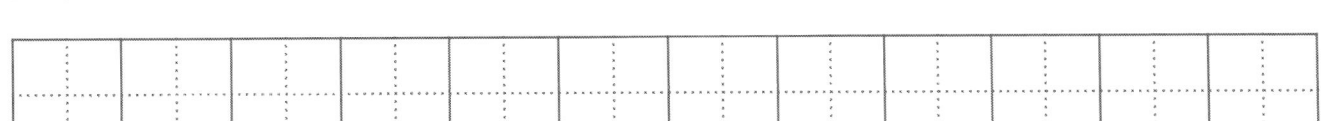

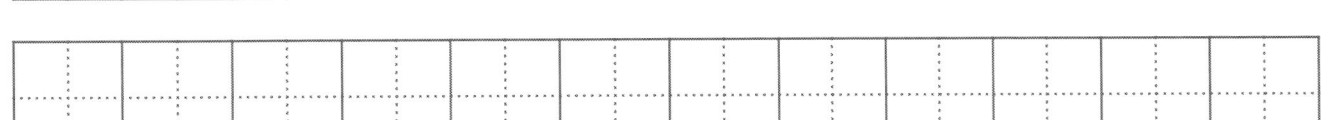

始 于 足 下

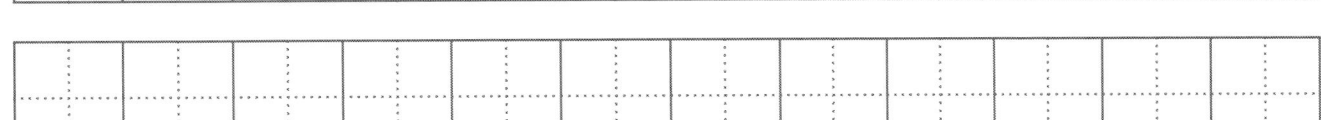

zì qiáng bù xī

自 强 不 息

One shall constantly striving for becoming better and stronger.

自 强 不 息

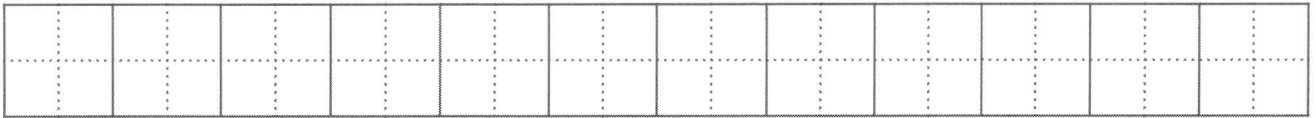

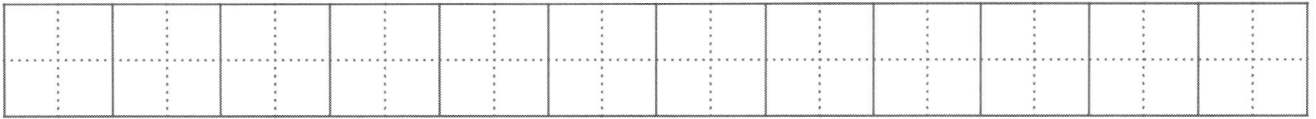

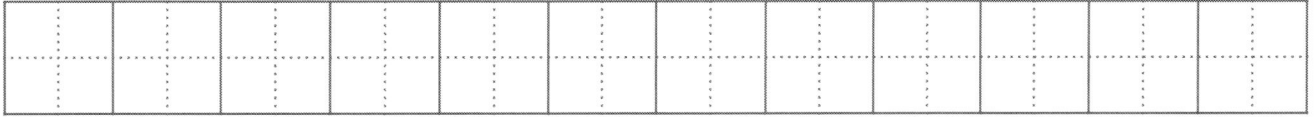

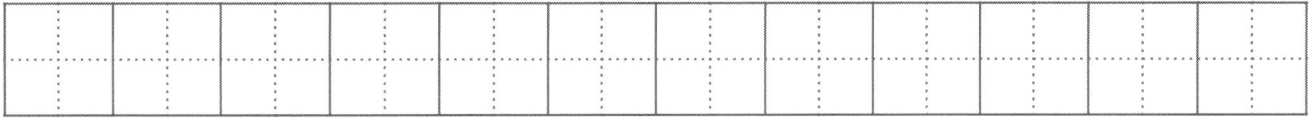

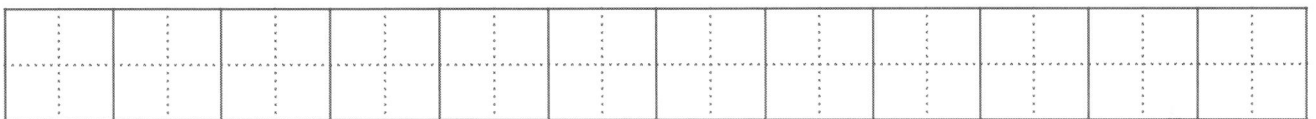

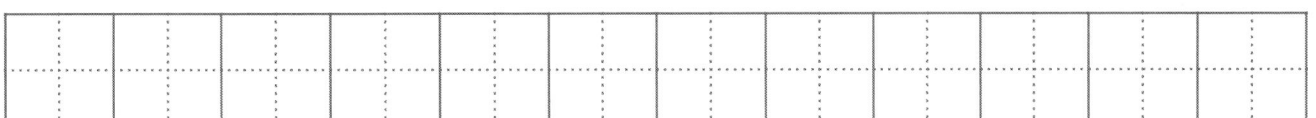

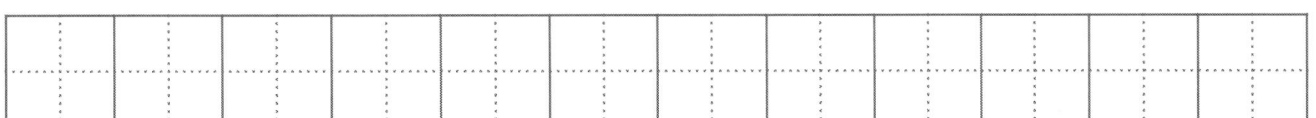

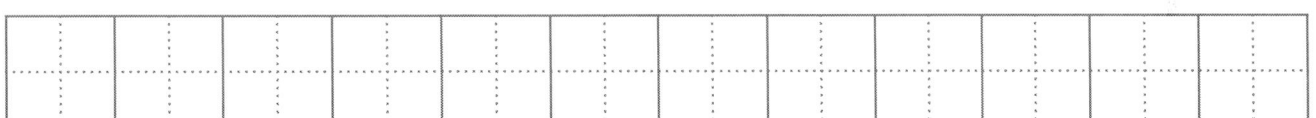

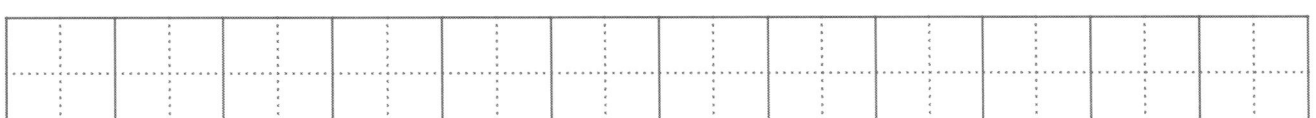

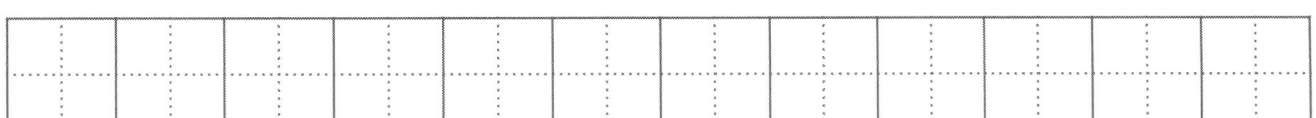

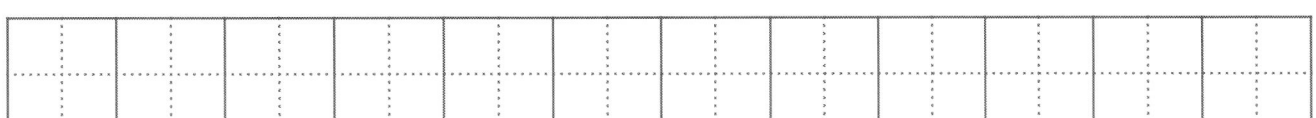

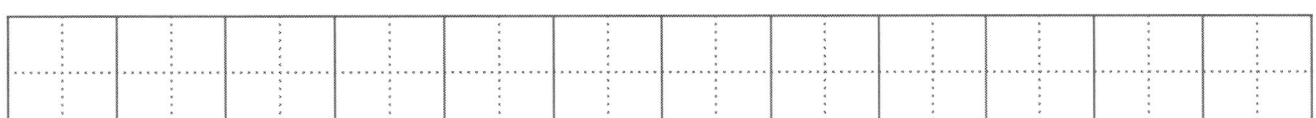

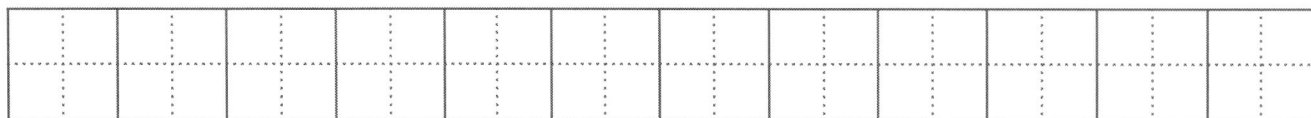
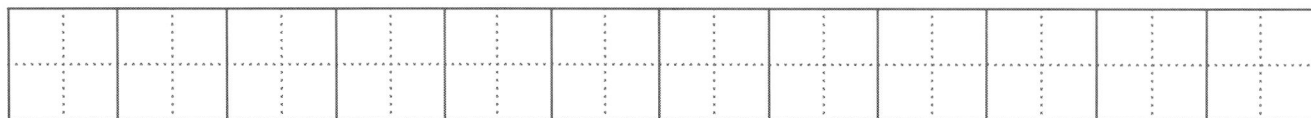
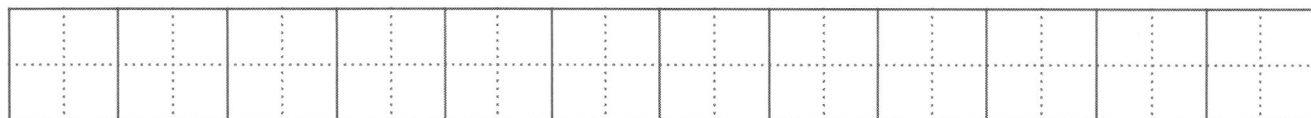
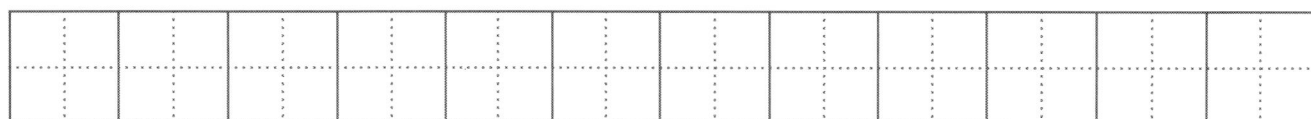
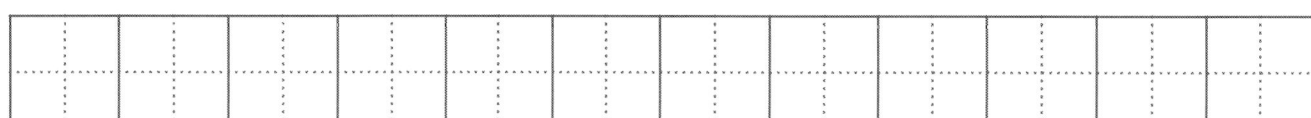
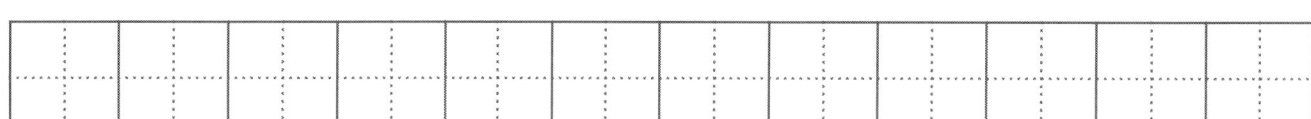
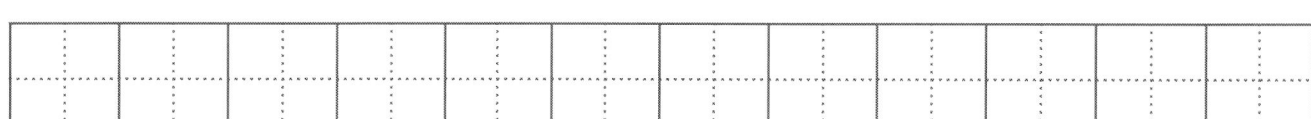
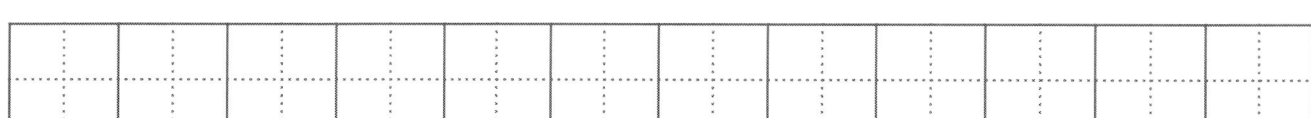
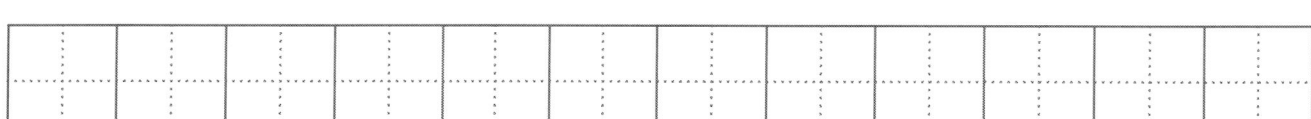
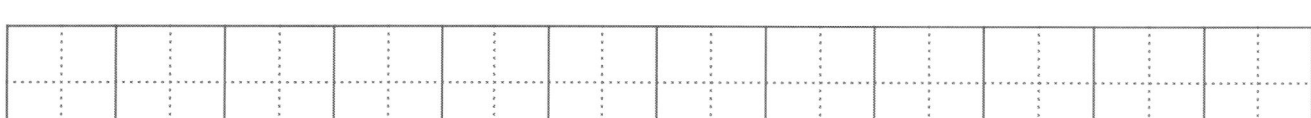
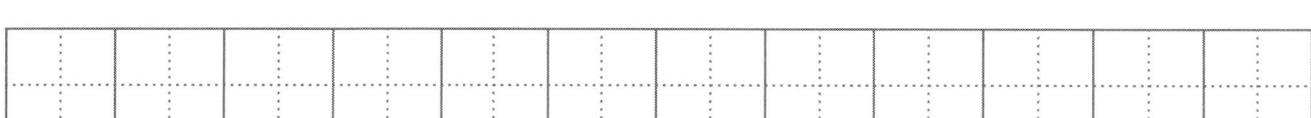
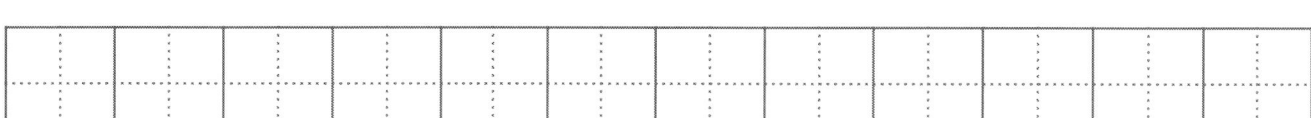

自　强　不　息

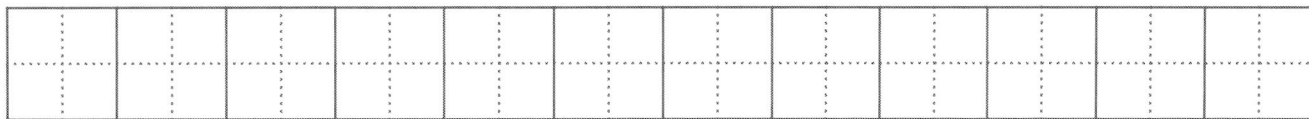

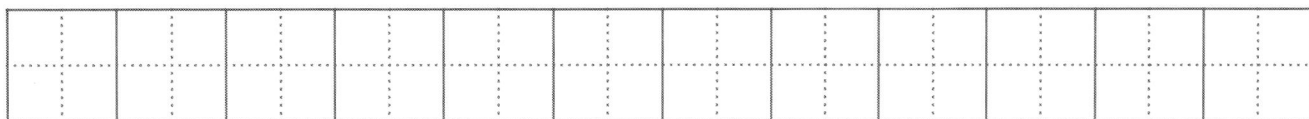

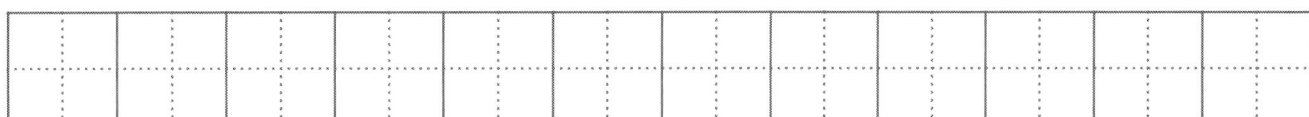

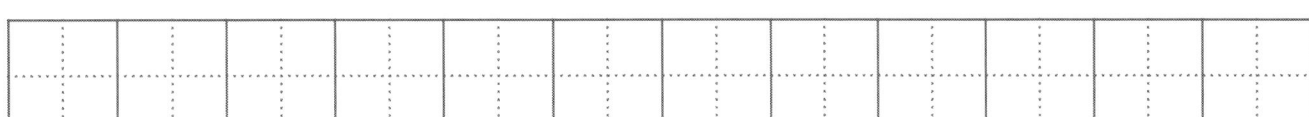

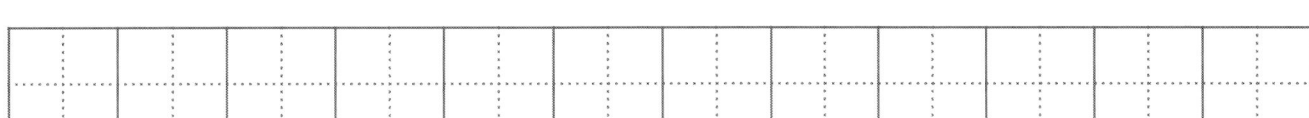

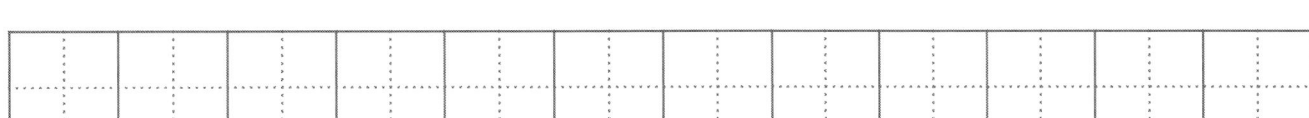

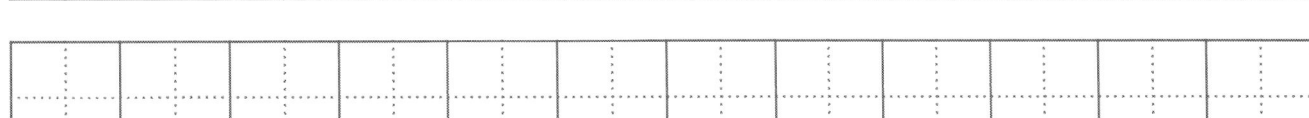

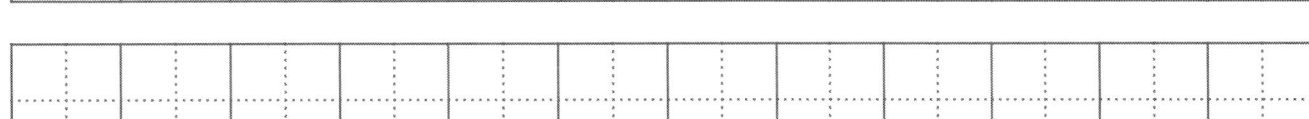

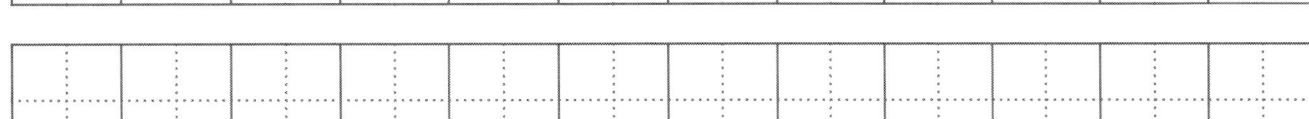

shì zài rén wéi

事 在 人 为

It all depends on one's own effort.

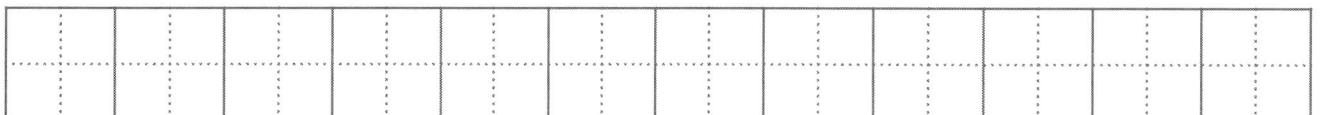

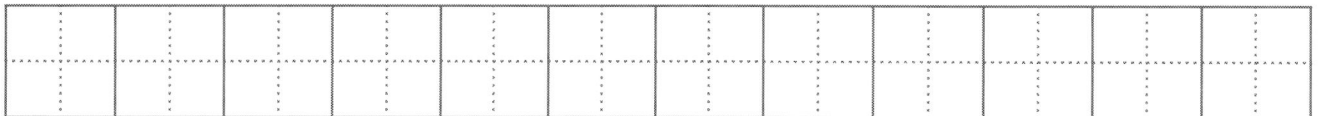

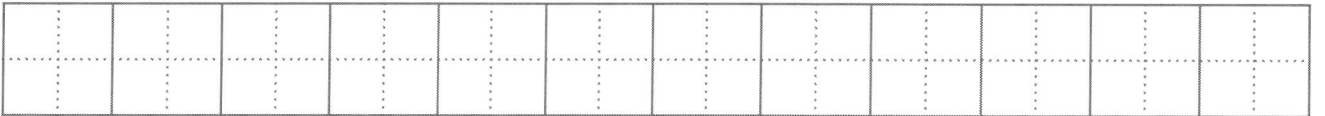

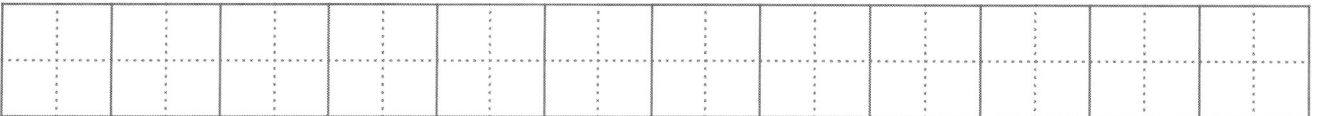

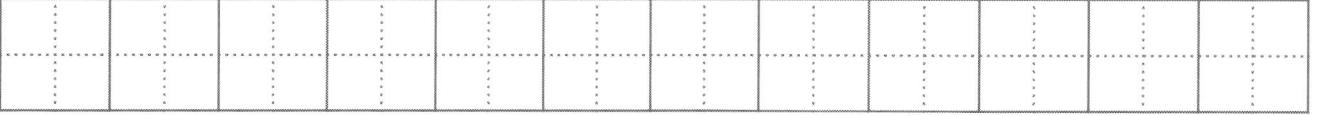

事在人为

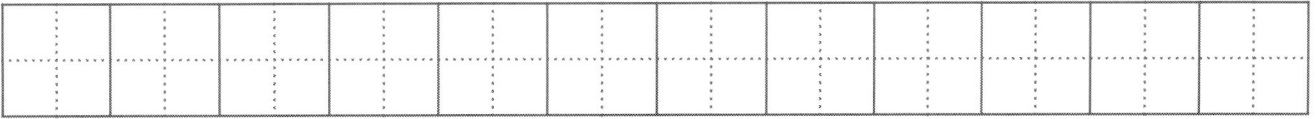
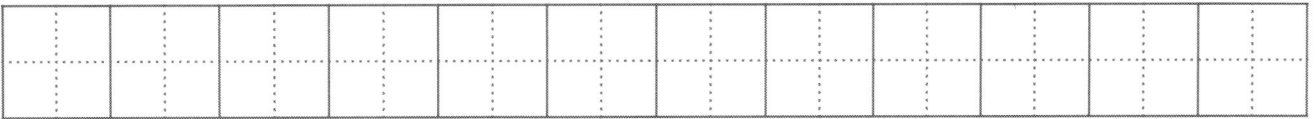

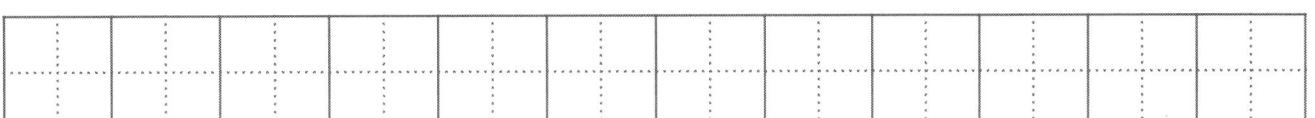
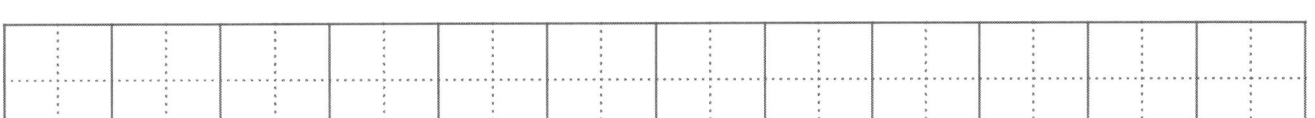
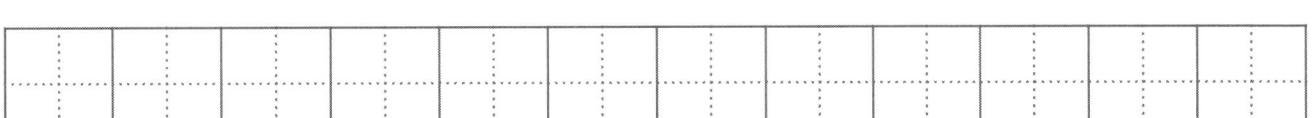
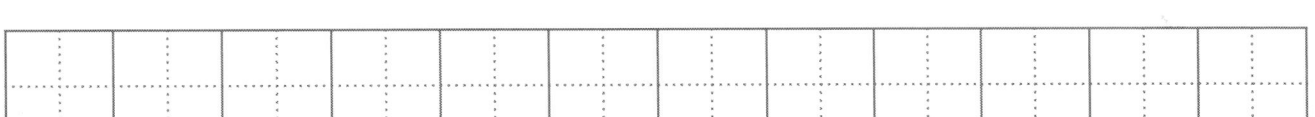
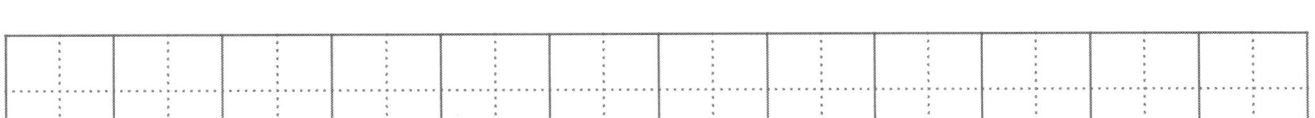
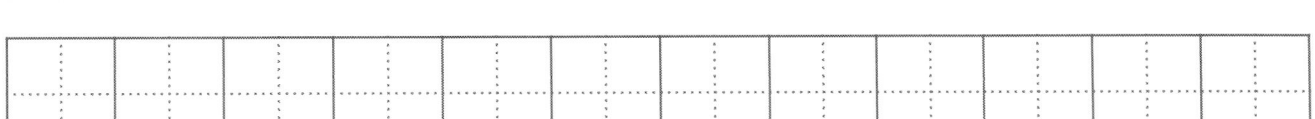
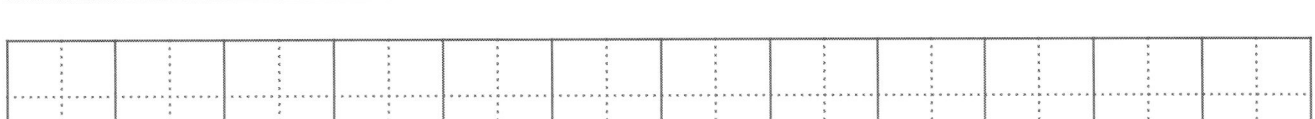

事 在 人 为
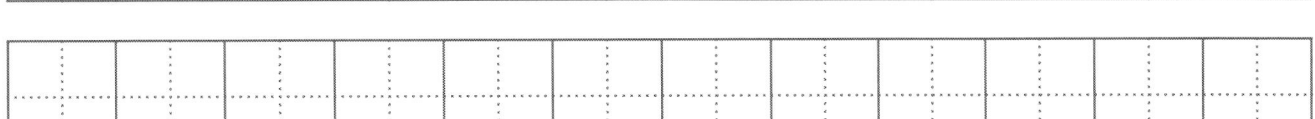

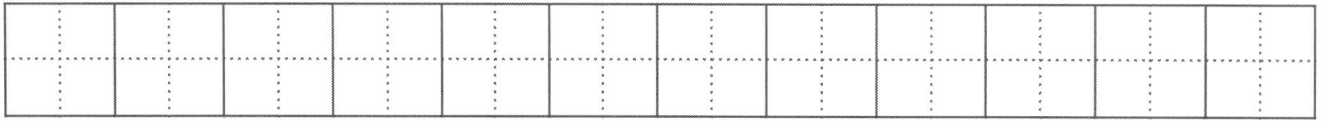
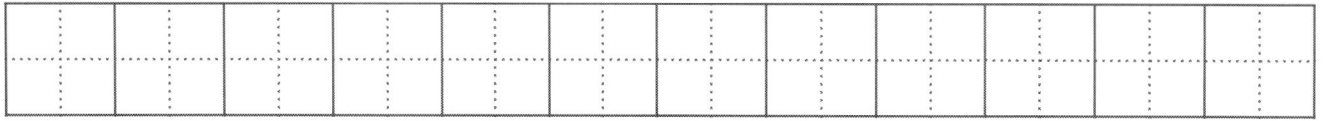
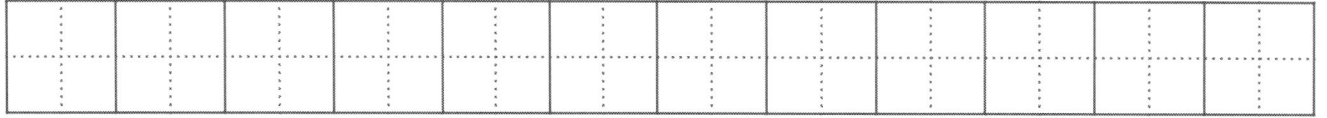
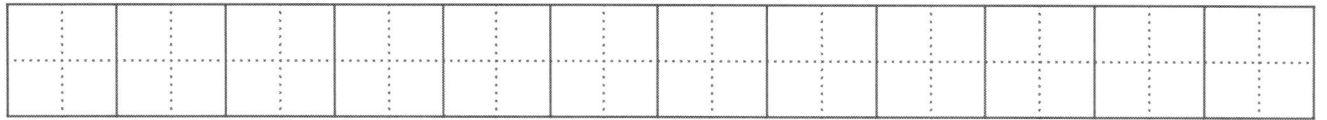
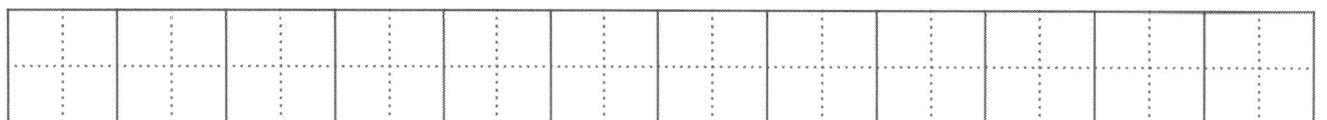
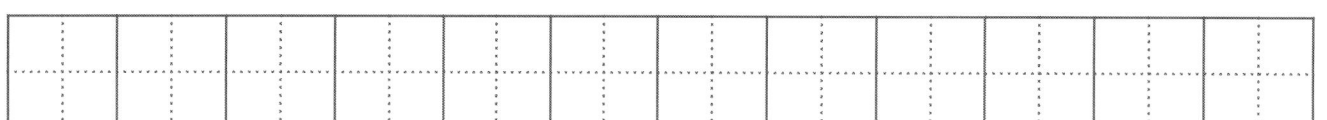
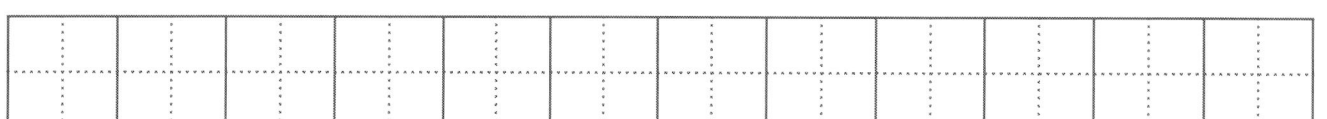
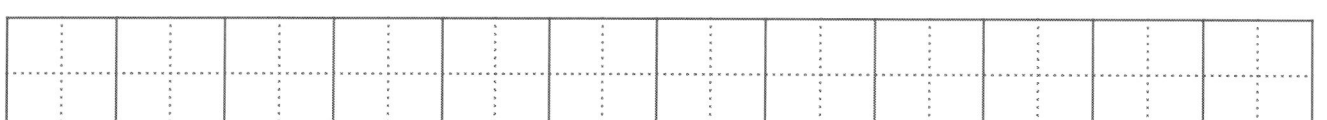
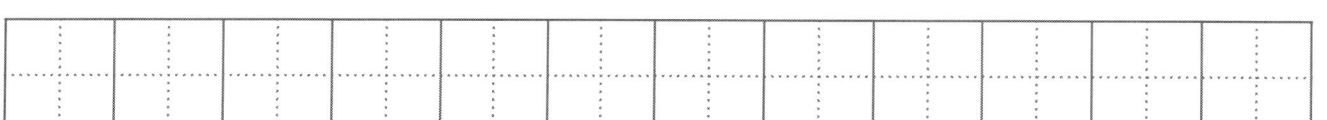
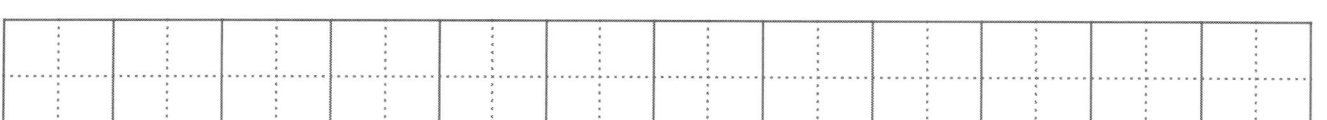
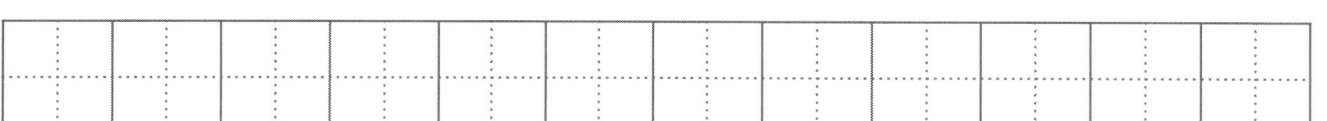
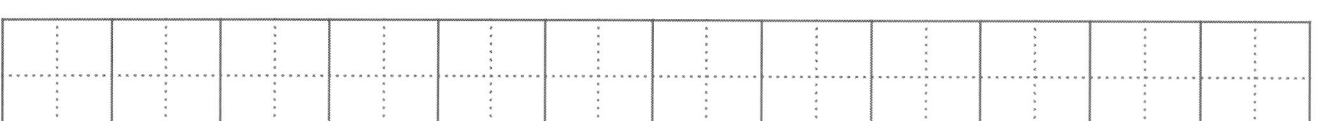

事 在 人 为

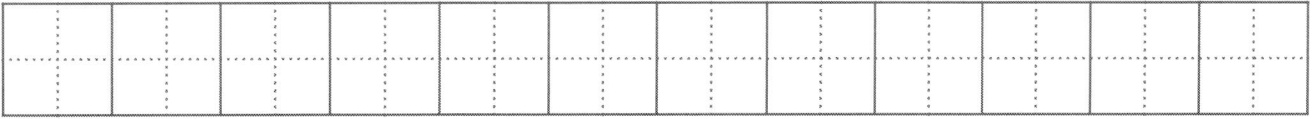

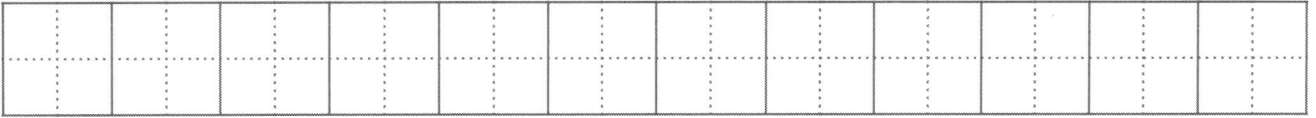

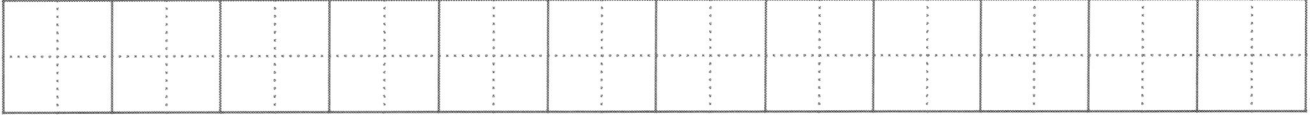

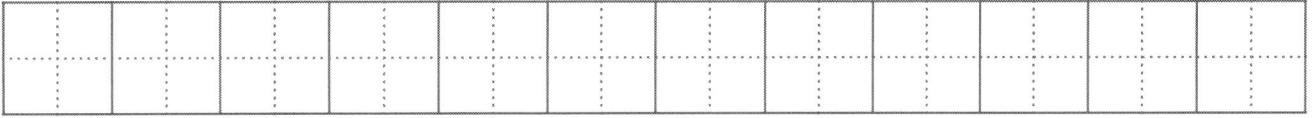

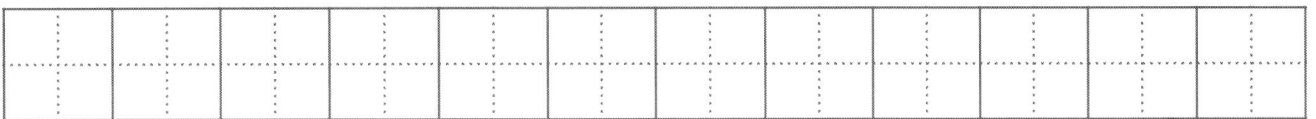

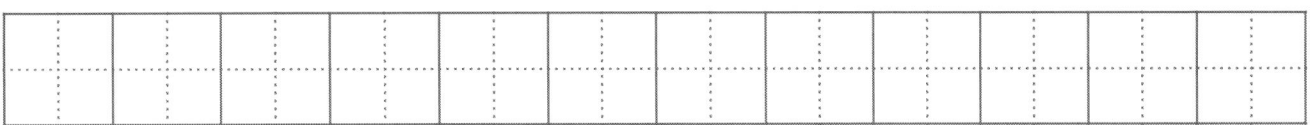

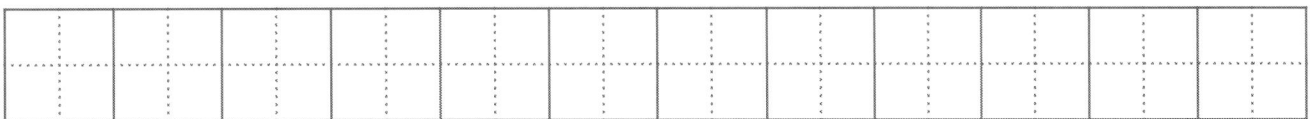

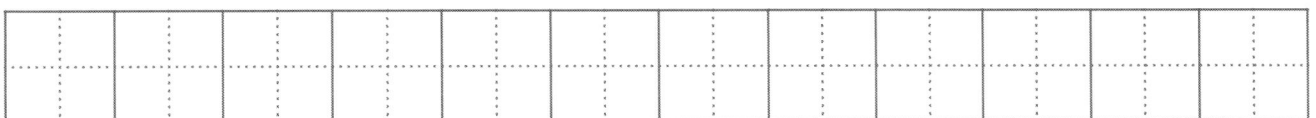

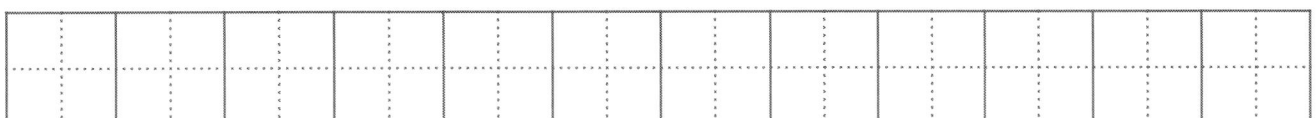

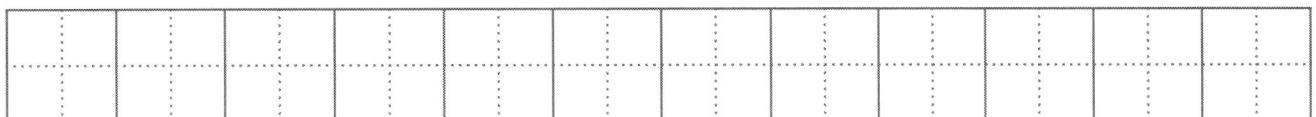

事 在 人 为

dú wàn juǎn shū　　xíng wàn lǐ lù

读 万 卷 书 ， 行 万 里 路 。

In order to attain wisdom,
it is not enough merely to read books,
One must be well-travelled as well.

有志者，事竟成！

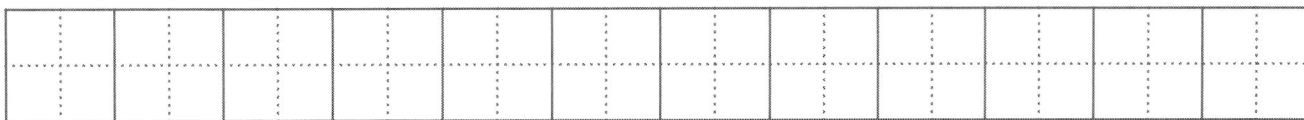

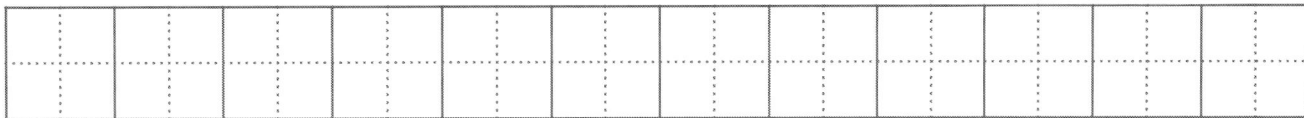

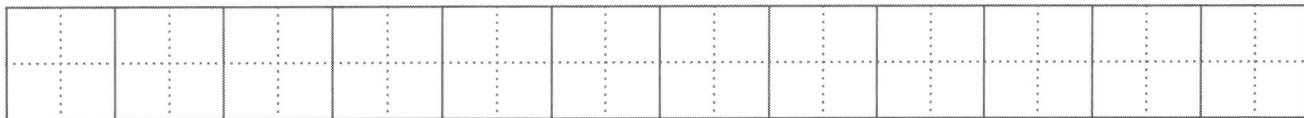

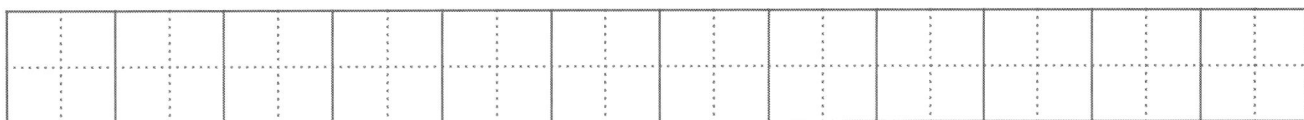

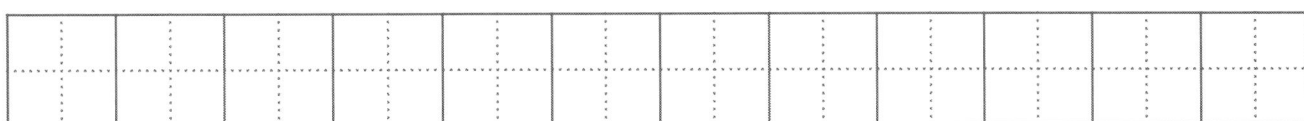

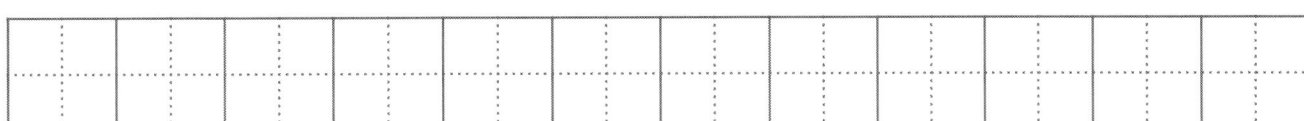

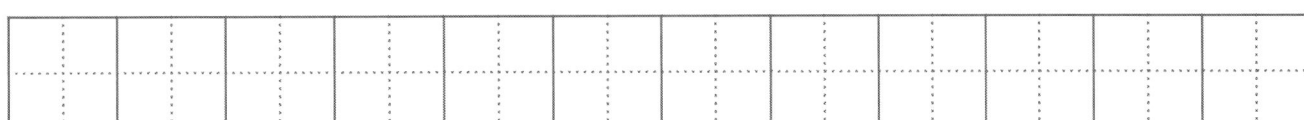

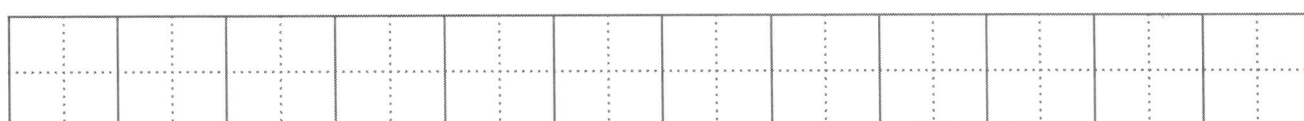

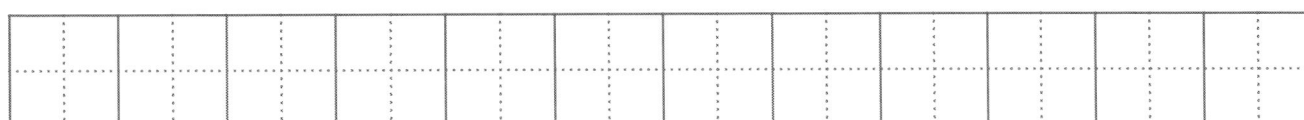

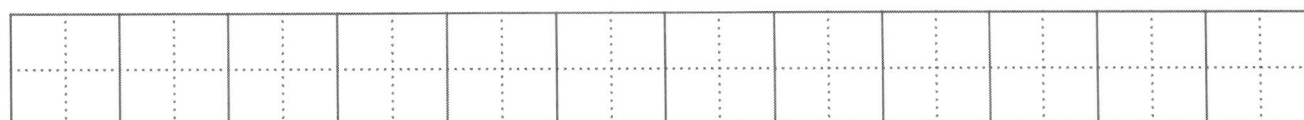

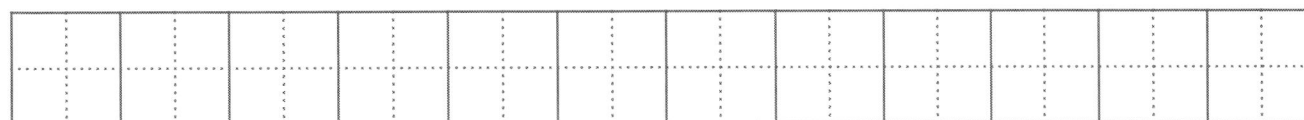

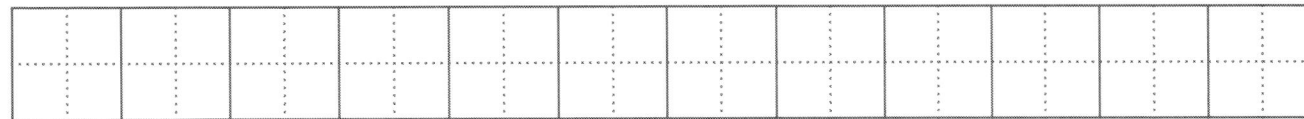

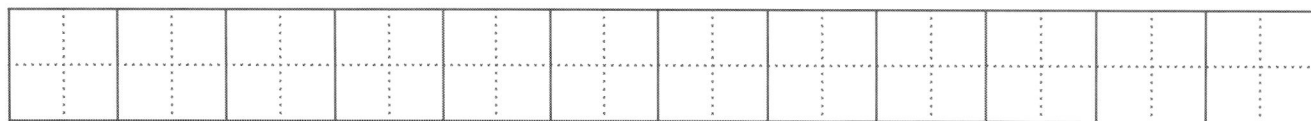
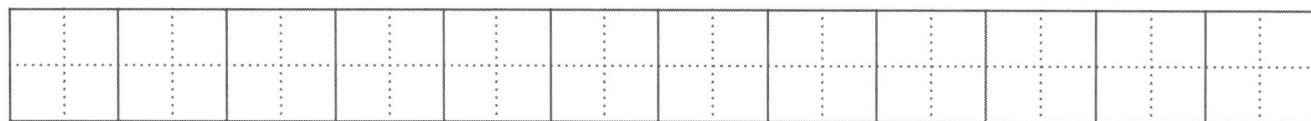
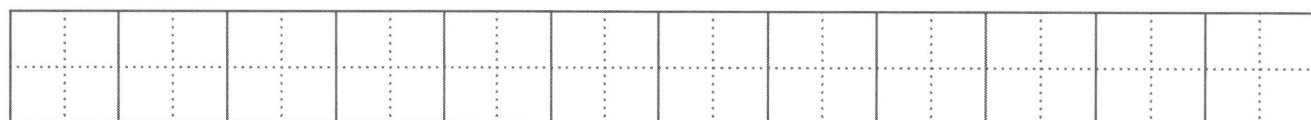
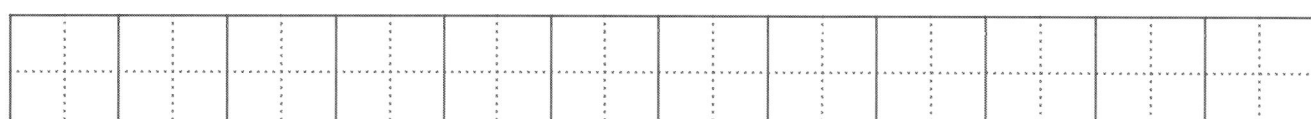
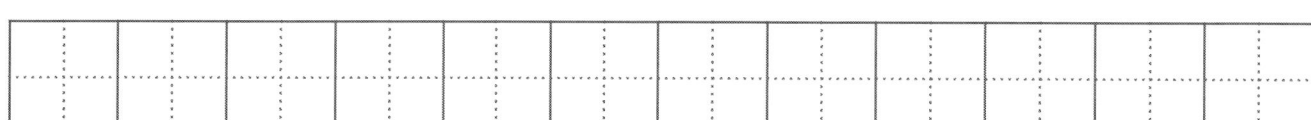
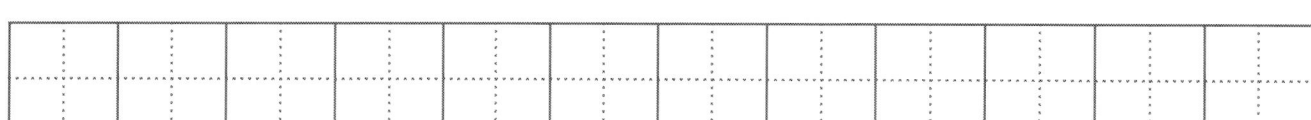
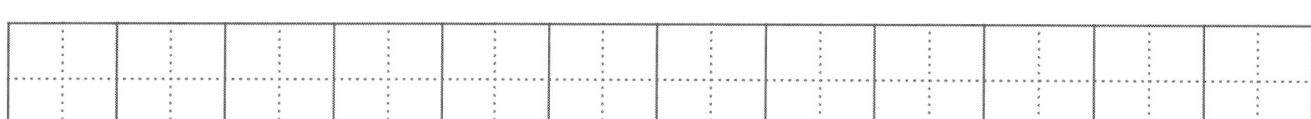
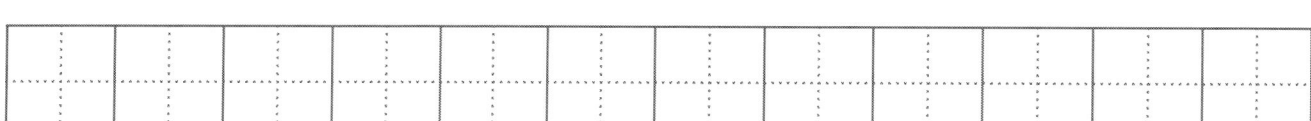
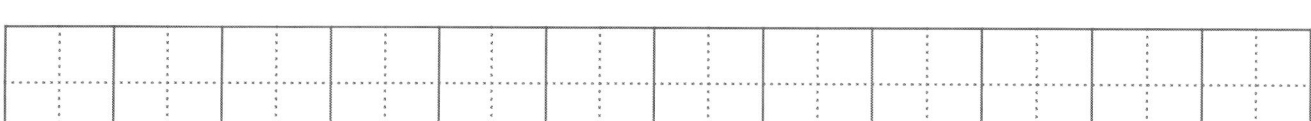
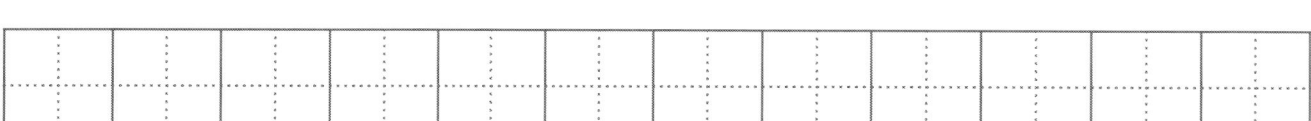
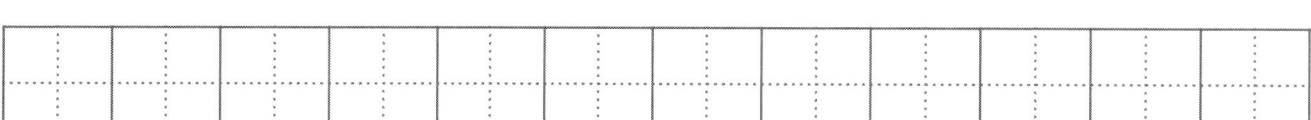

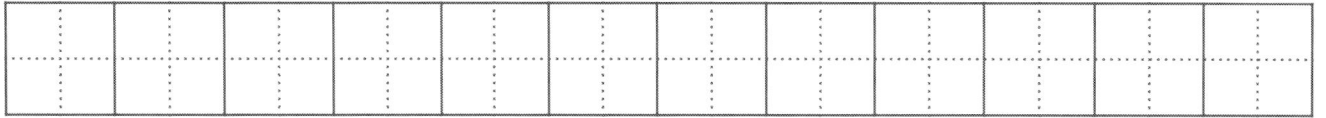
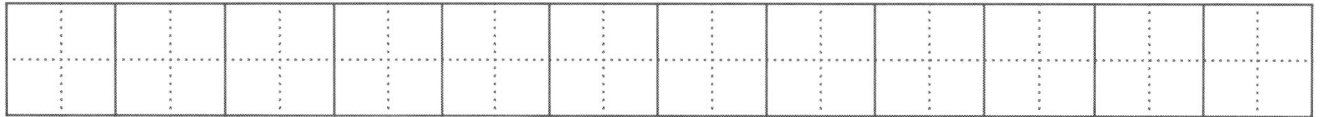
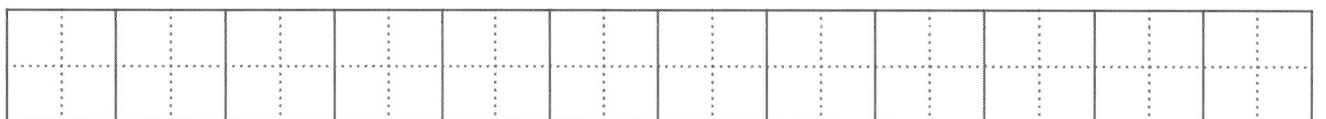
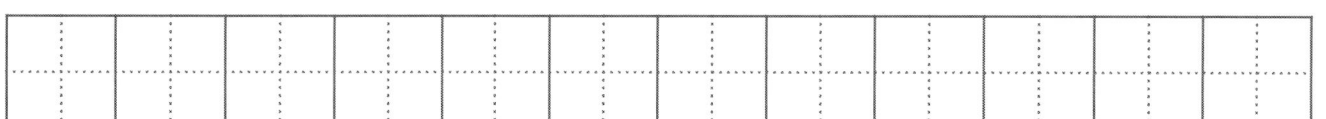
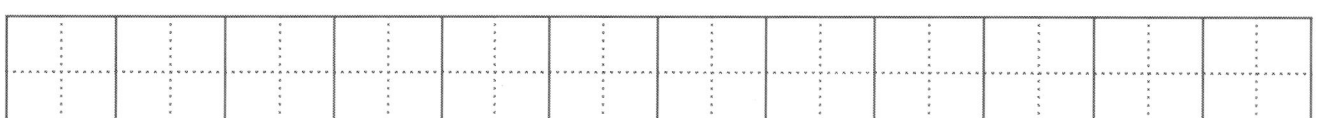
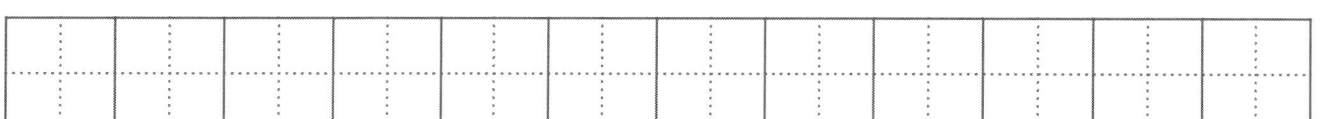
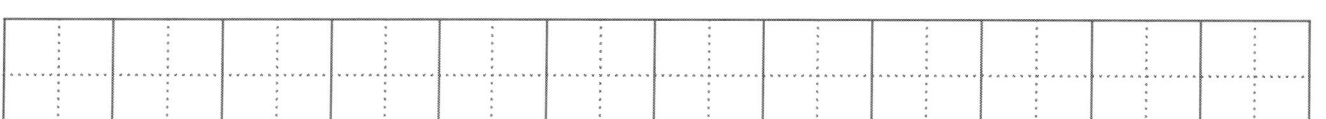
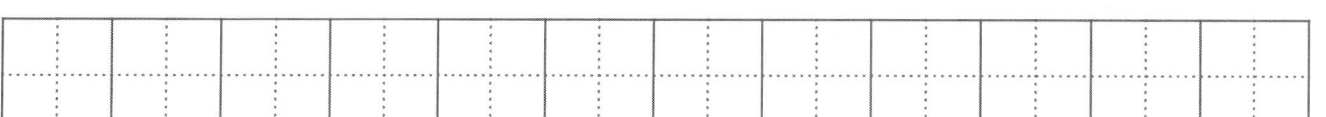
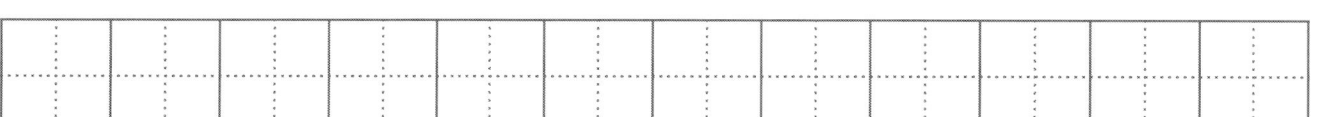
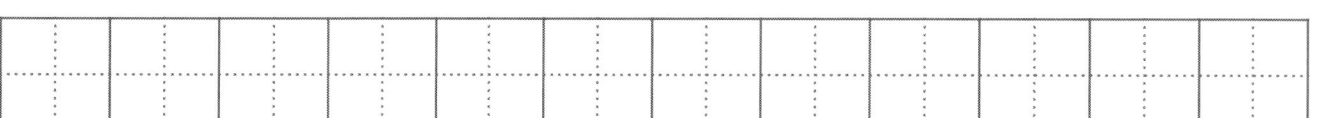

读 万 卷 书

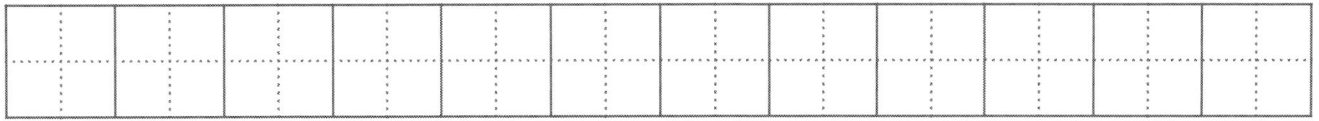
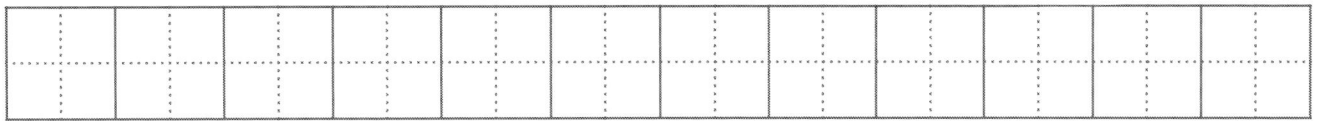
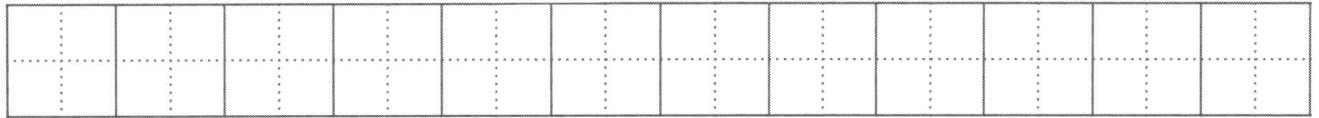

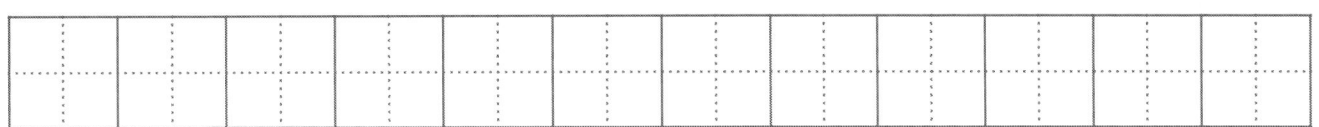
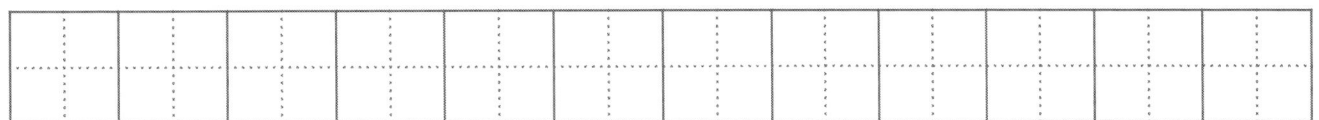
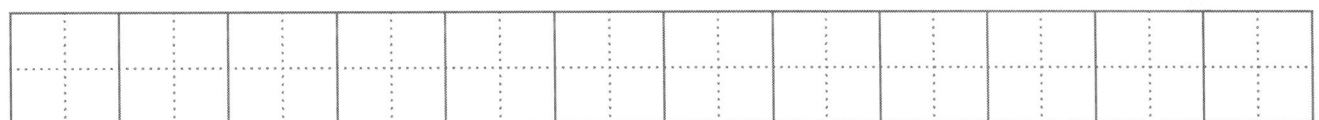
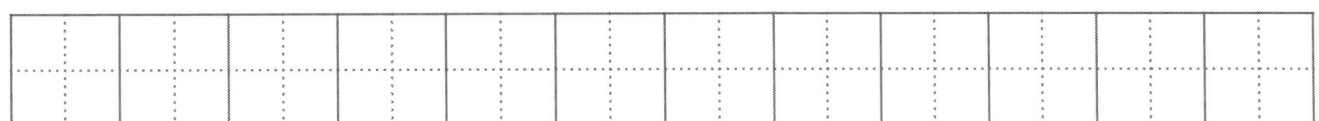
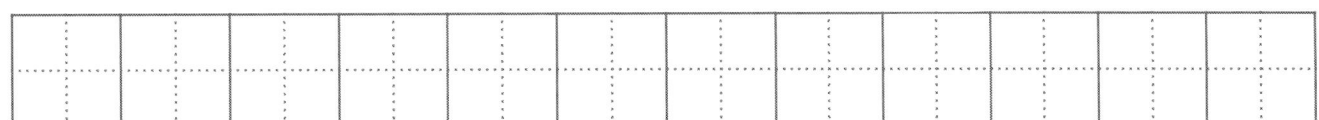
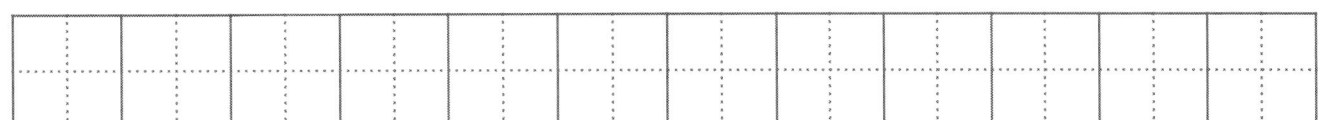
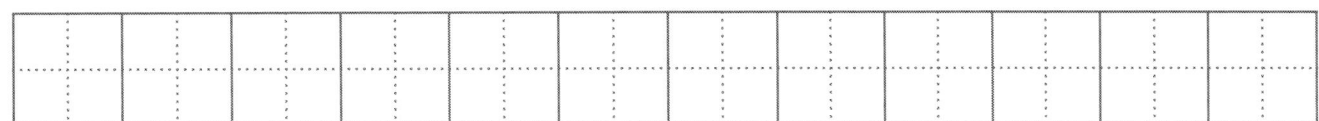

水 滴 石 穿

Dripping water penetrates the stone.
- Persistent effort overcomes any difficulty.

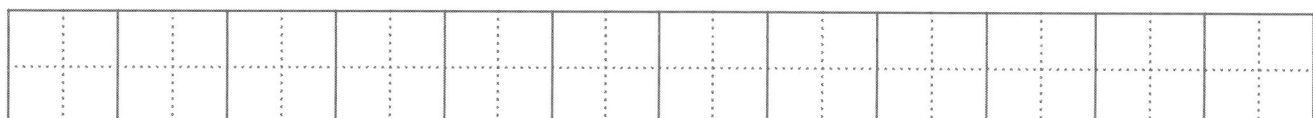

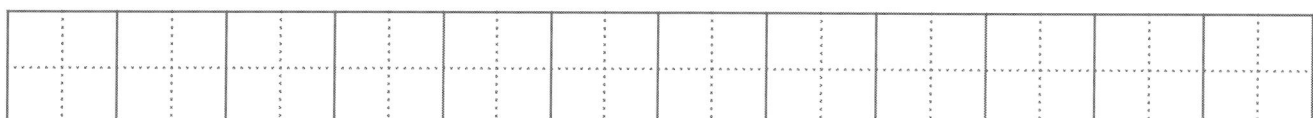

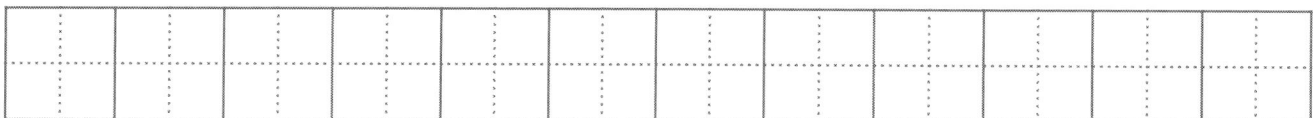

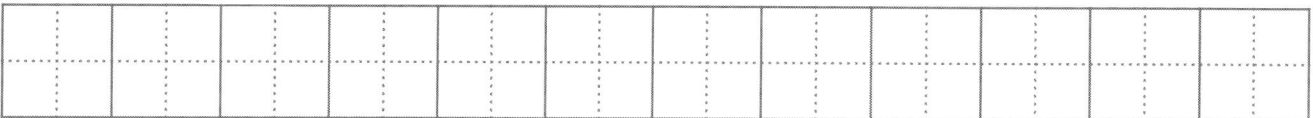

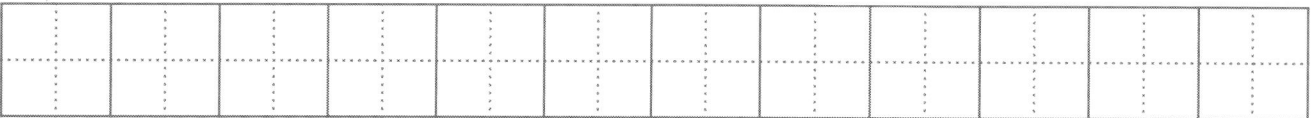

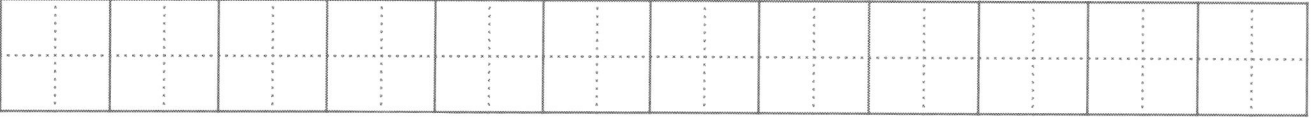

水 滴 石 穿

水 滴 石 穿

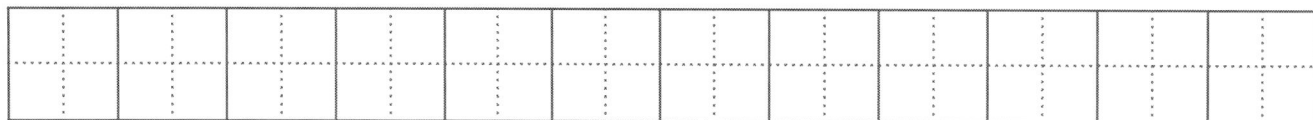

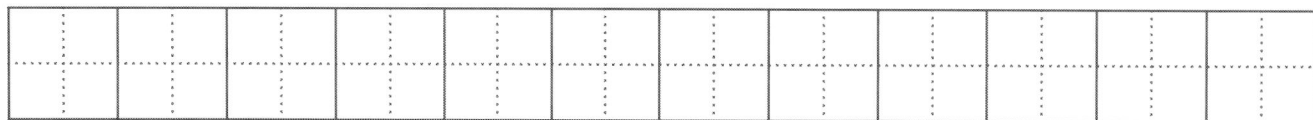

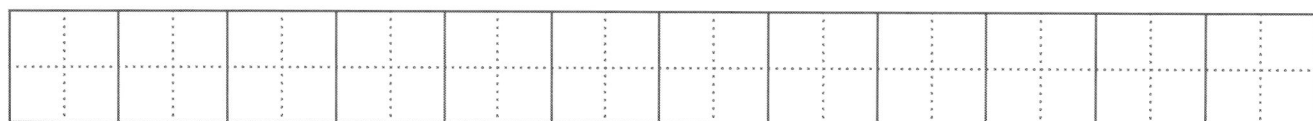

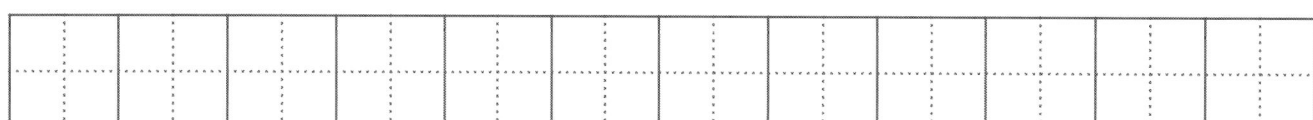

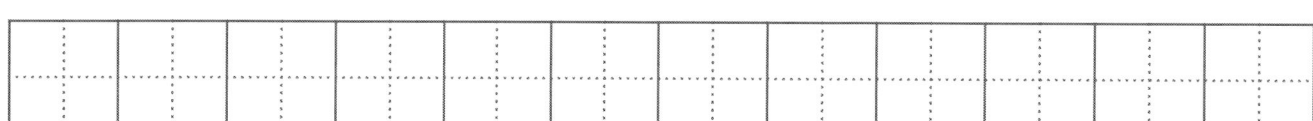

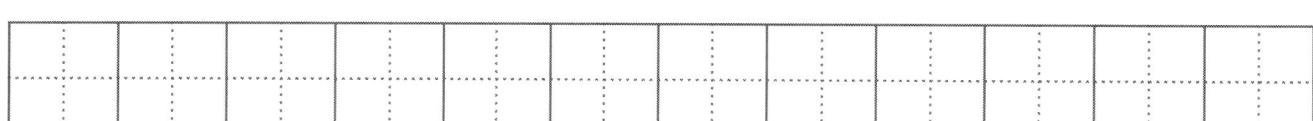

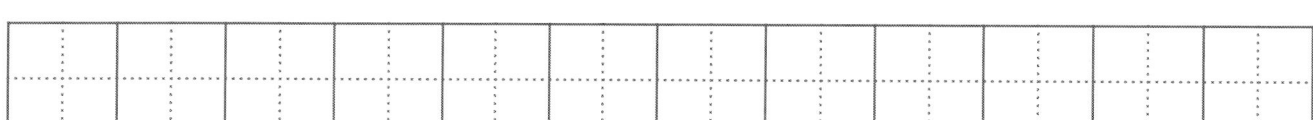

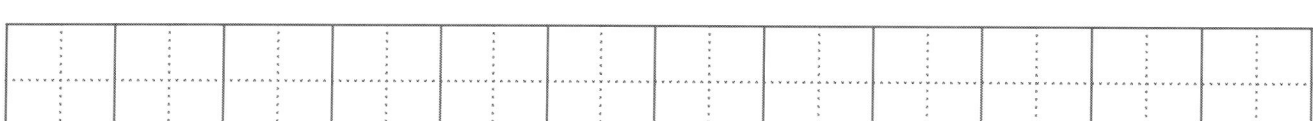

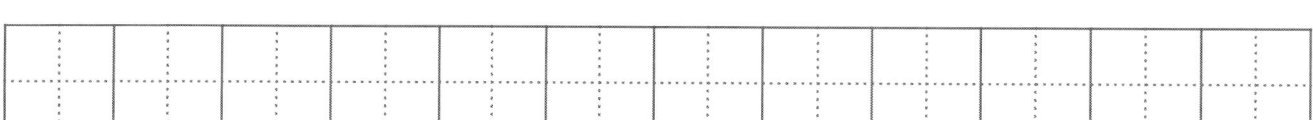

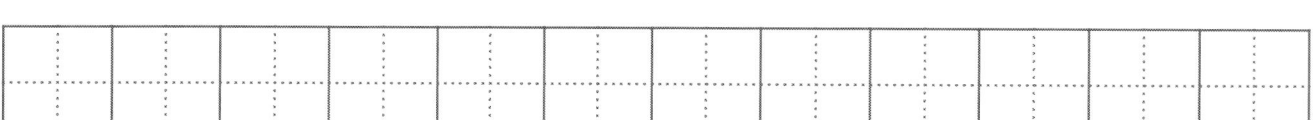

水 滴 石 穿

水滴石穿

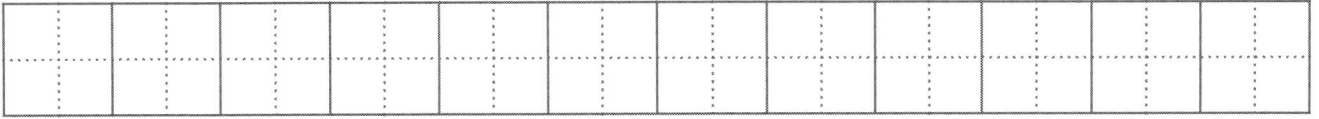

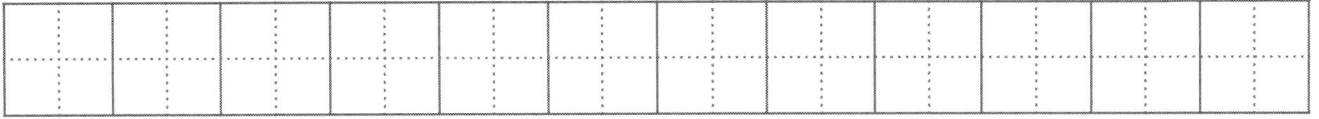

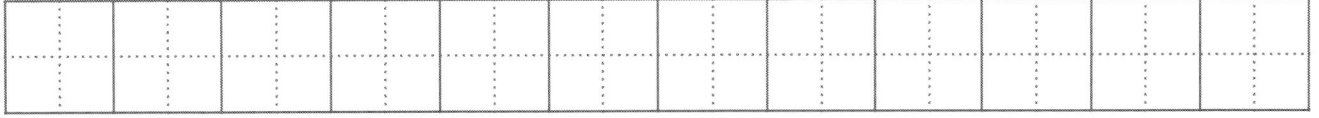

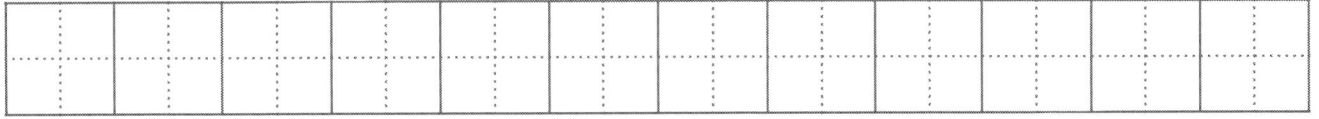

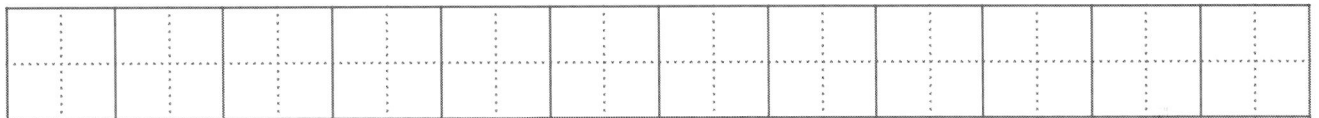

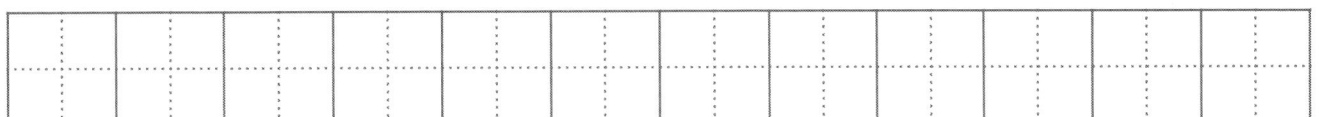

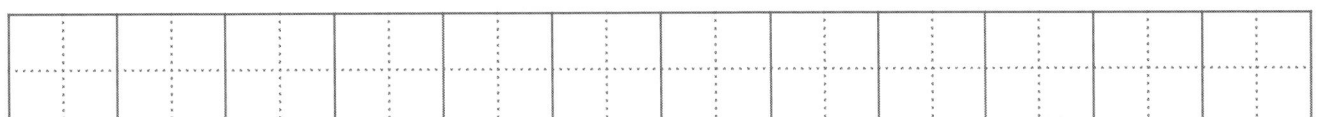

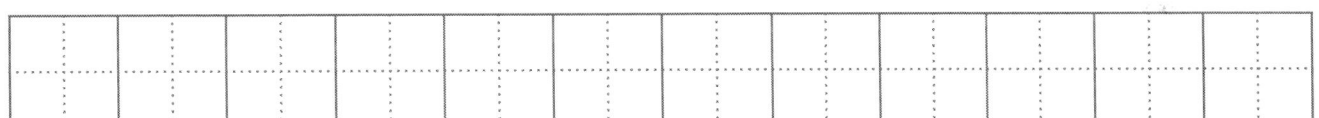

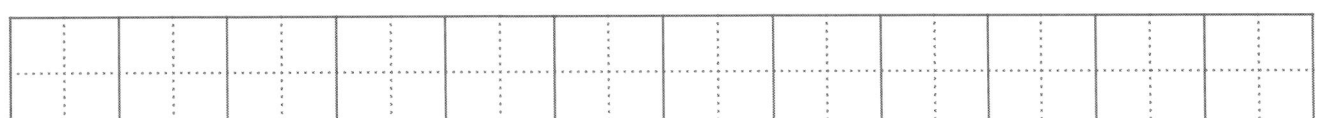

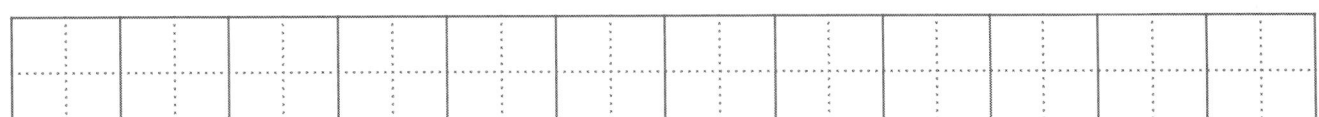

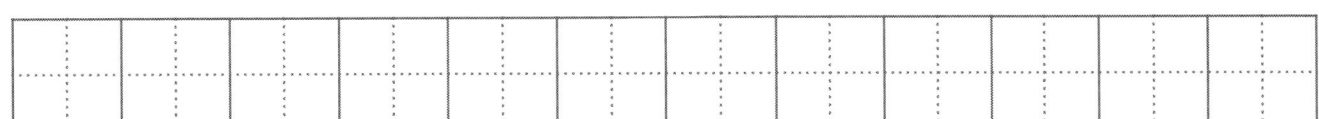

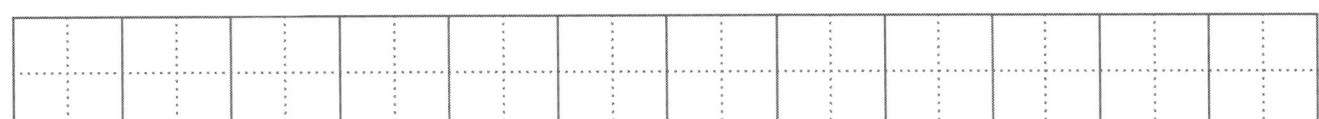

	zhī	jǐ	zhī	bǐ		bǎi	zhàn	bù	dài		
	知	己	知	彼	，	百	战	不	殆	。	

If you know both yourself and your enemy,
you can win a hundred battles without a single loss.

千里之行，始于足下。

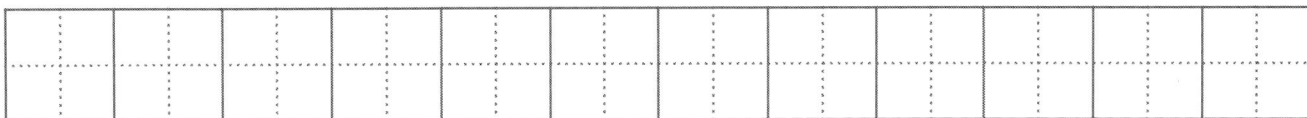

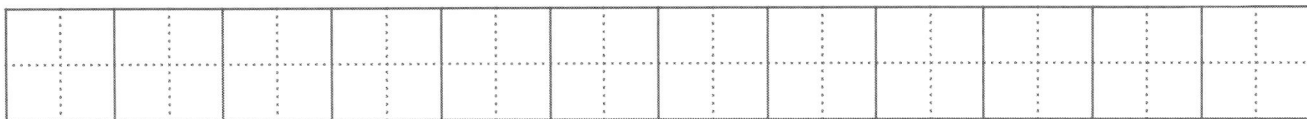

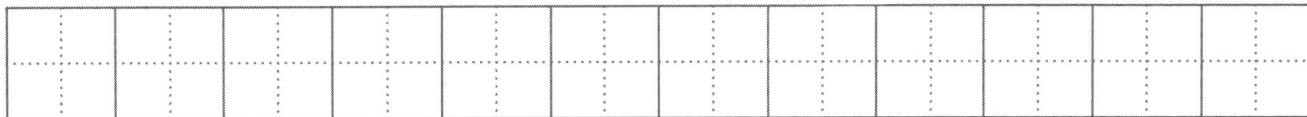

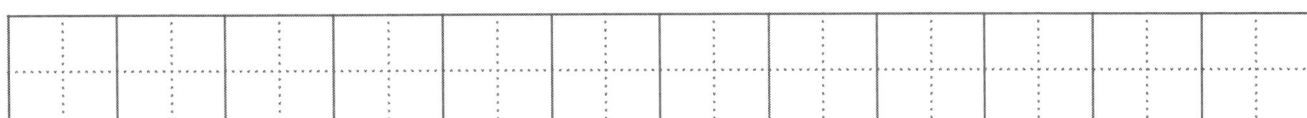

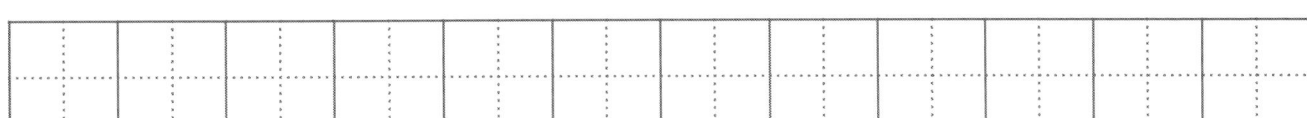

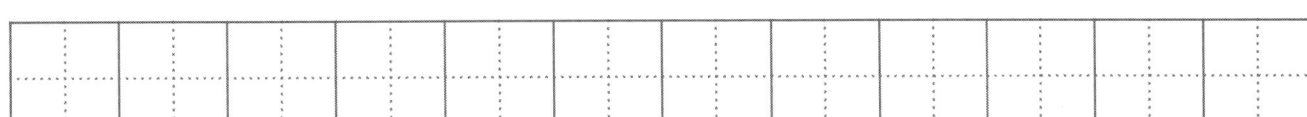

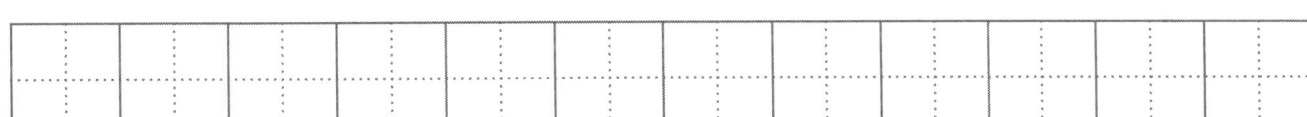

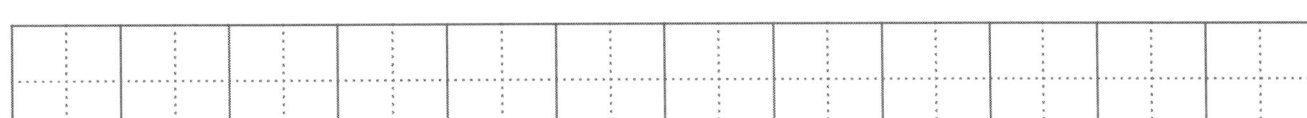

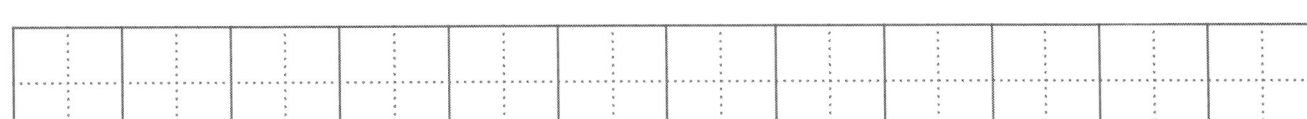

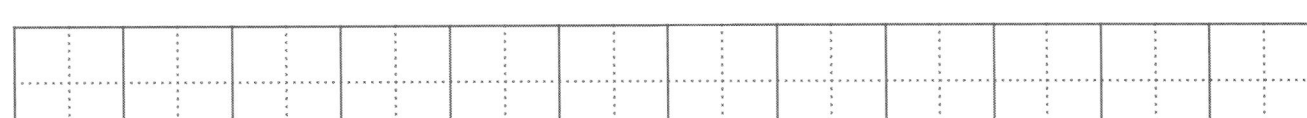

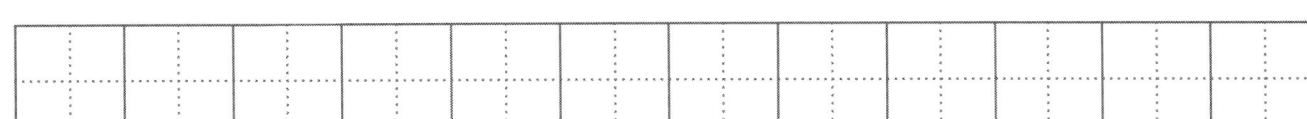

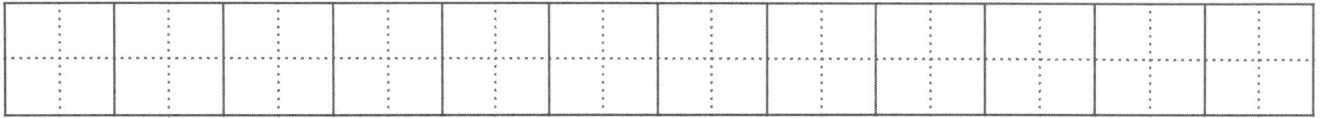

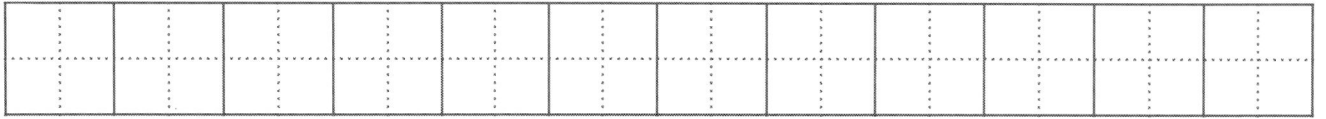

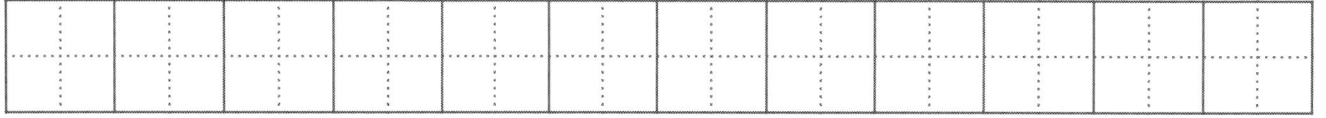

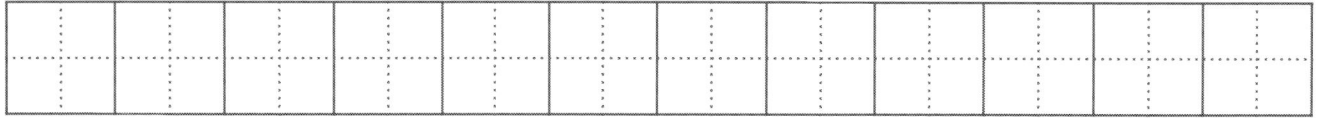

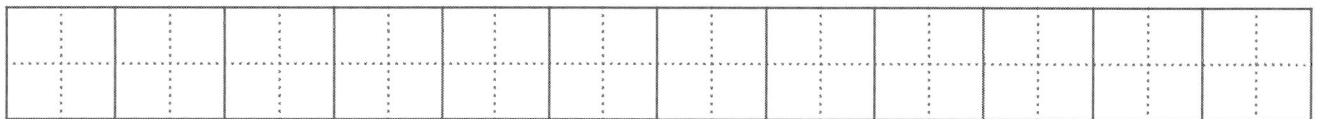

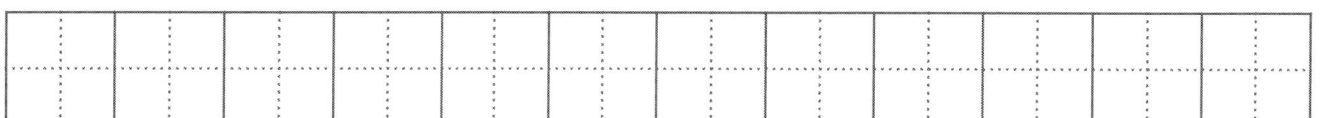

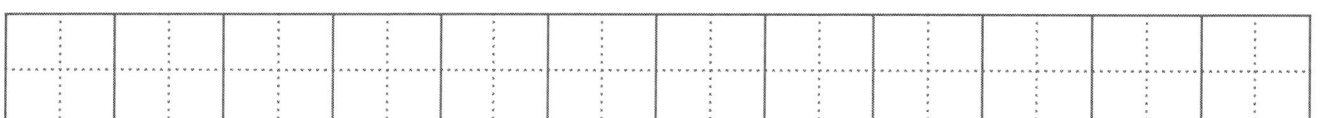

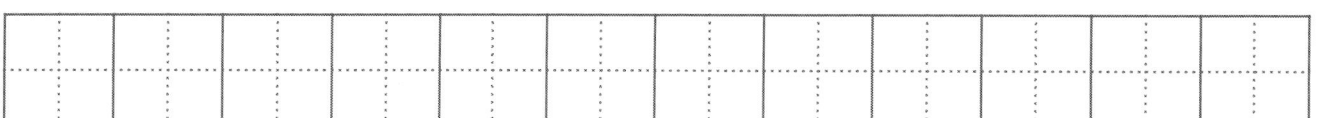

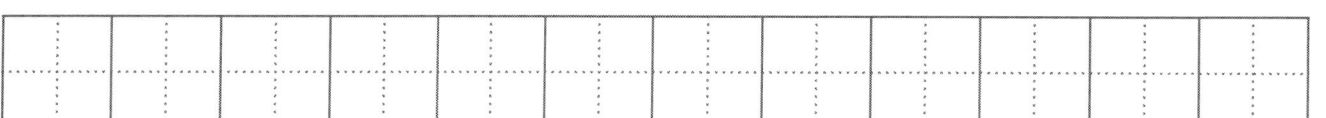

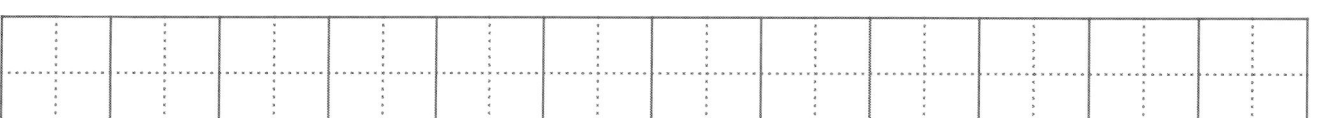

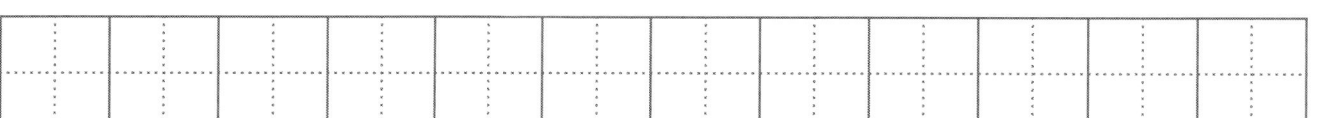

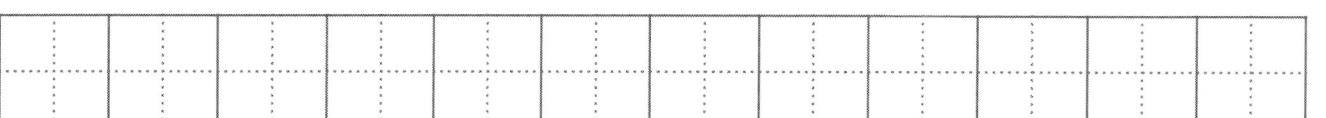

百 战 不 殆

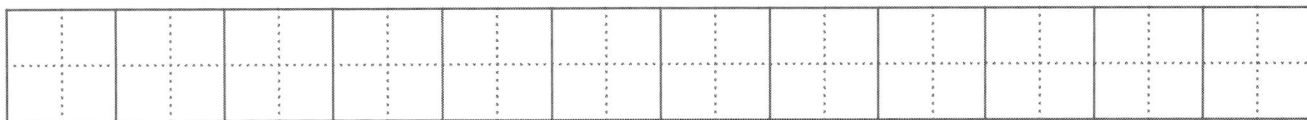
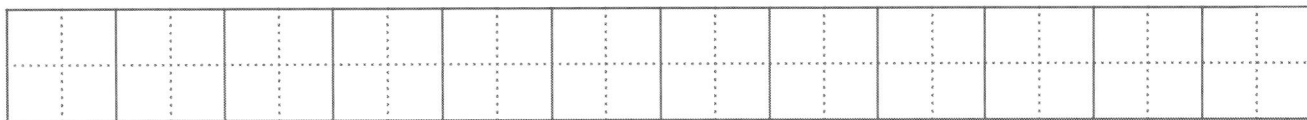
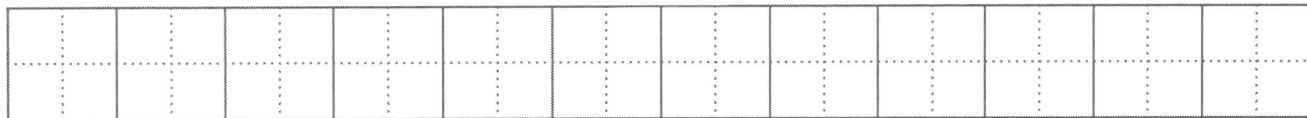
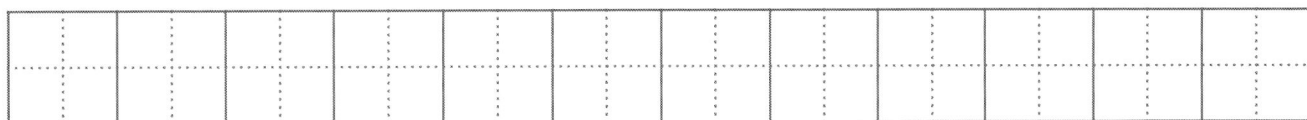
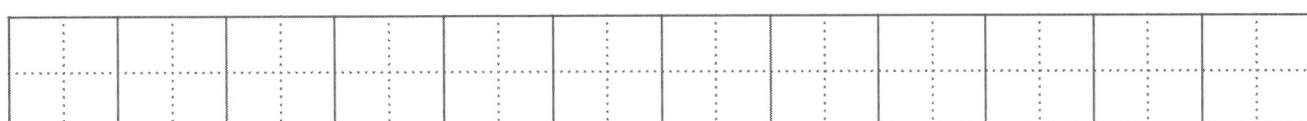
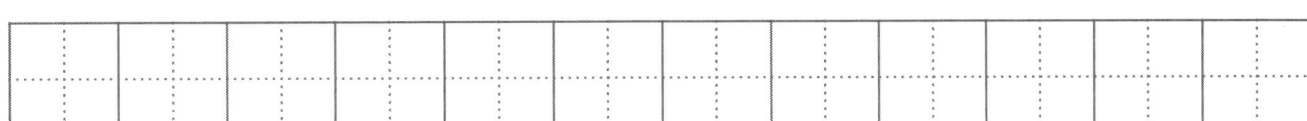
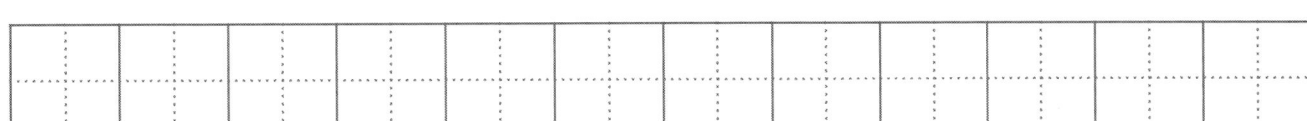
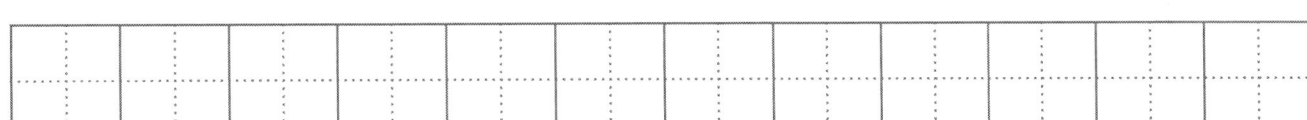
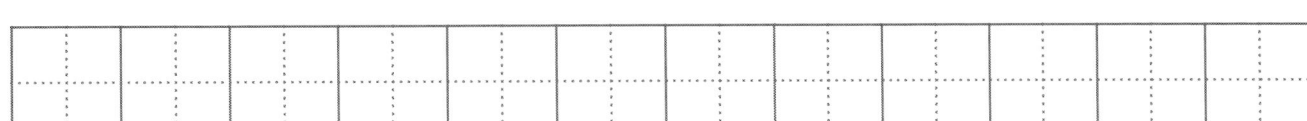

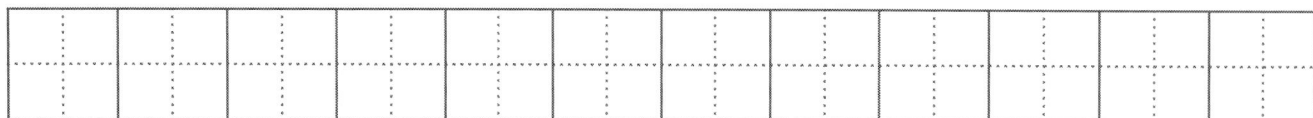

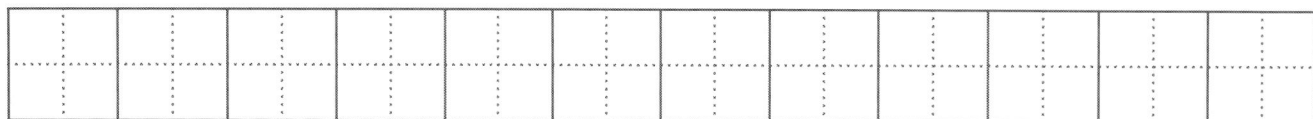

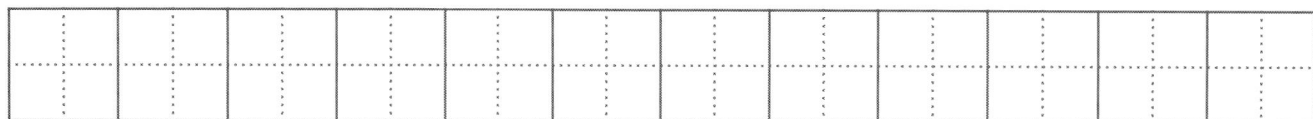

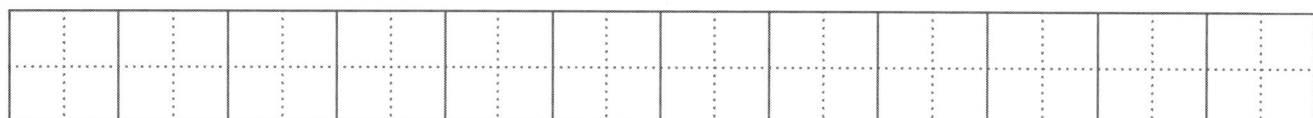

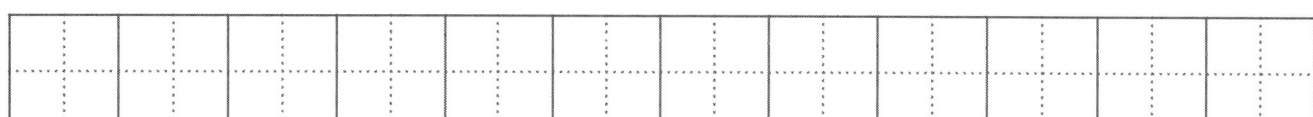

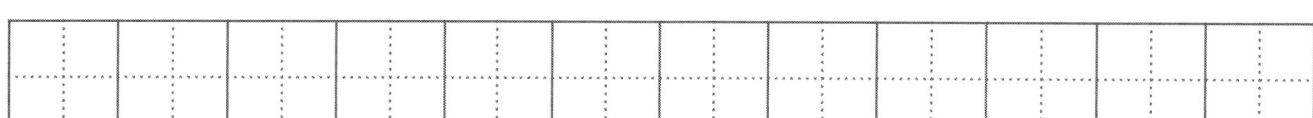

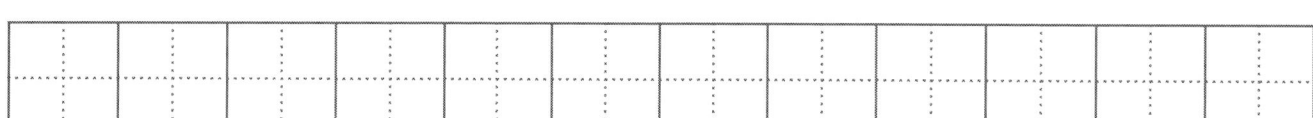

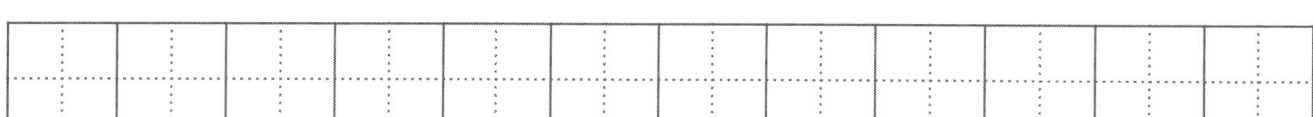

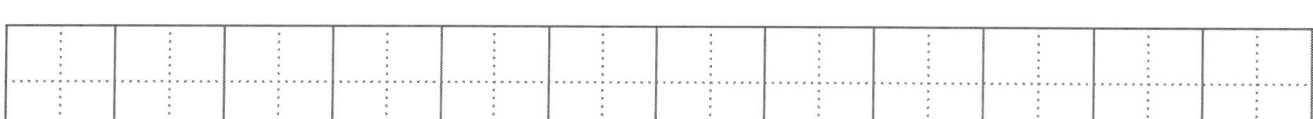

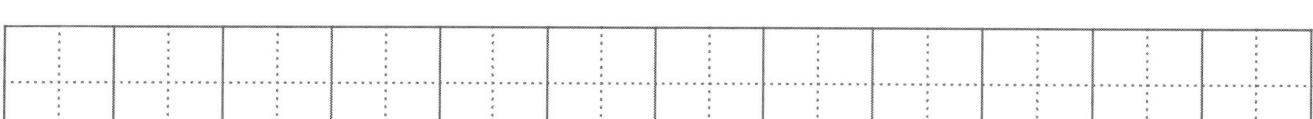

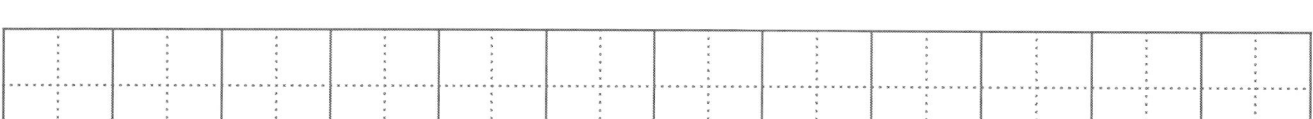

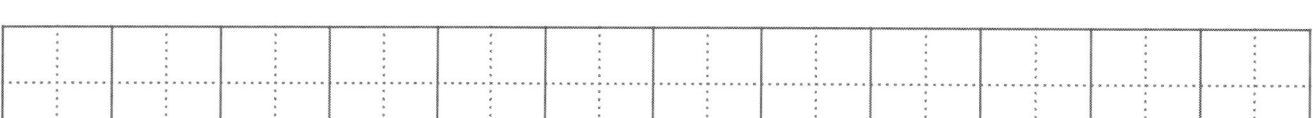

百 战 不 殆

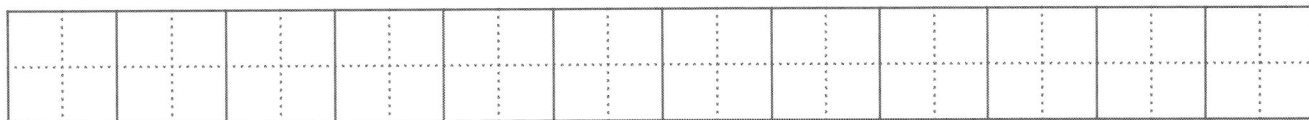

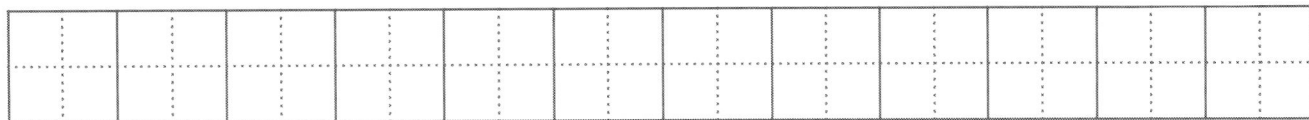

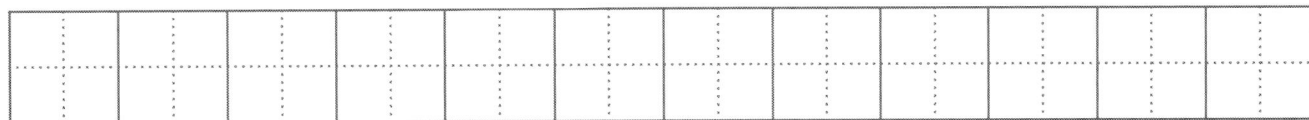

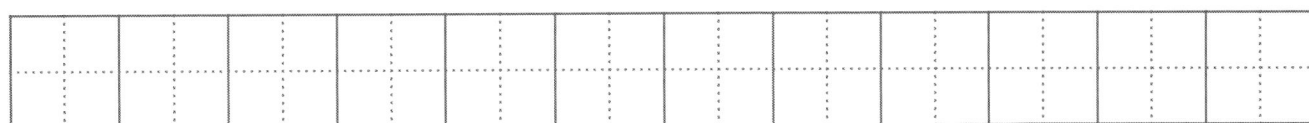

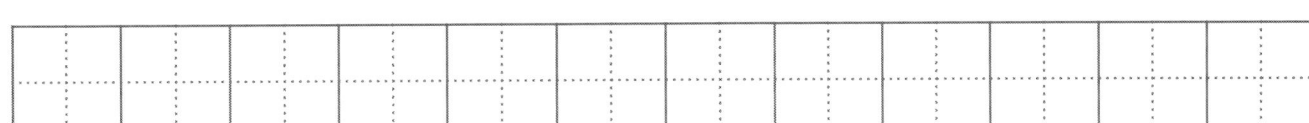

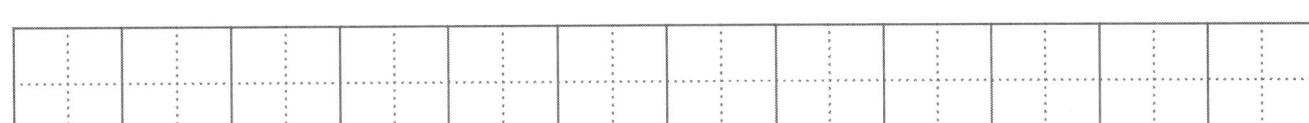

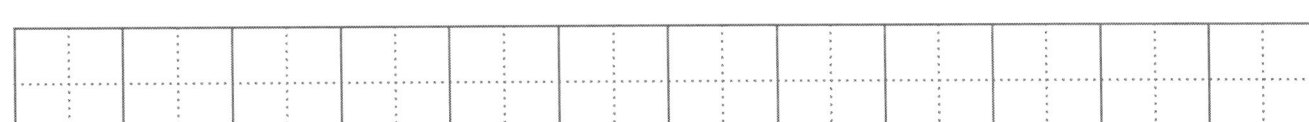

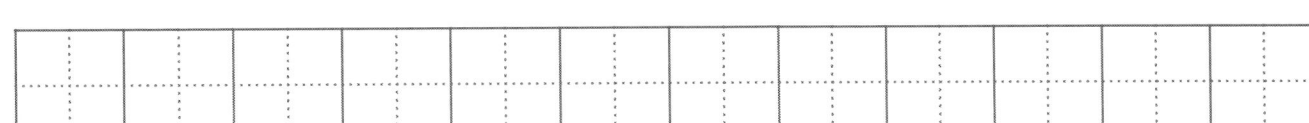

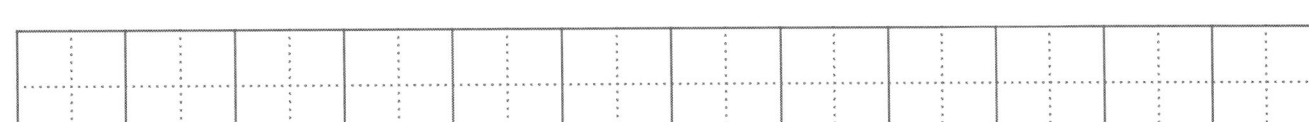

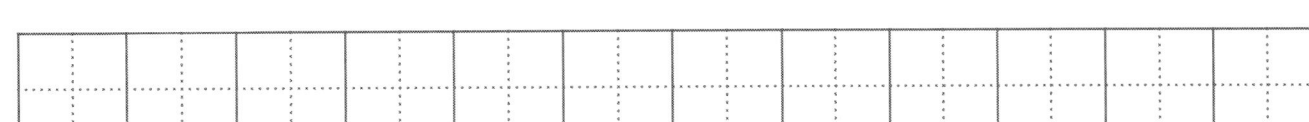

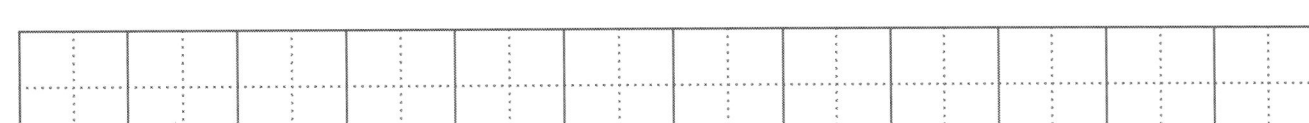

tiān shēng wǒ cái bì yǒu yòng

天 生 我 材 必 有 用 ！

Everybody has something that they were born to be good at.

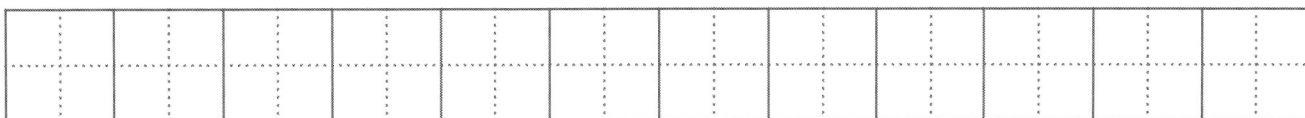

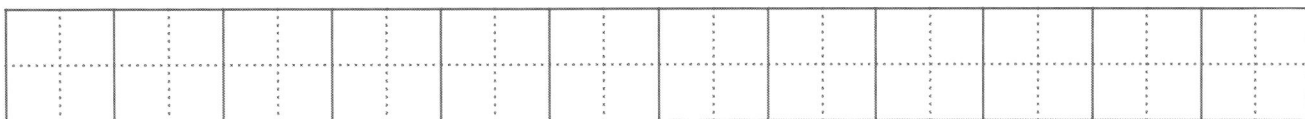

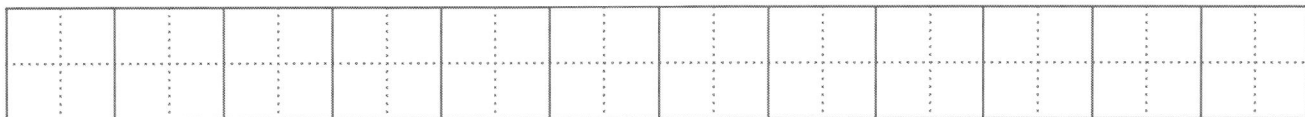

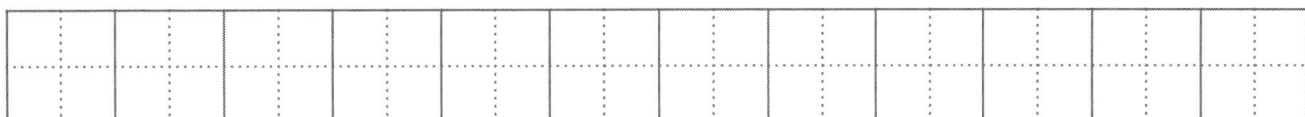

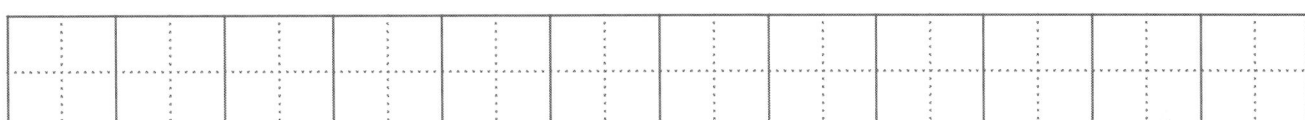

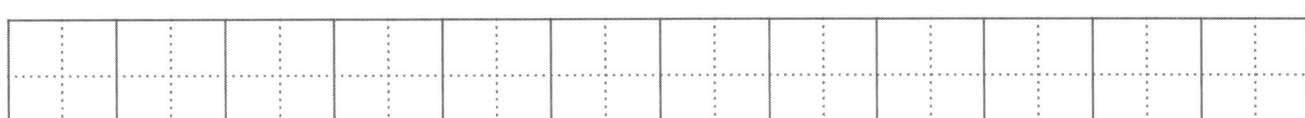

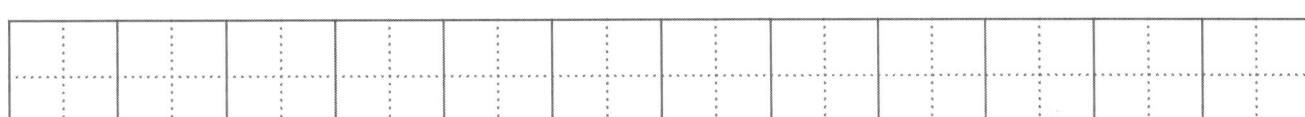

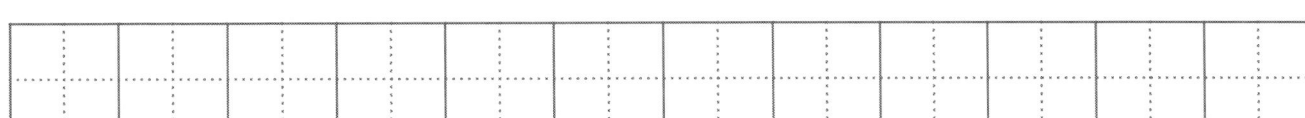

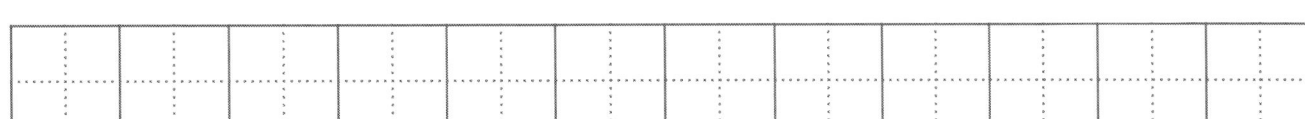

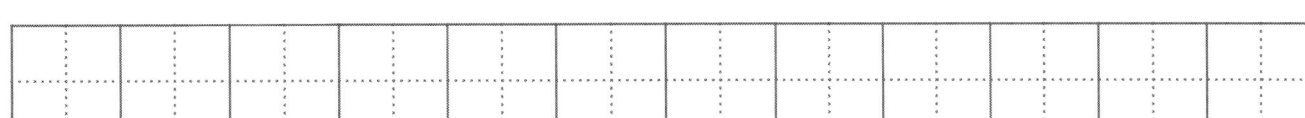

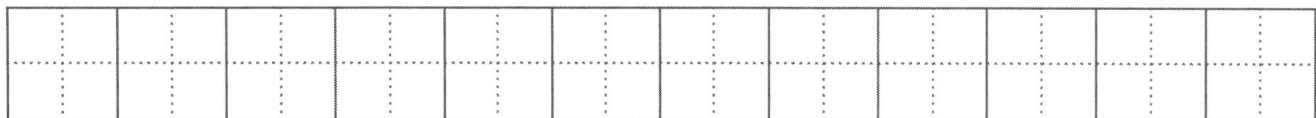

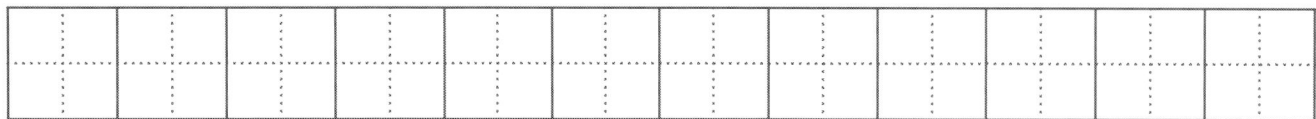

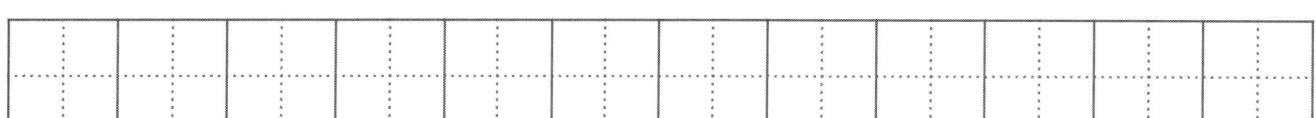

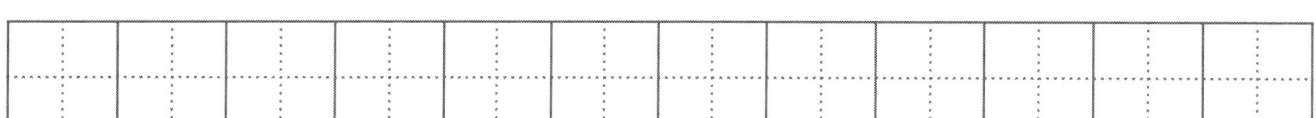

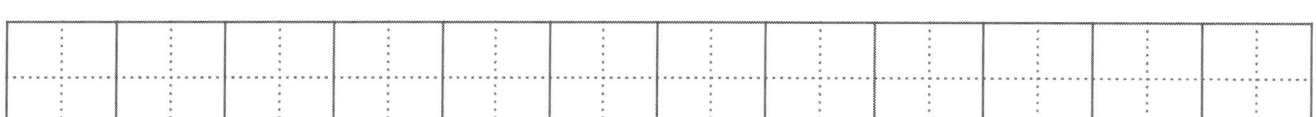

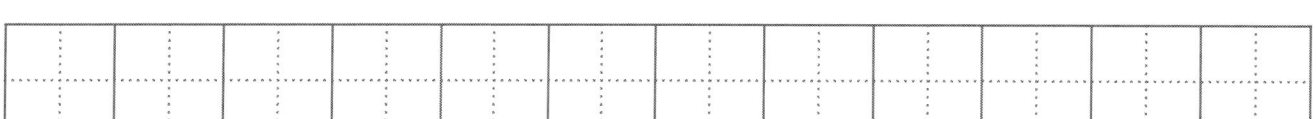

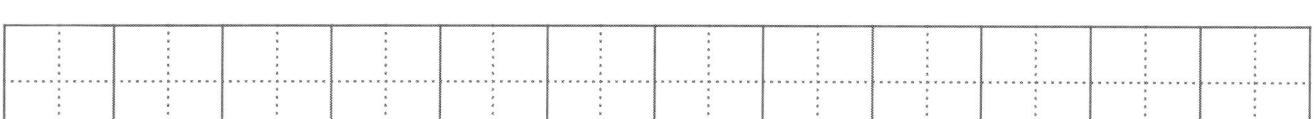

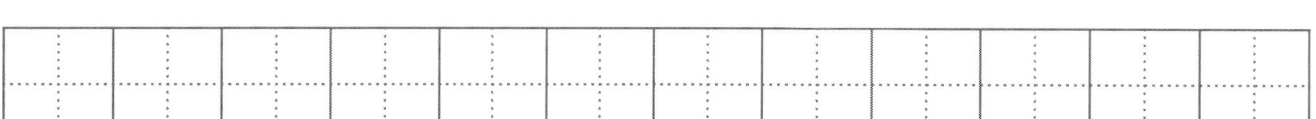

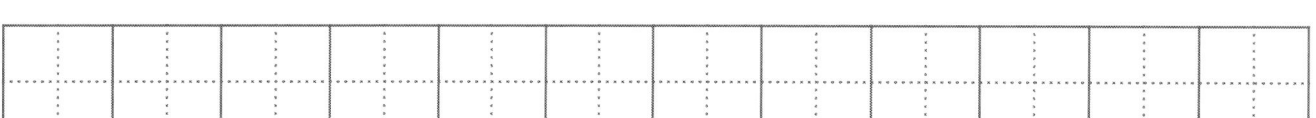

天生我材必有用

rén	wú	yuǎn	lǜ		bì	yǒu	jìn	yōu	
人	无	远	虑	，	必	有	近	忧	。

If a man is not far-sighted

he is bound to encounter difficulties in the near future.

读万卷书，行万里路。

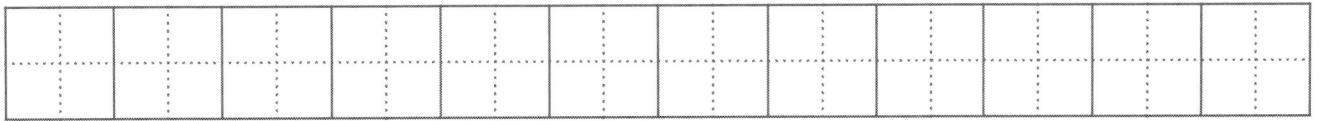

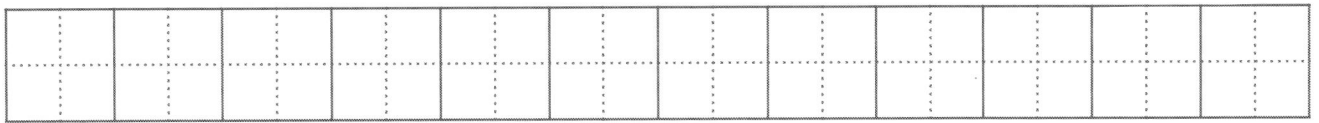

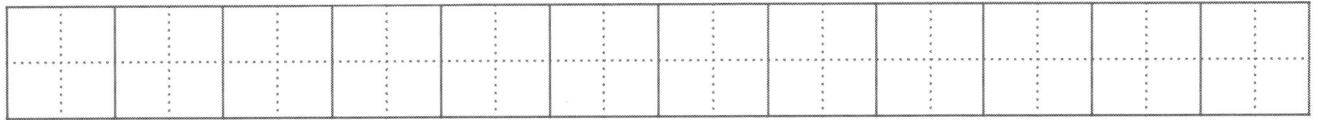

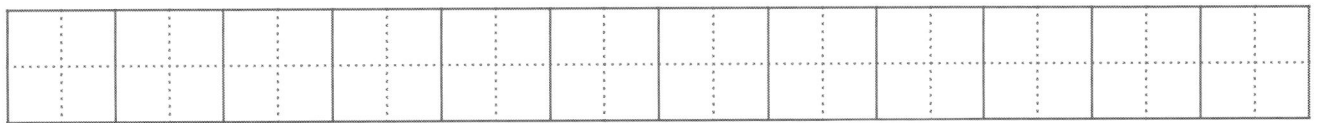

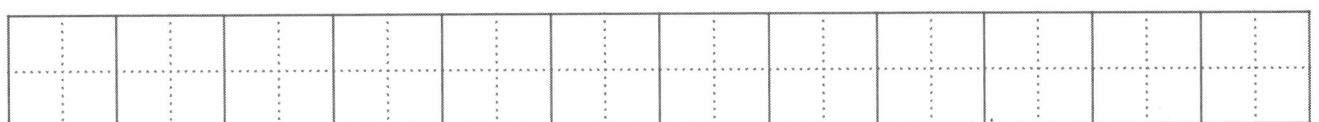

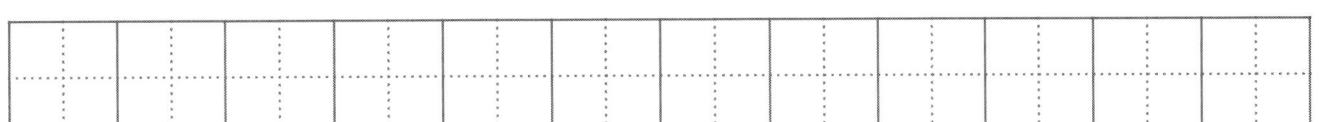

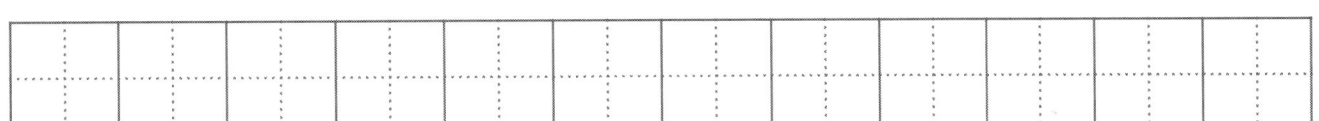

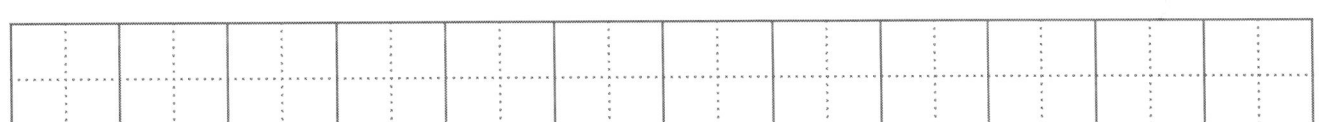

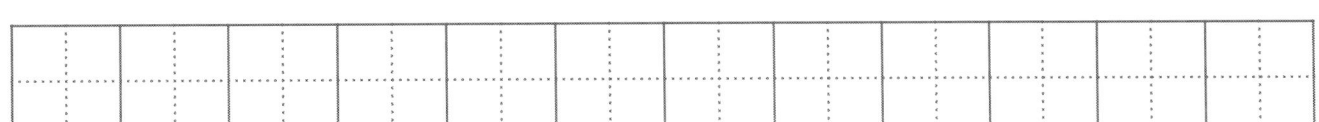

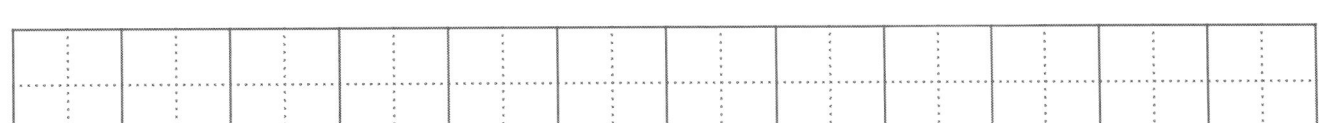

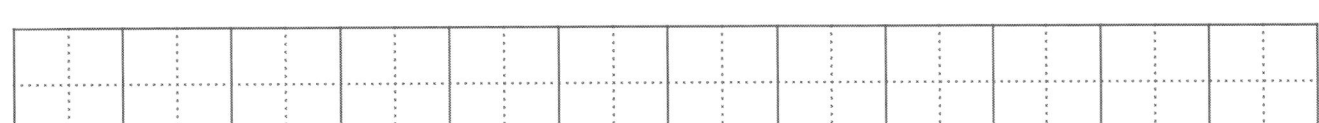

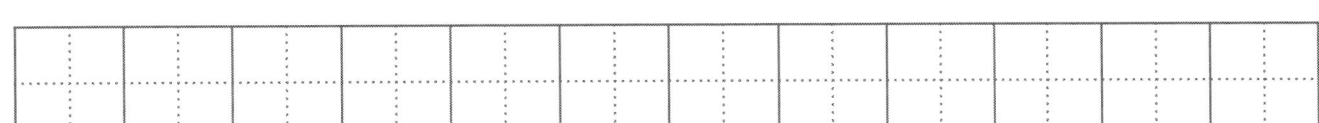

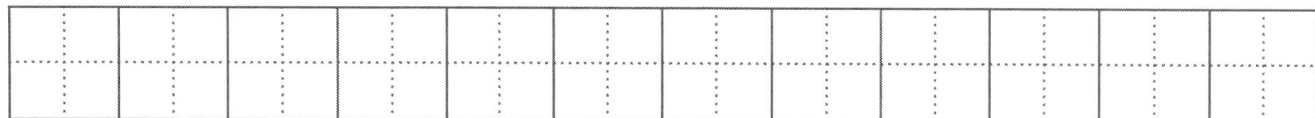
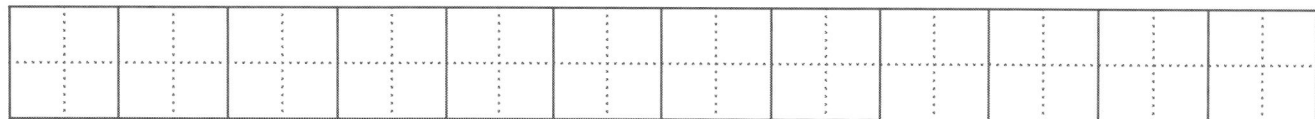

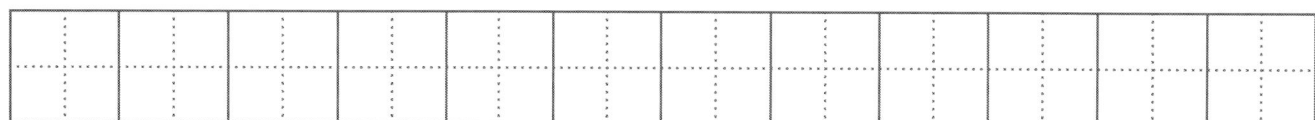
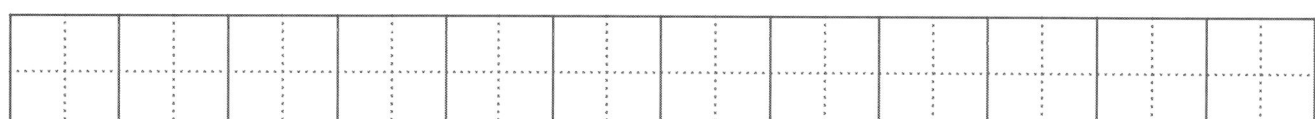
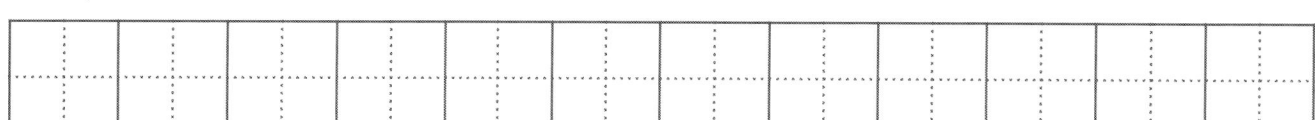
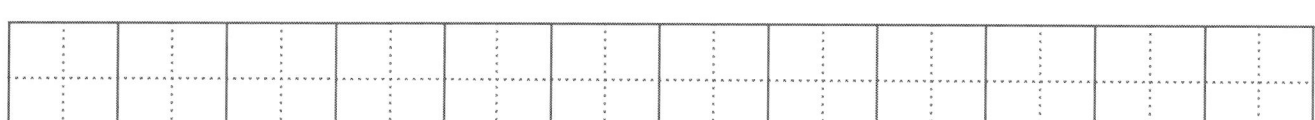
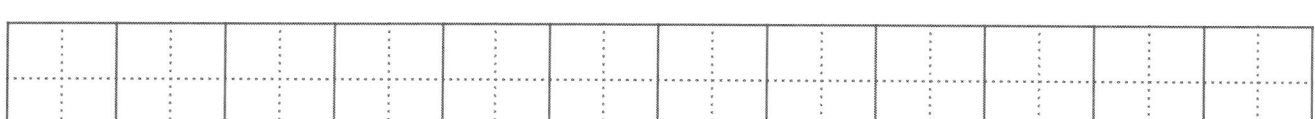
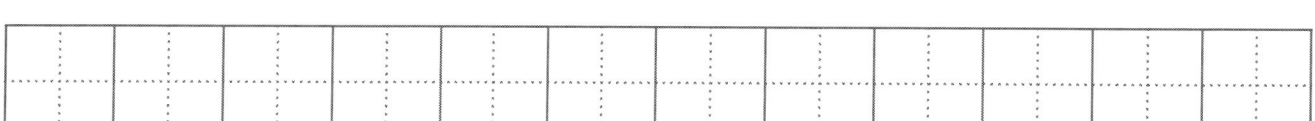
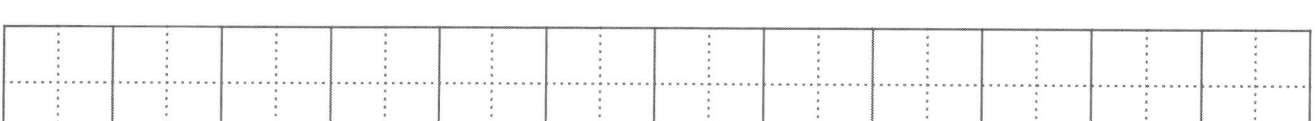
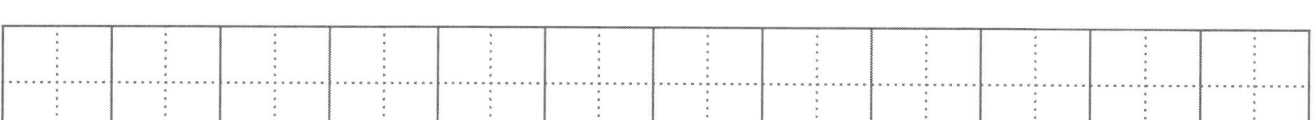

必 有 近 忧

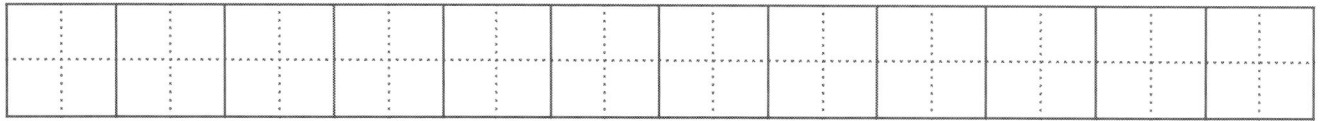
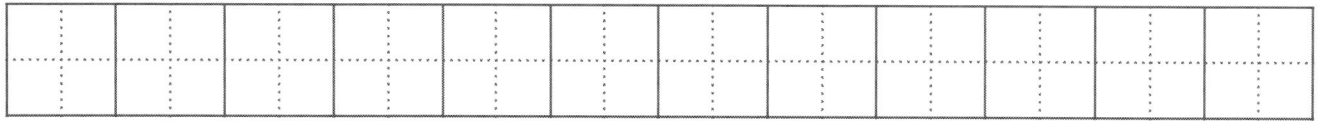
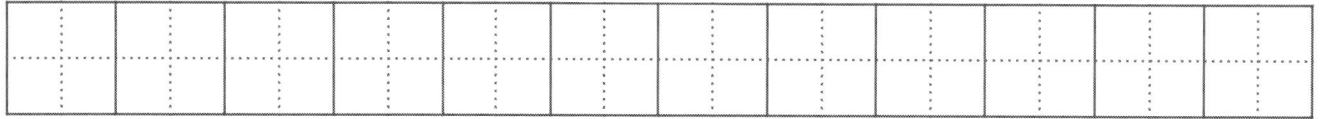
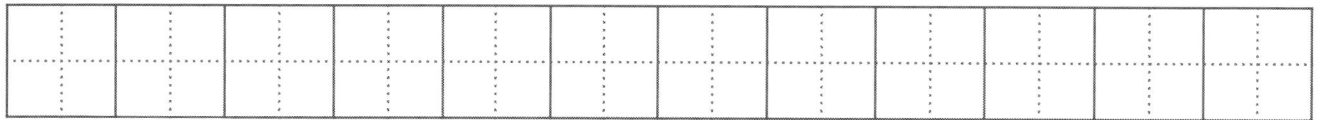
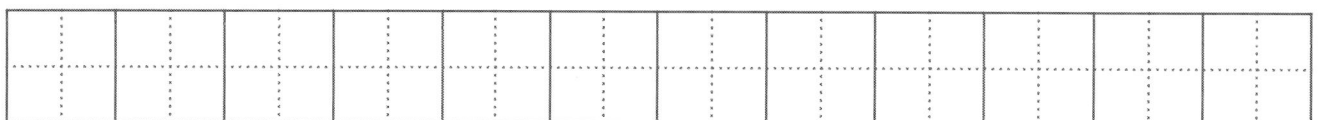
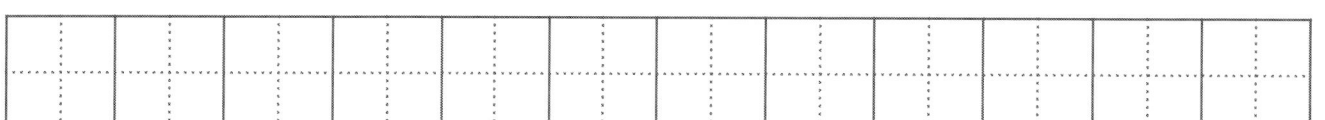
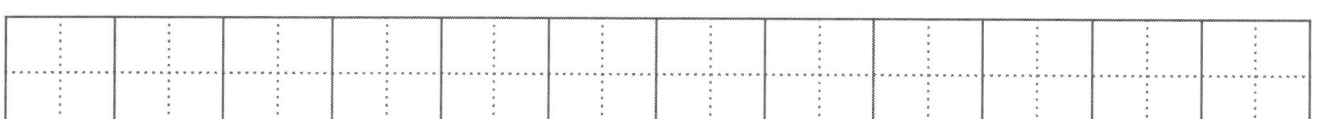
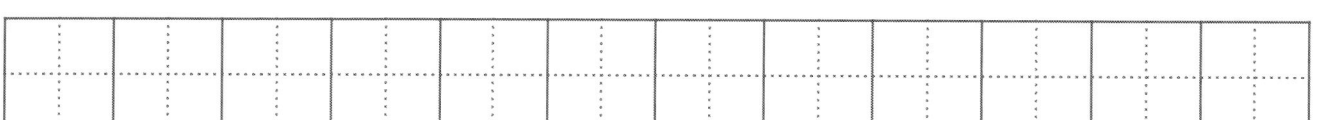
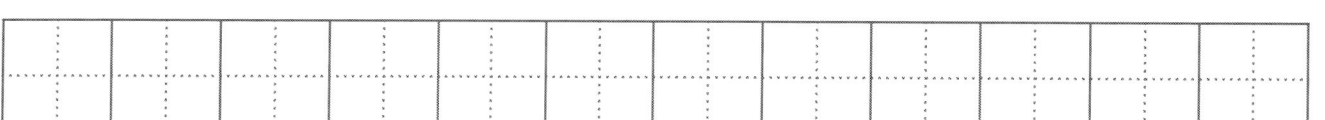
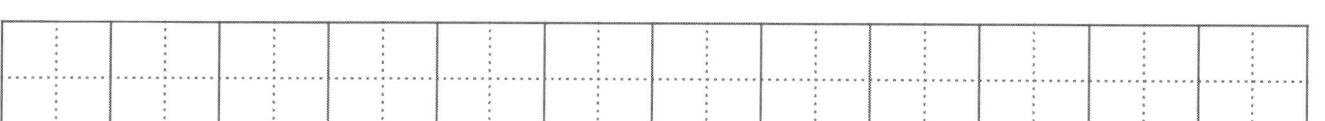
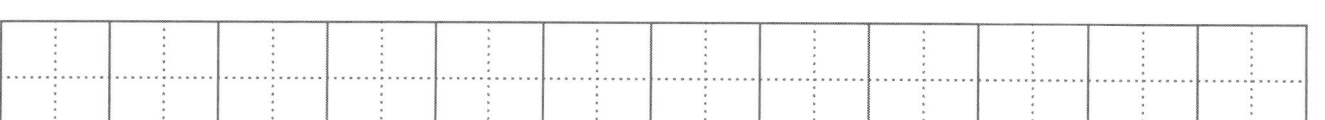
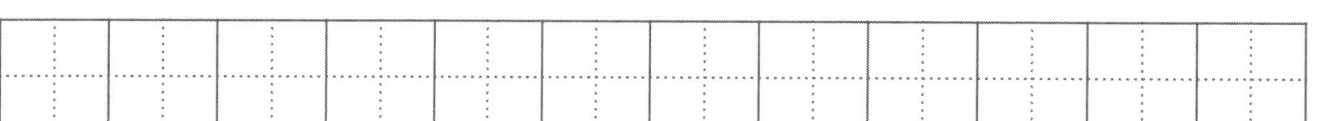

必 有 近忧

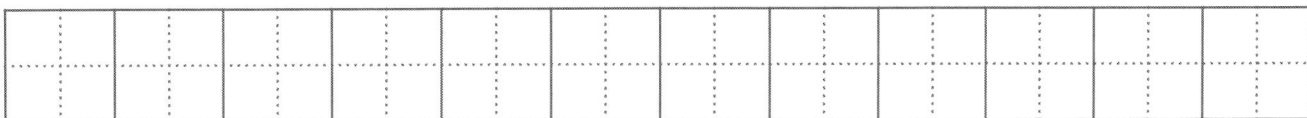

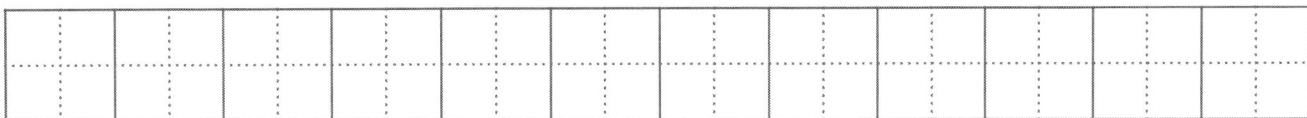

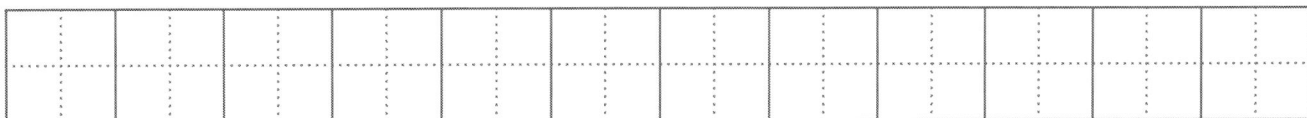

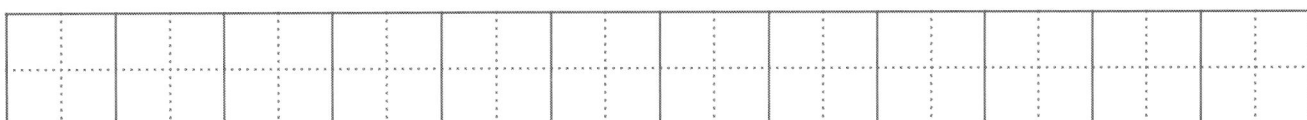

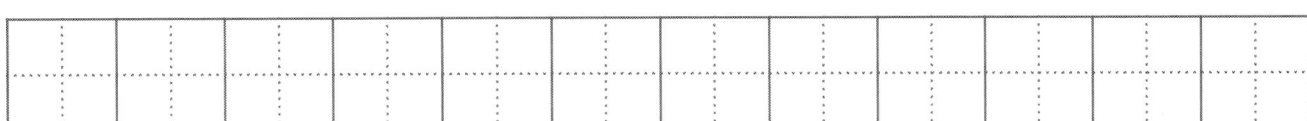

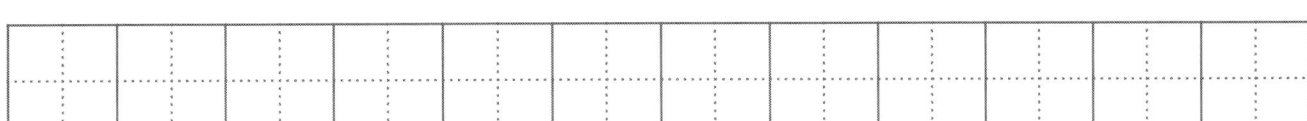

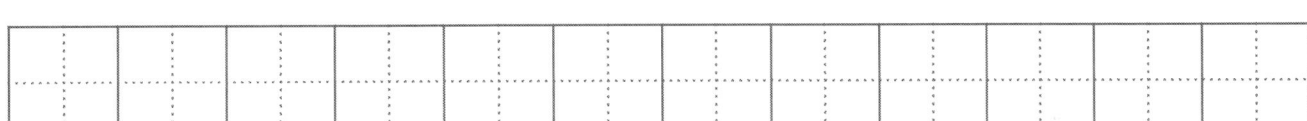

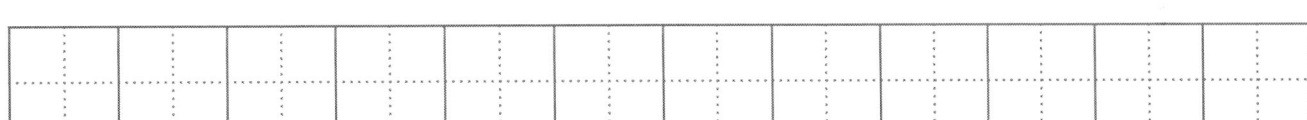

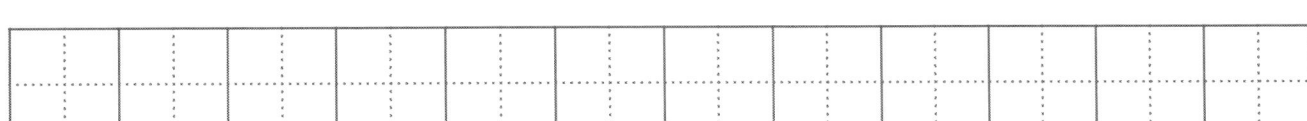

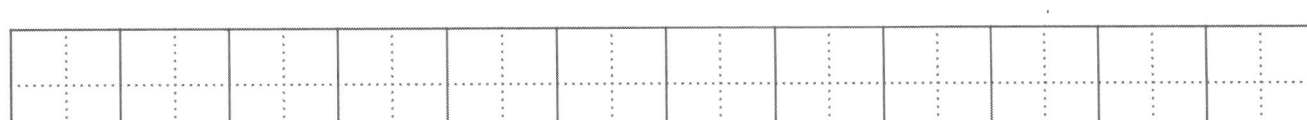

必 有 近忧

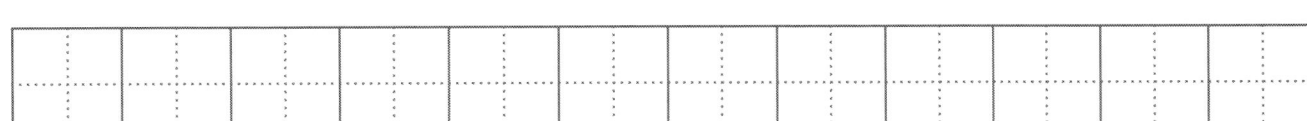

	tiān	xià	xīng	wáng		pǐ	fū	yǒu	zé		
	天	下	兴	亡	，	匹	夫	有	责	。	

For the rise and fall of the nation,
every citizen has his obligation.

知己知彼，百战不殆。

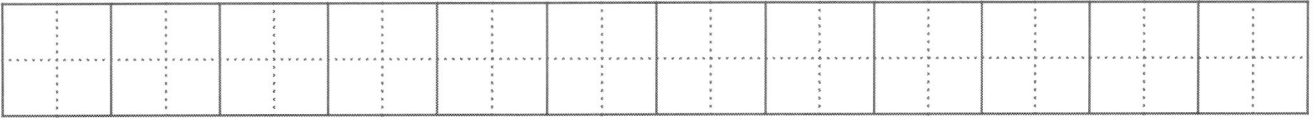

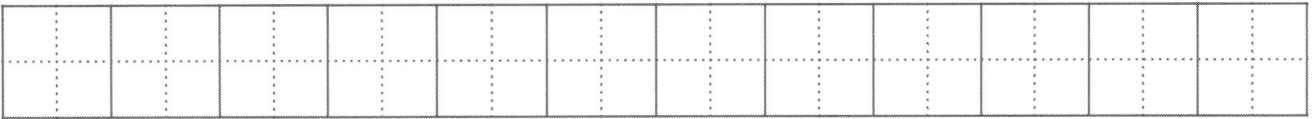

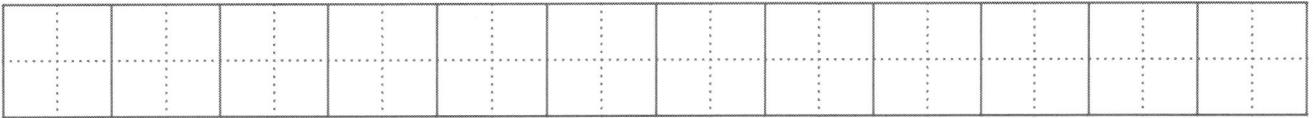

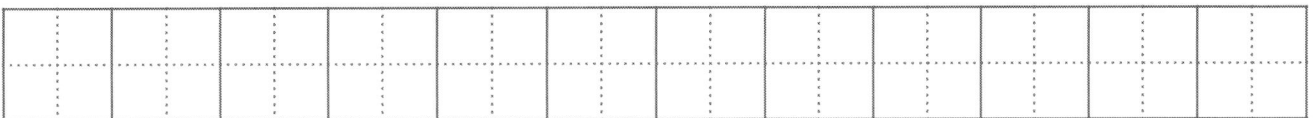

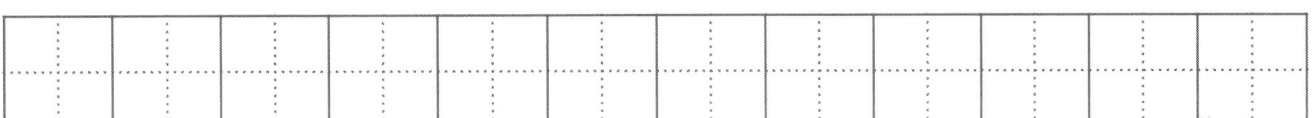

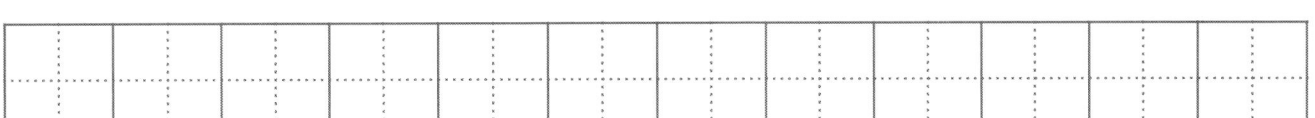

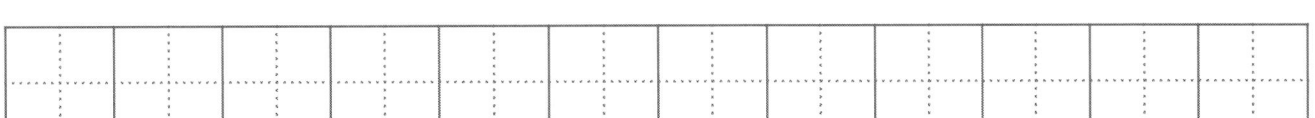

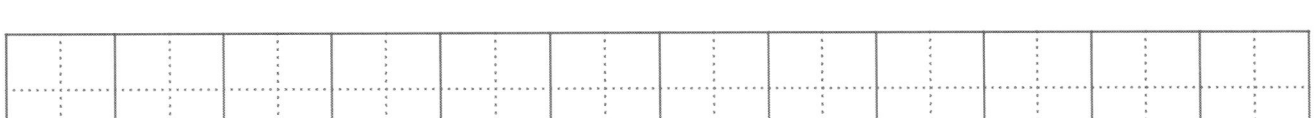

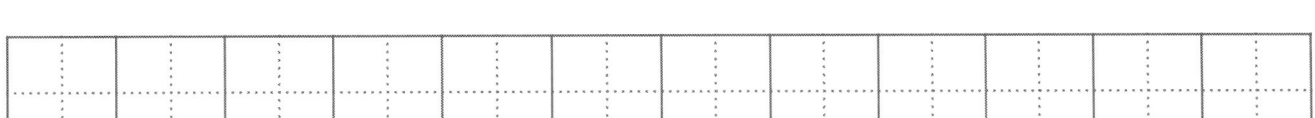

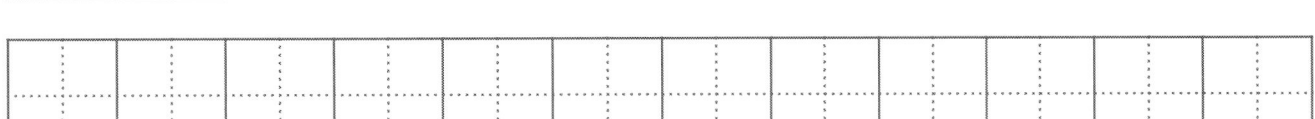

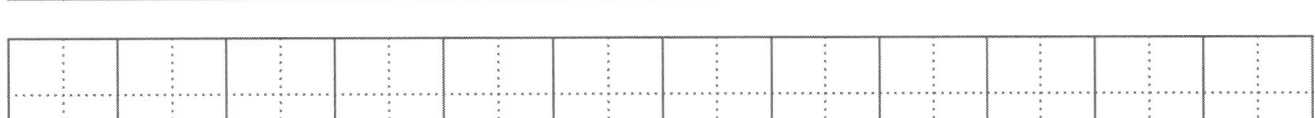

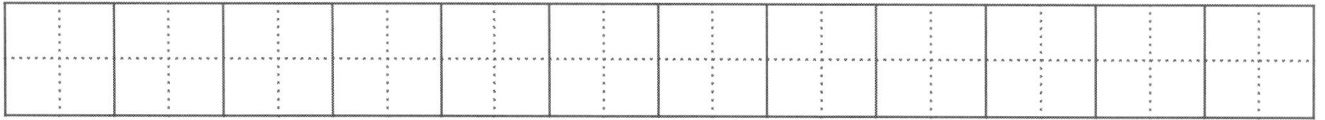
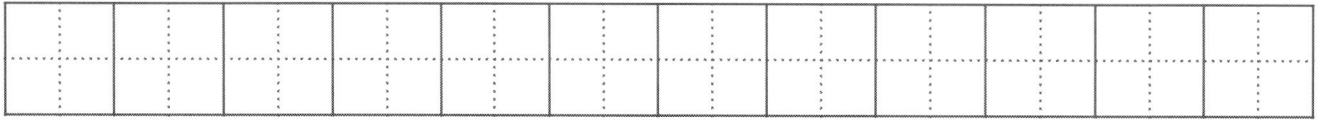
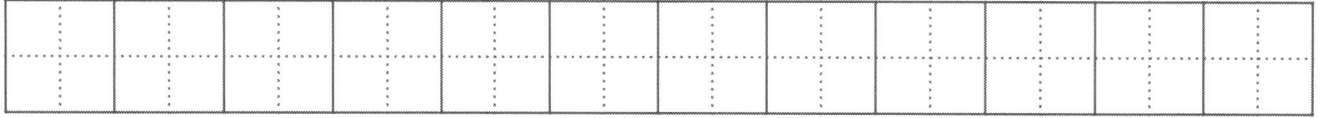
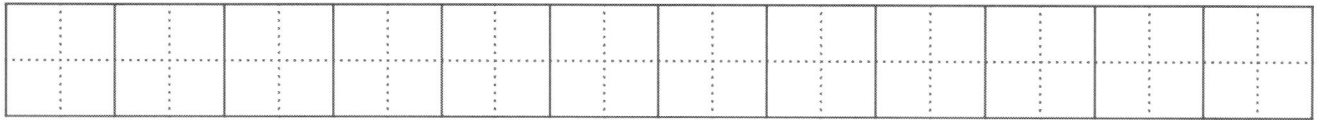

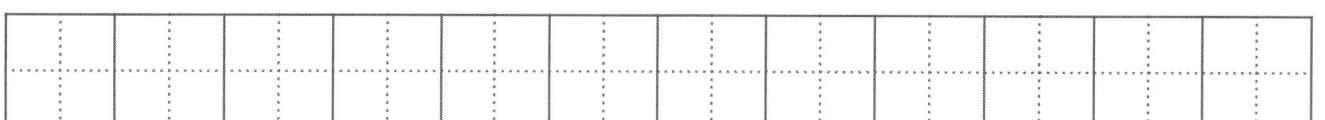
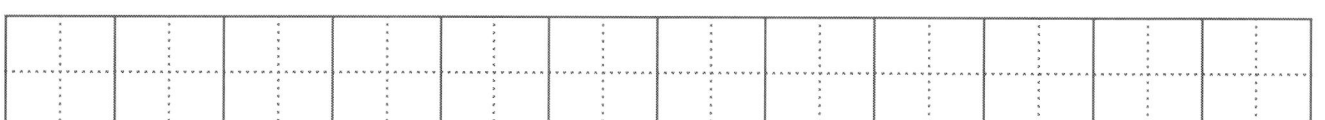
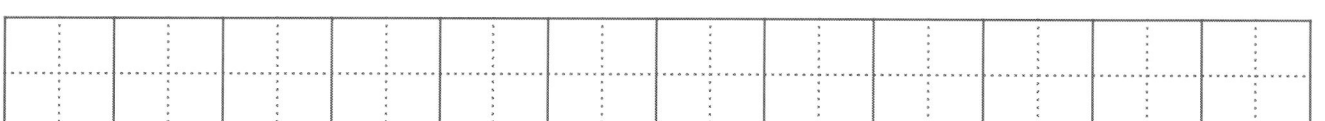
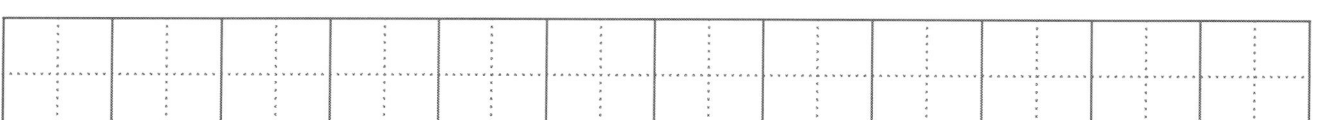
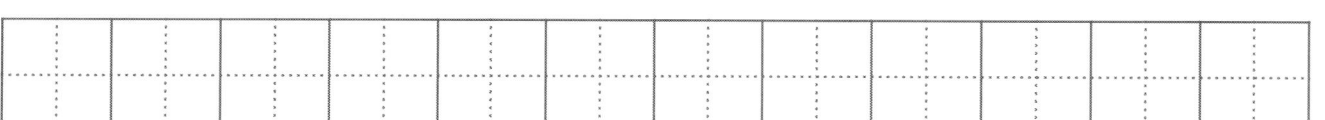
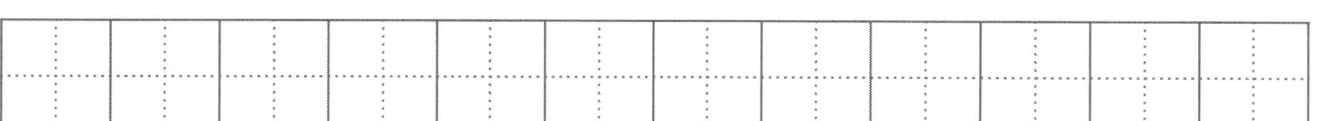
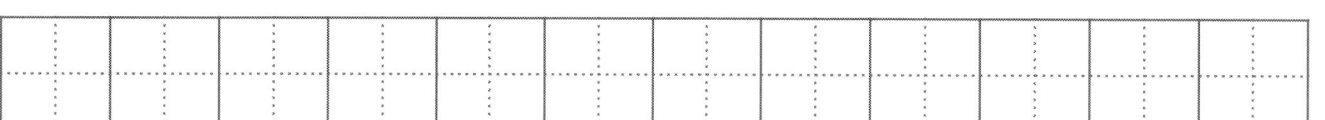

匹夫有责

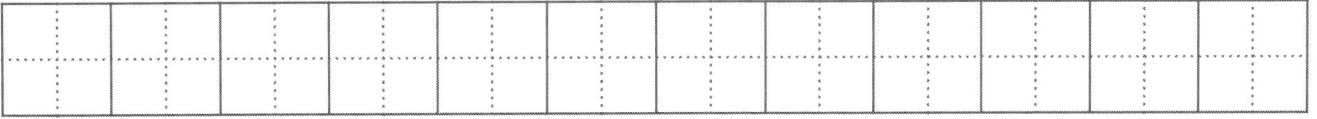

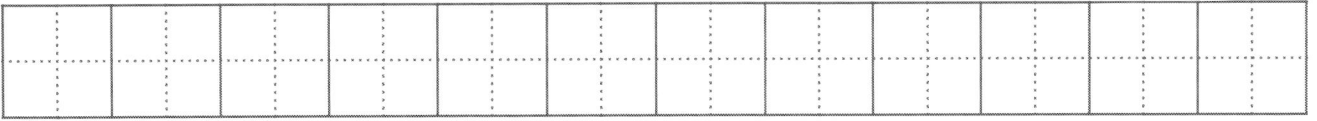

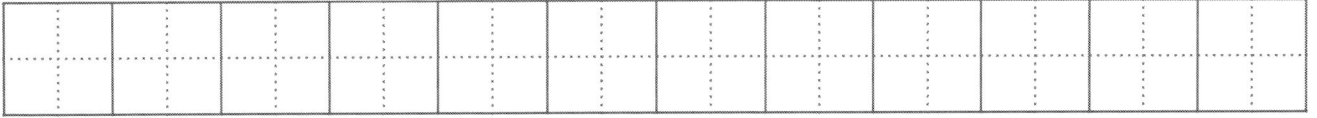

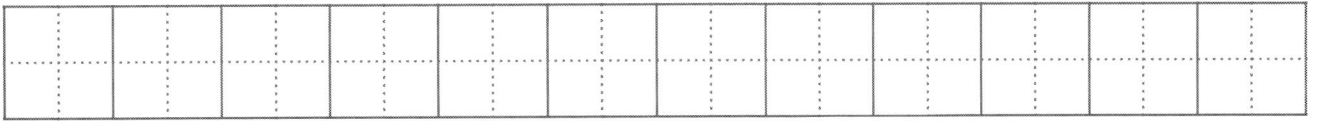

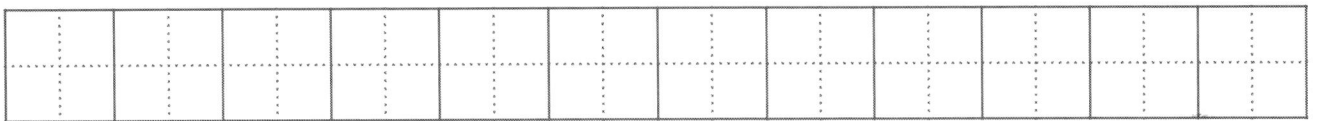

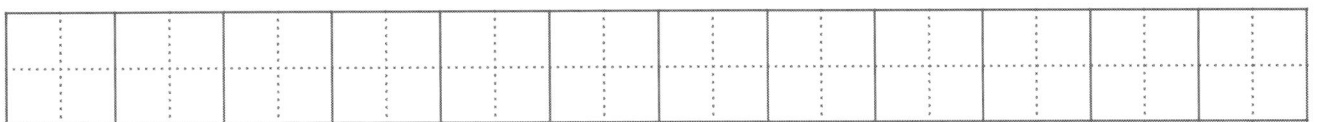

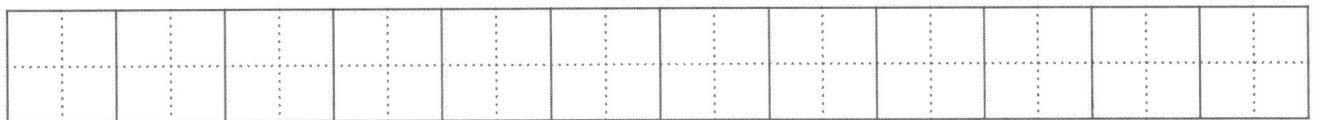

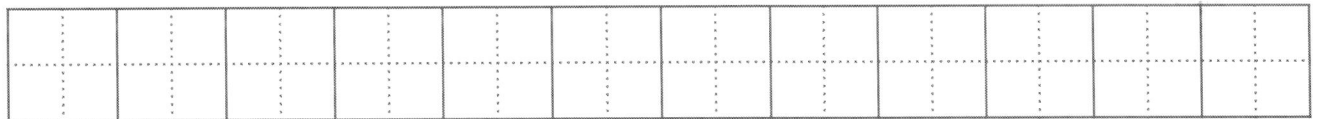

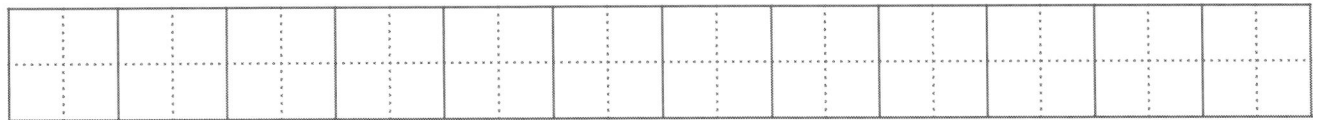

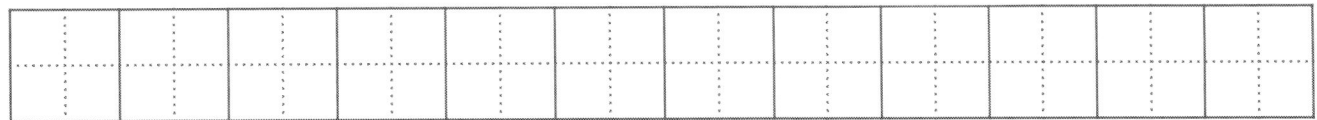

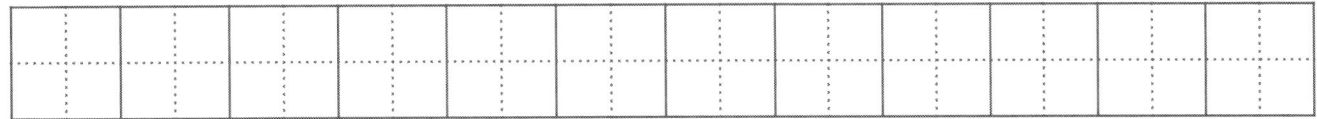

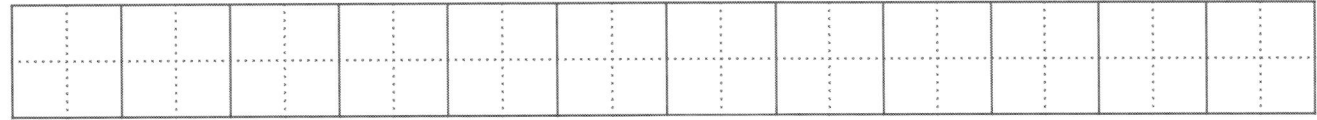

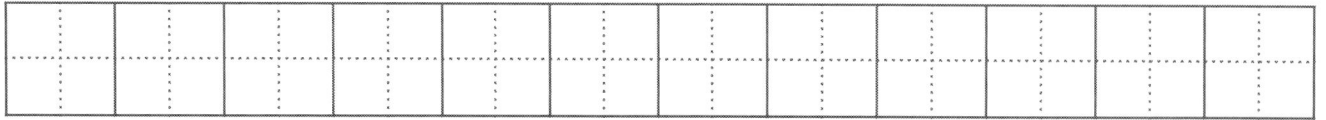

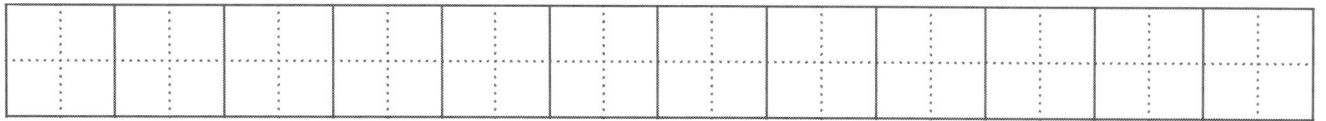

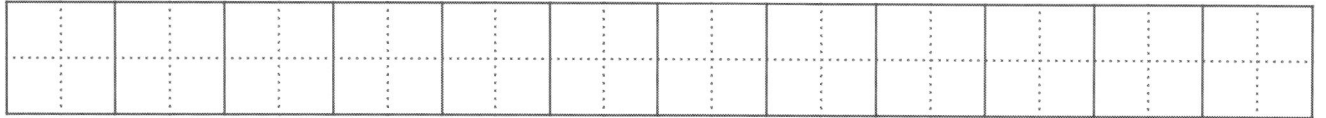

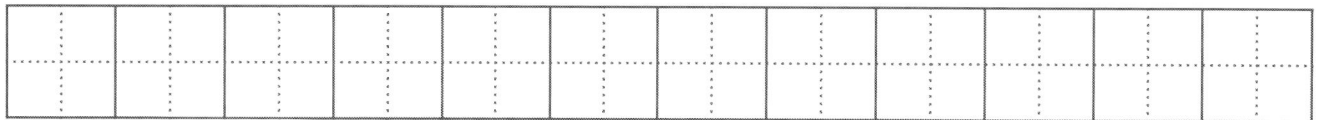

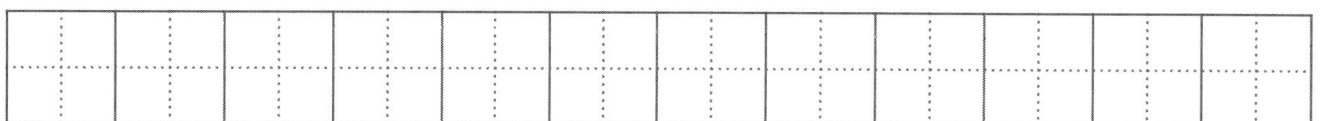

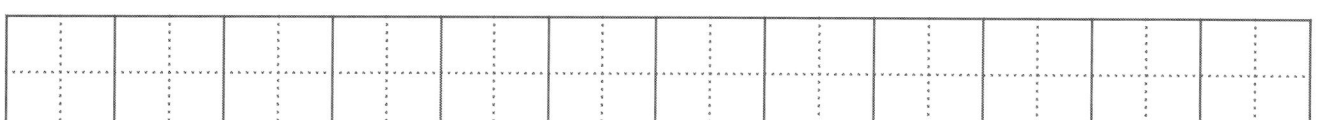

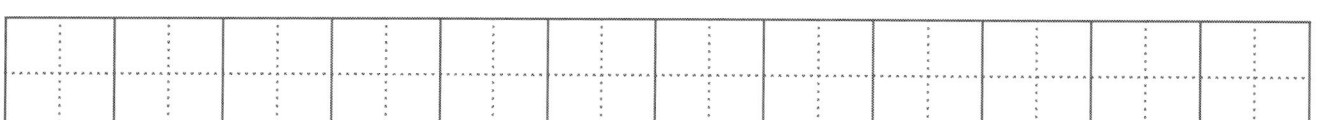

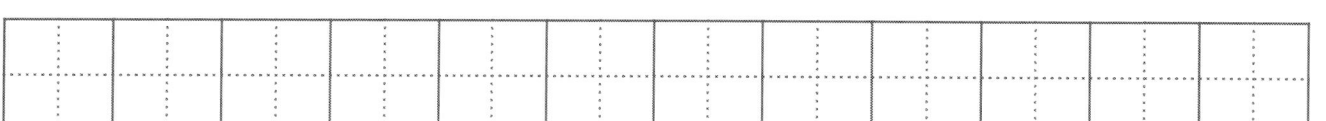

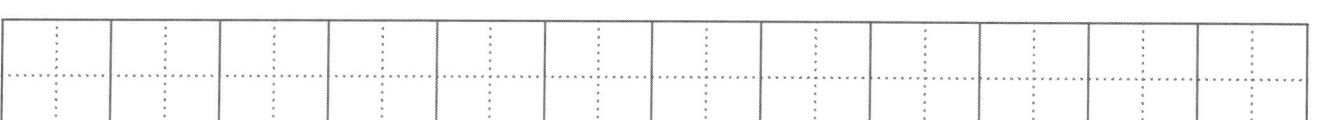

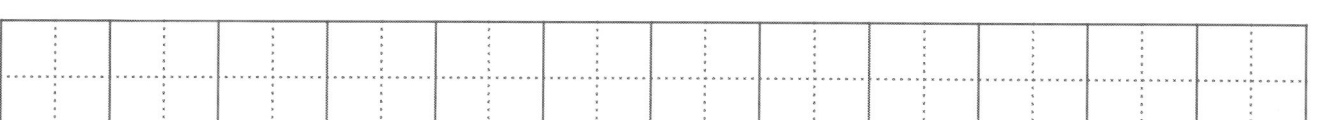

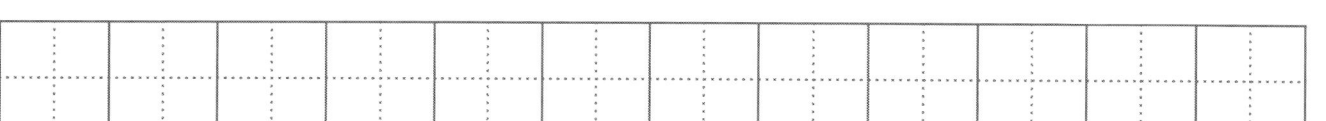

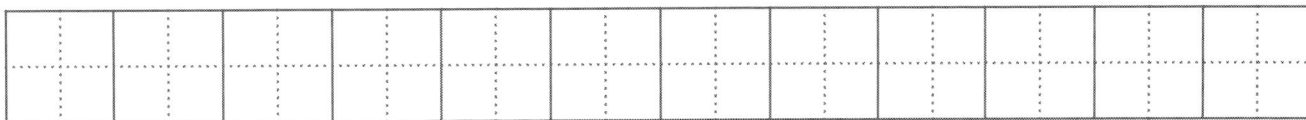
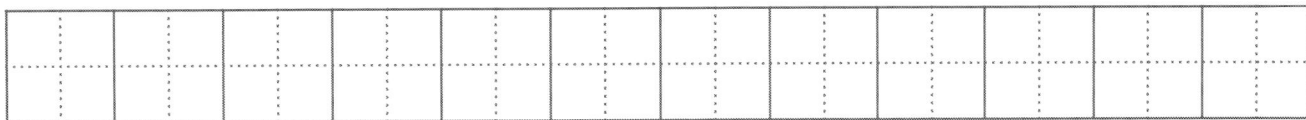
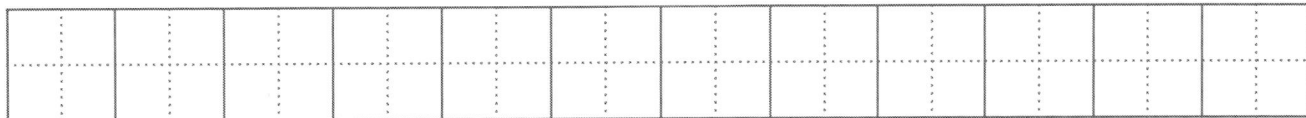
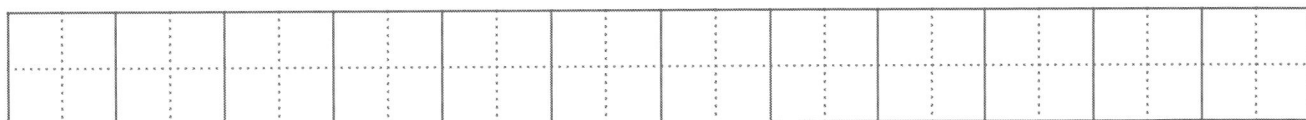
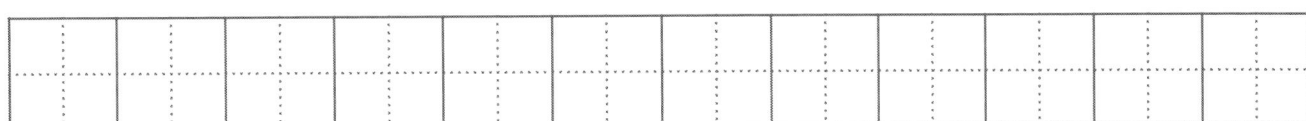

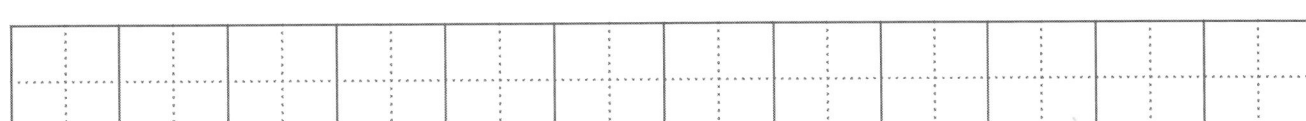
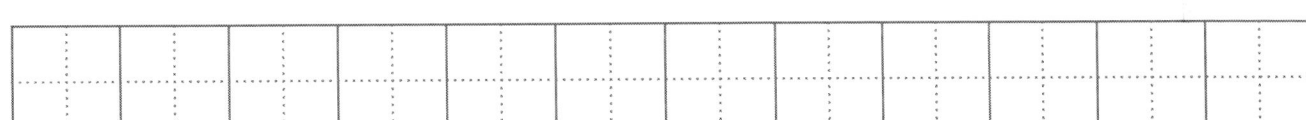
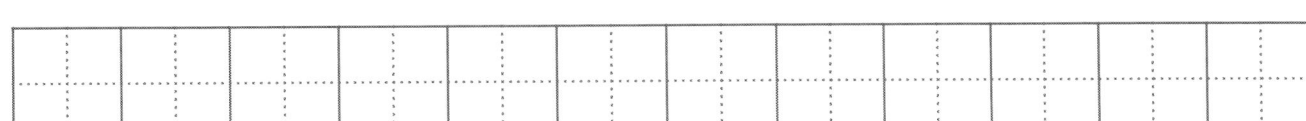
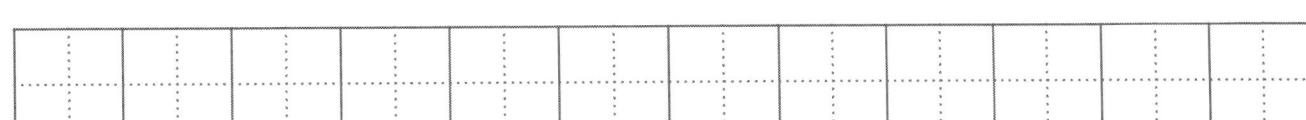
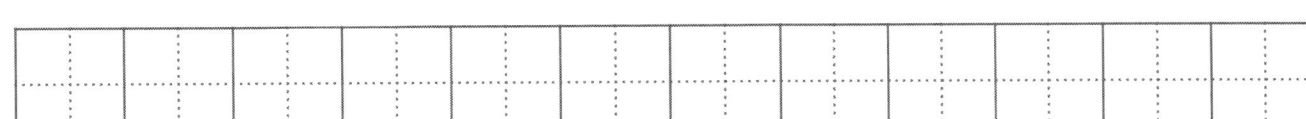
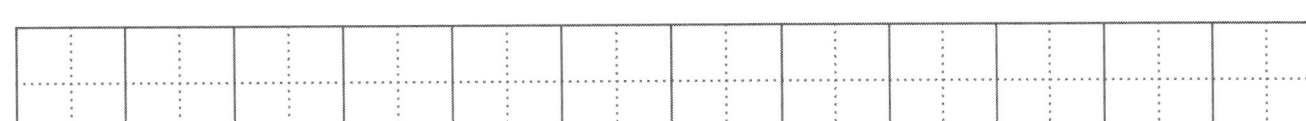

言 必 信 ， 行 必 果 ！

One must be a man of his words and resolute in his actions !

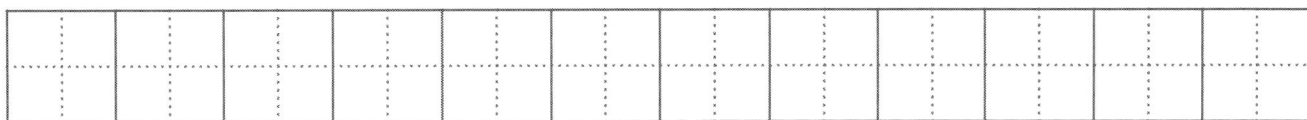
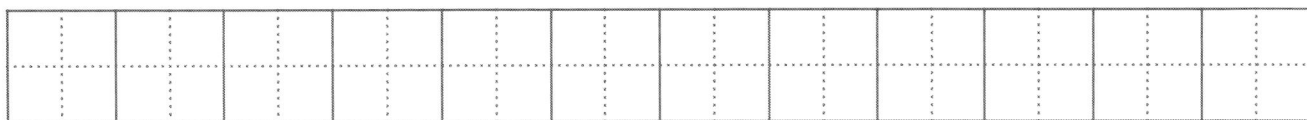
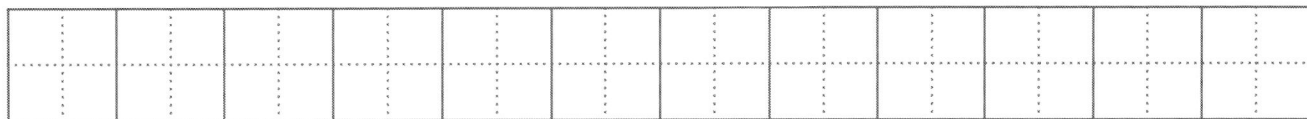
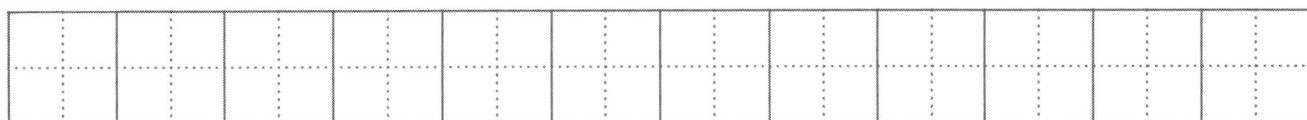
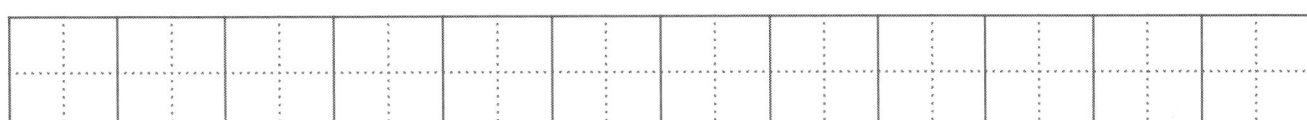
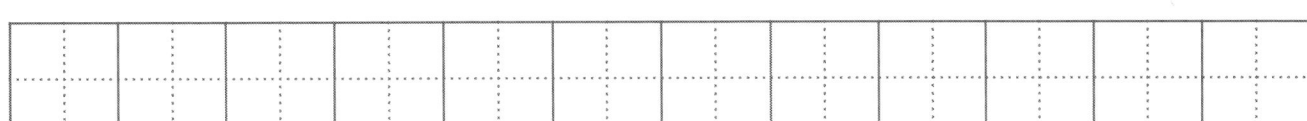
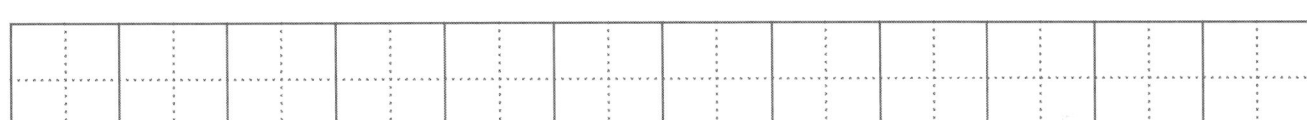
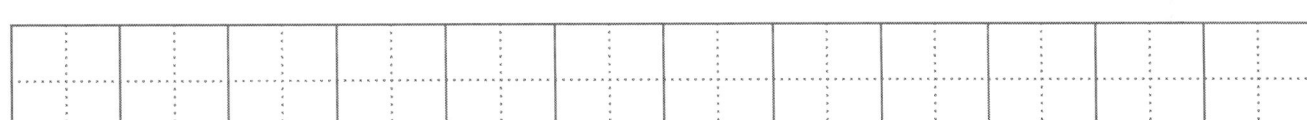
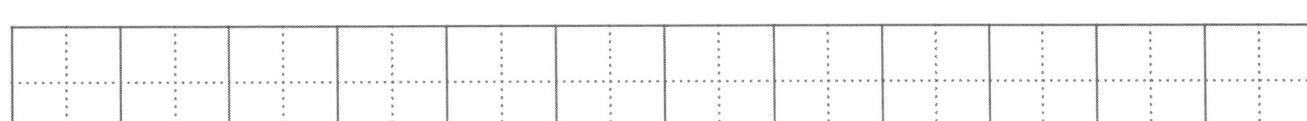

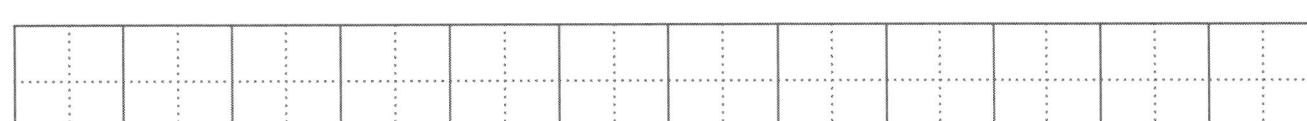

近朱者赤，近墨者黑。

jìn zhū zhě chì　　jìn mò zhě hēi

He who stays near vermillion gets stained red, and he who stays near ink
gets stained black.
- People are easily influenced by their surroundings and the companions
they hang around with.

千里之行，始于足下。

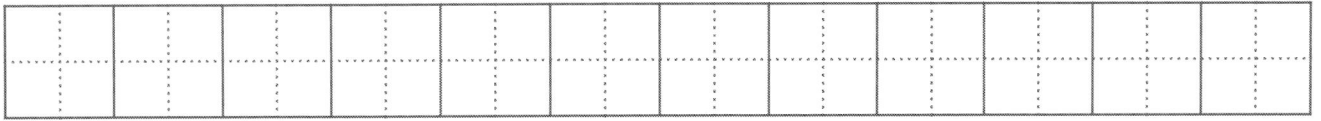

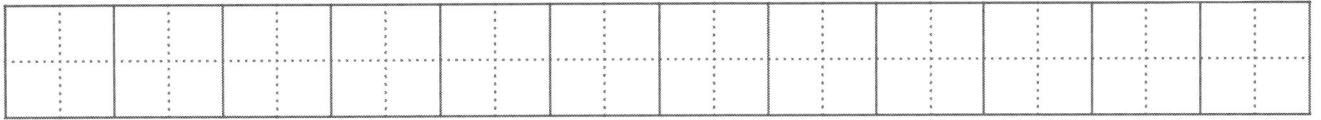

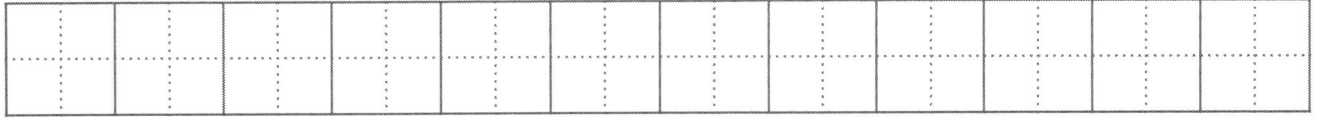

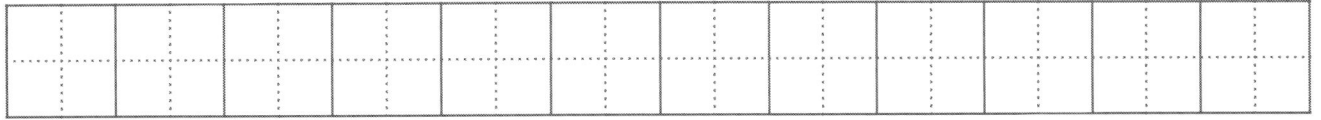

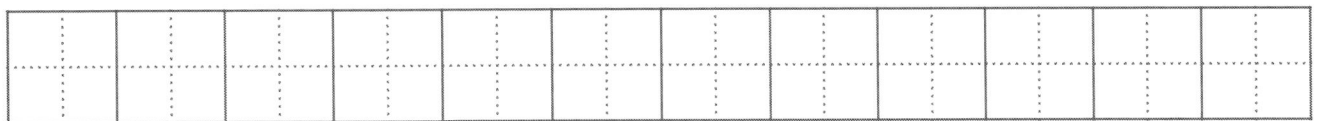

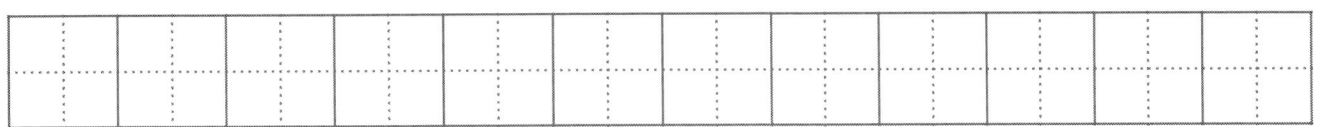

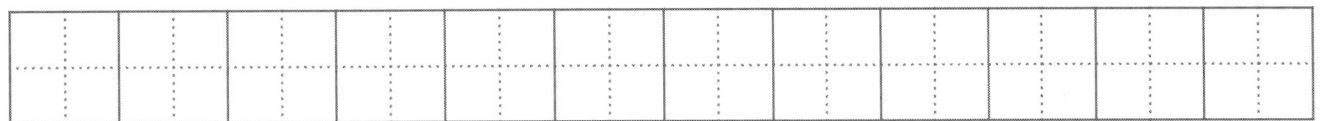

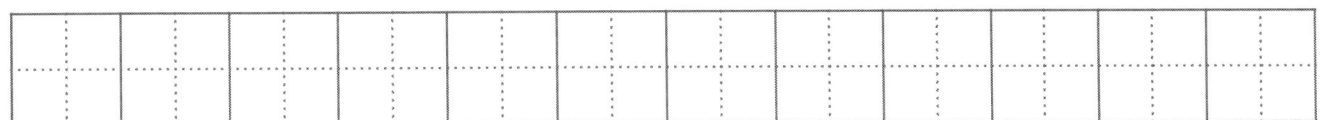

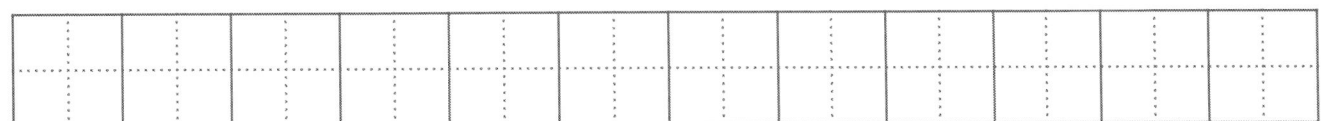

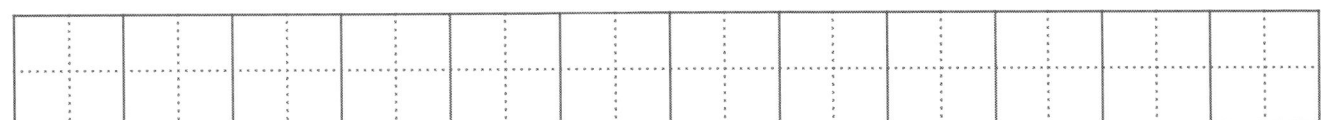

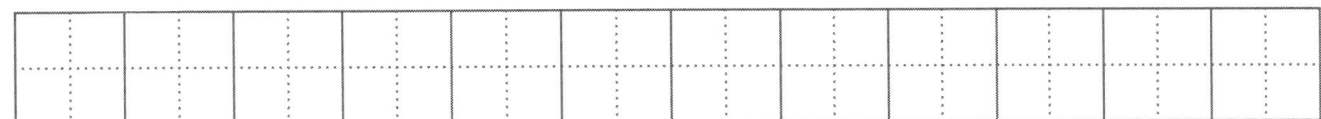

49

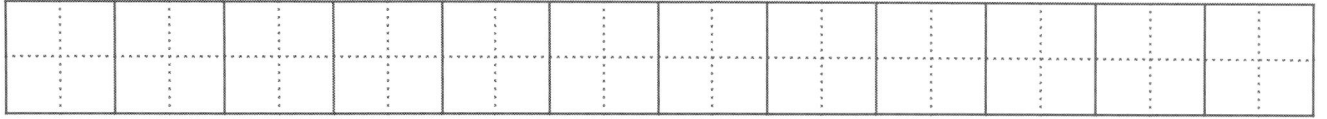
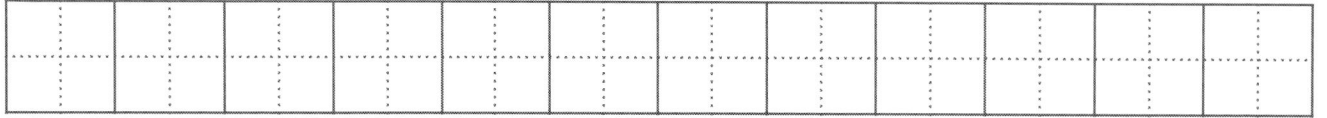

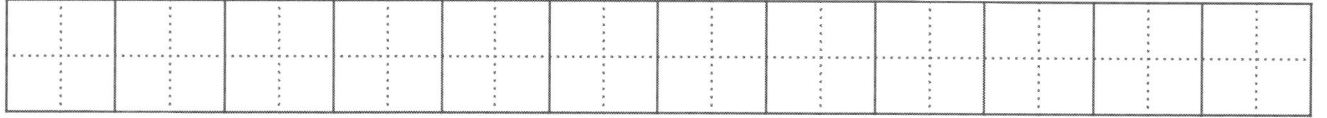
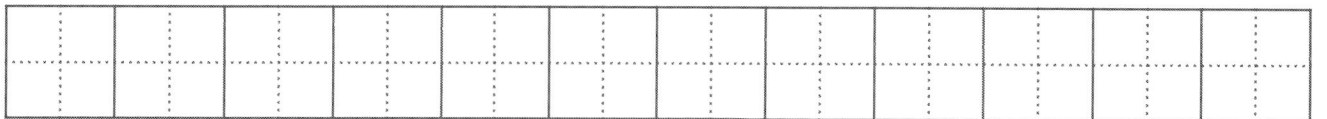
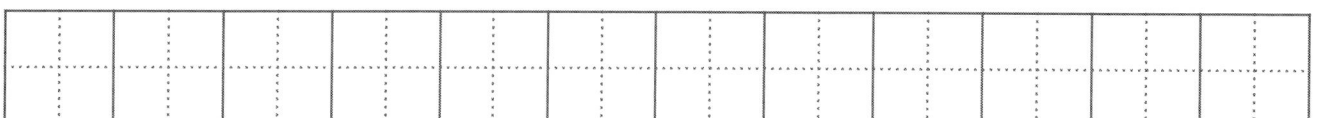
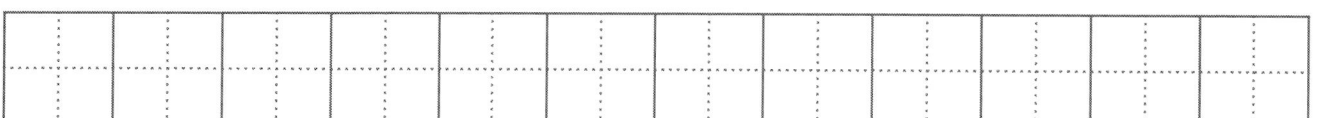
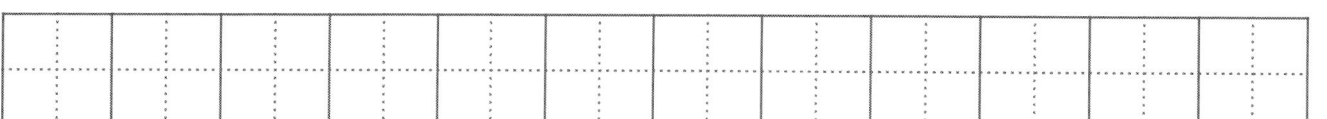
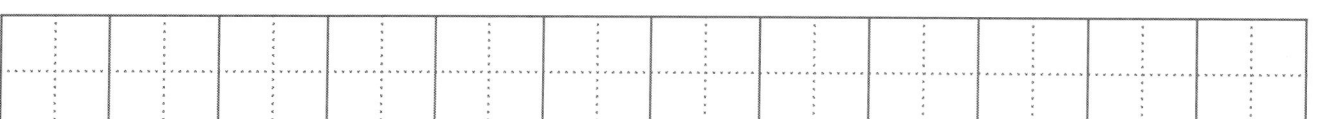
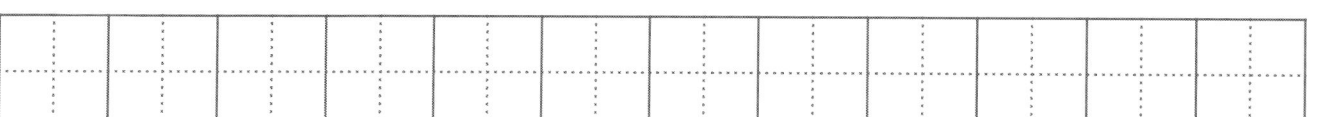
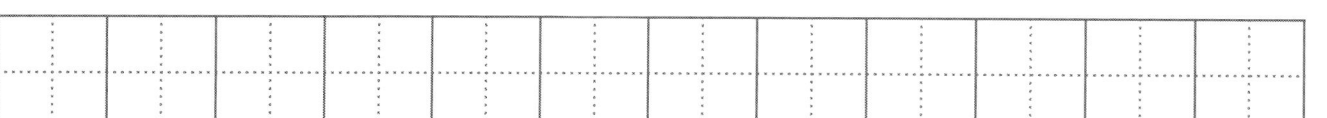
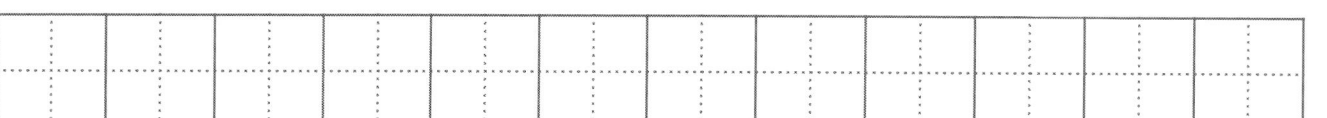

近墨者黑

近墨者黑

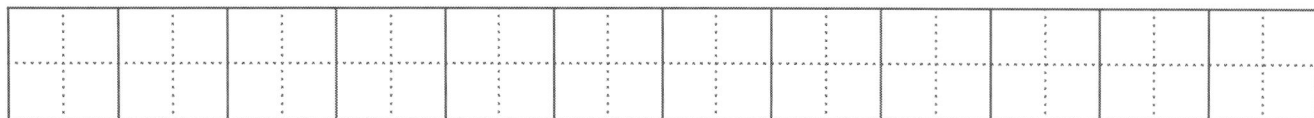
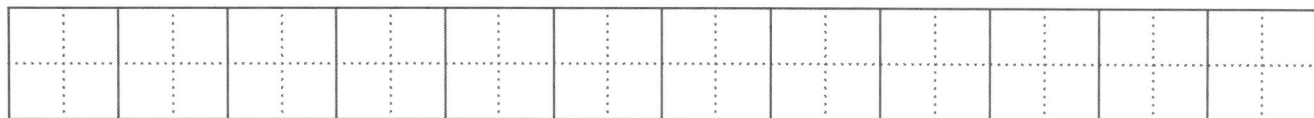
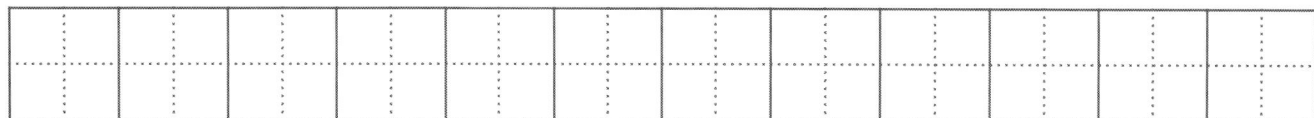
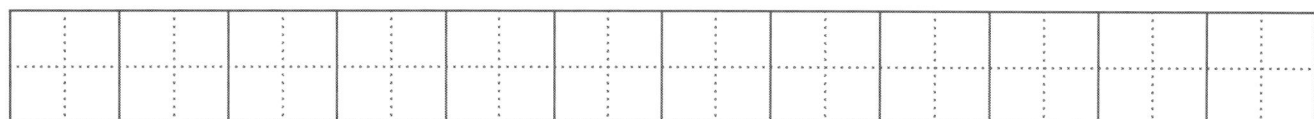
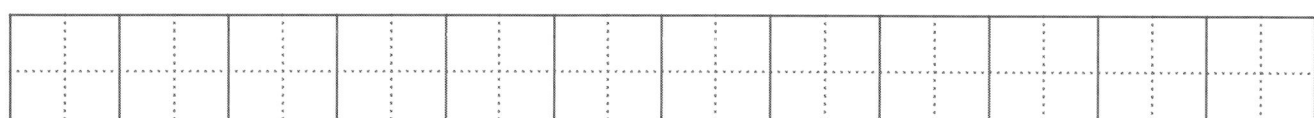
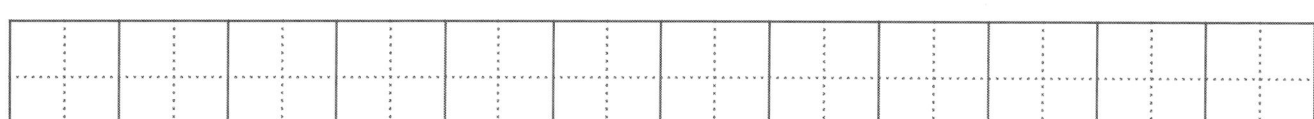
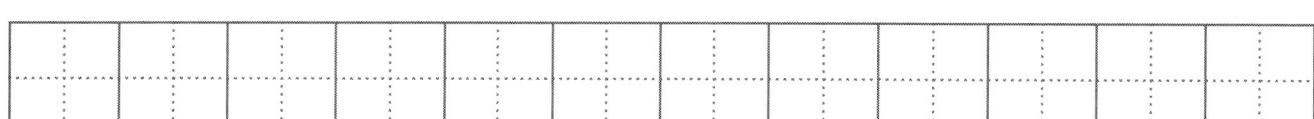
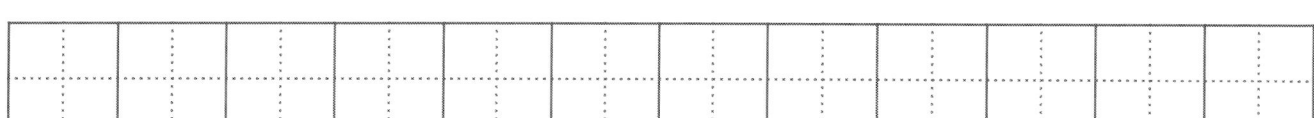
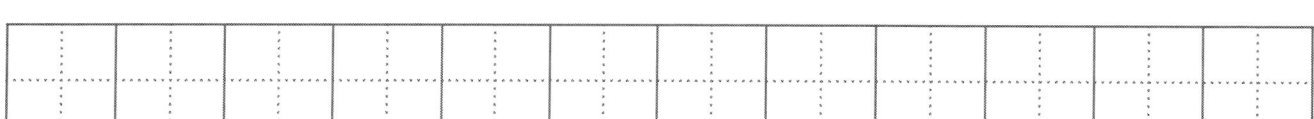
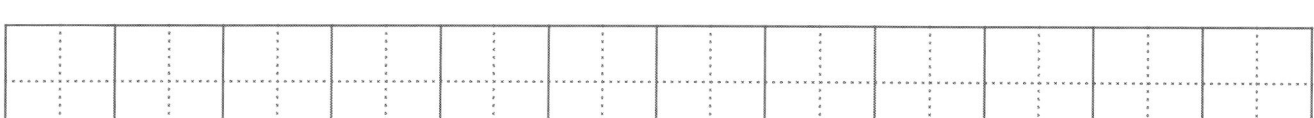
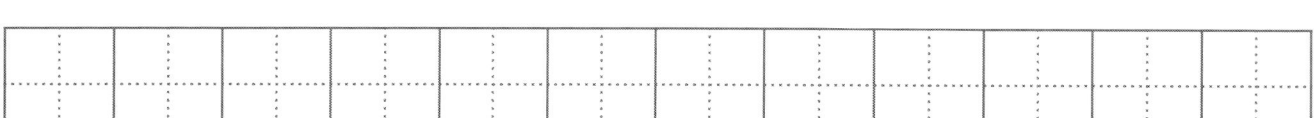
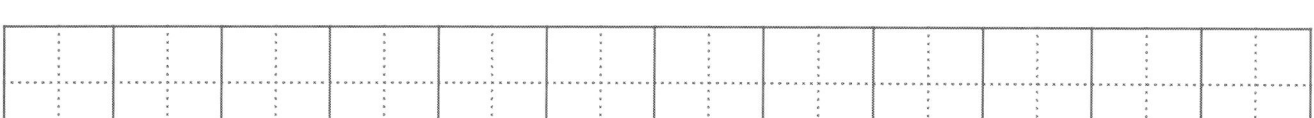

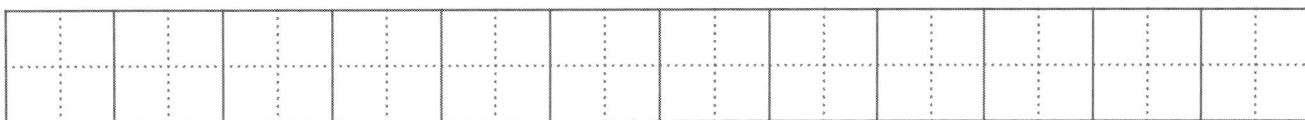

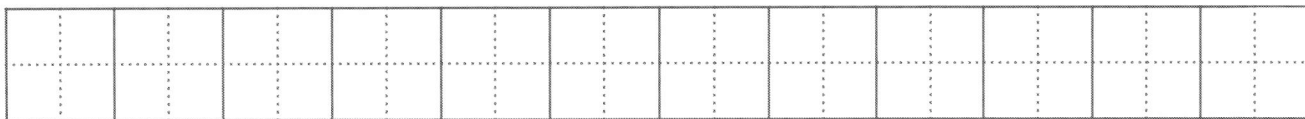

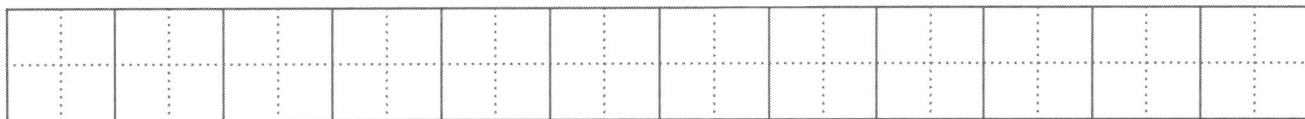

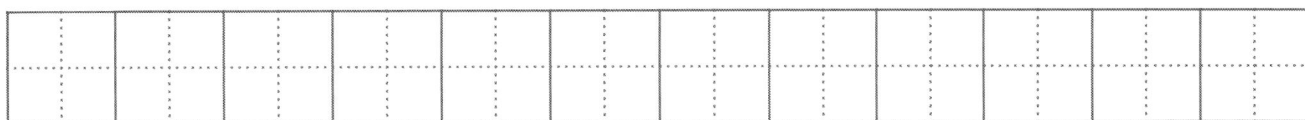

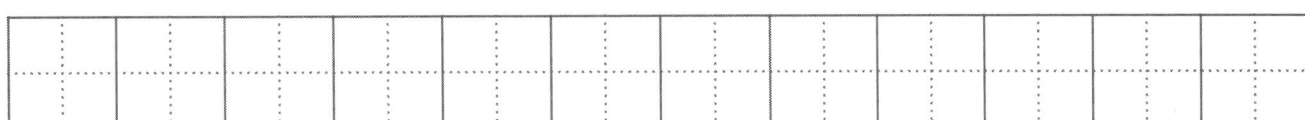

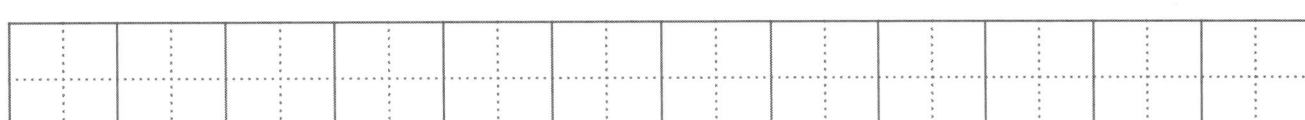

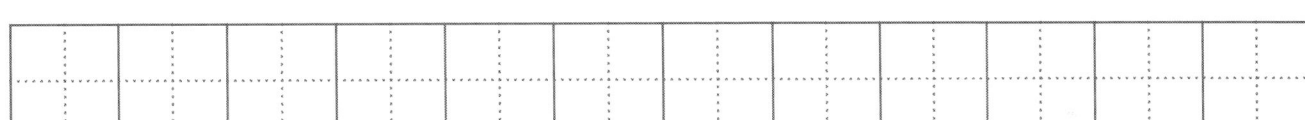

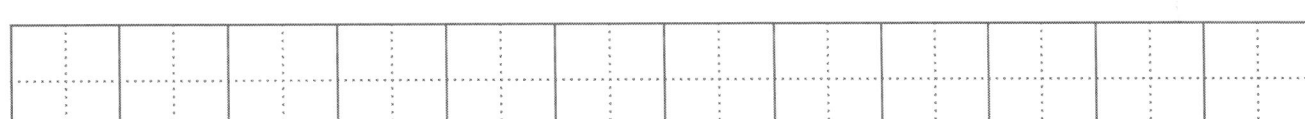

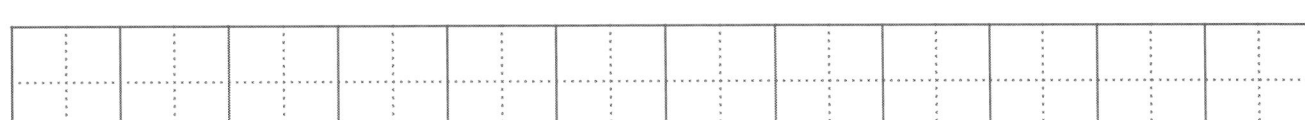

近墨者黑

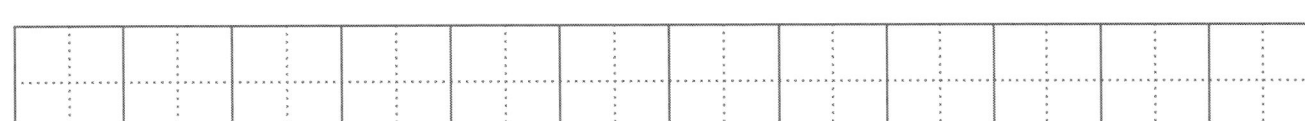

qīng chū yú lán　　　ér shèng yú lán

青 出 于 蓝 ， 而 胜 于 蓝 。

The color blue is made out of indigo but is more vivid than indigo.
- The student surpasses the master.

言必信，行必果！

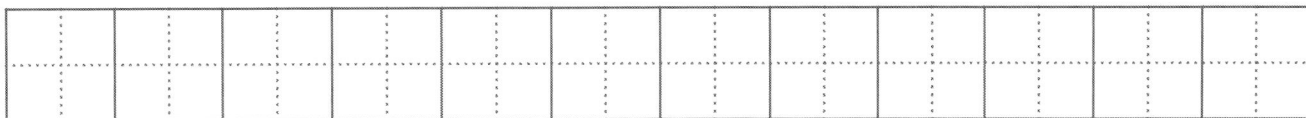

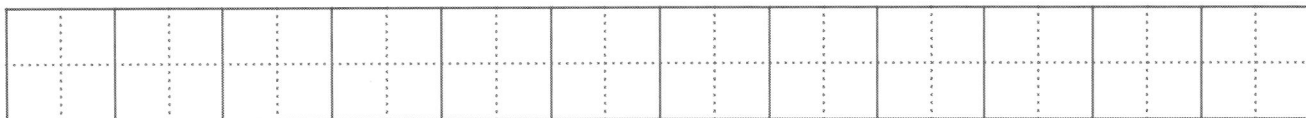

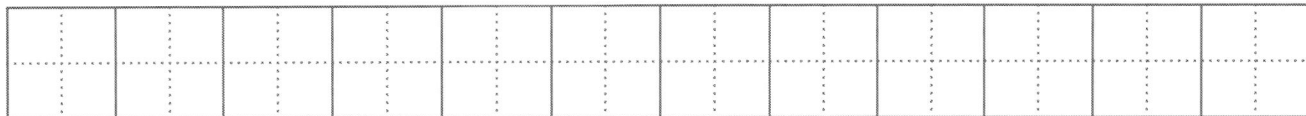

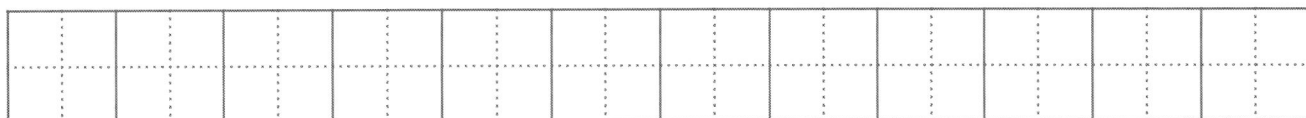

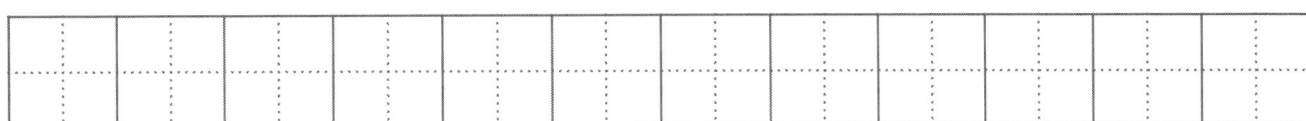

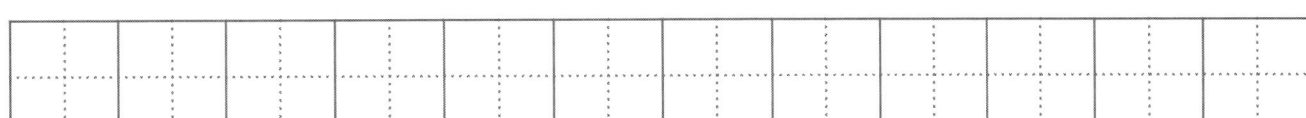

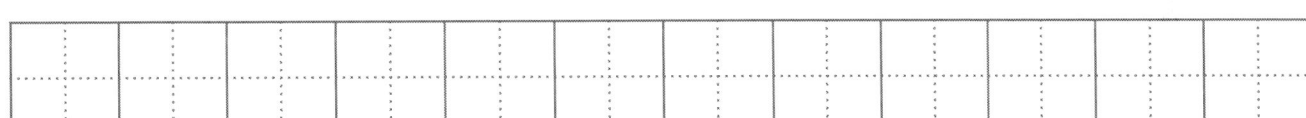

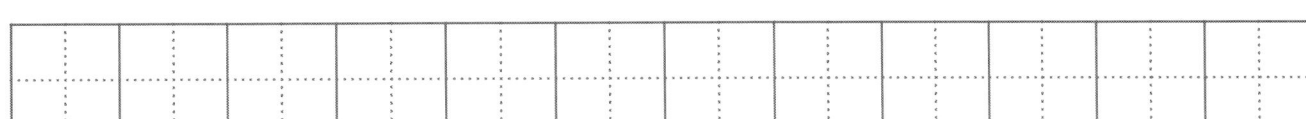

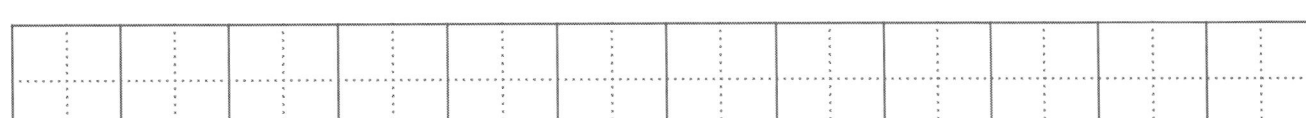

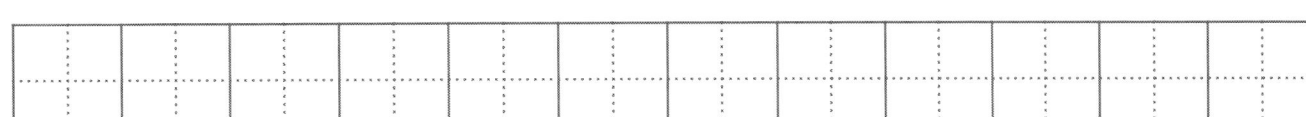

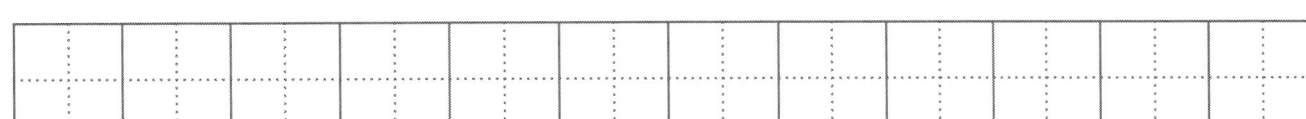

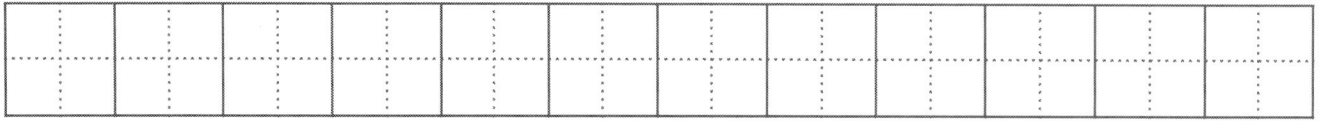

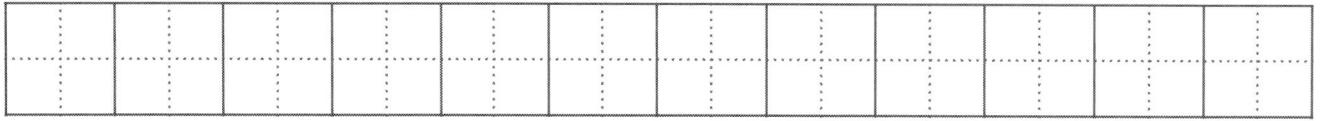

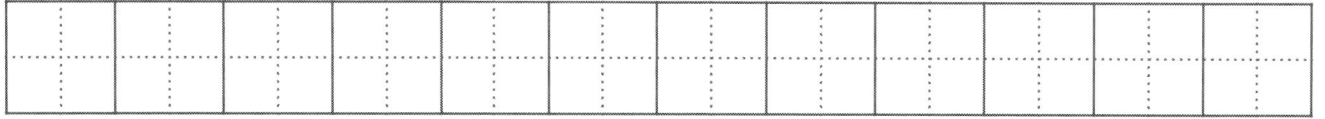

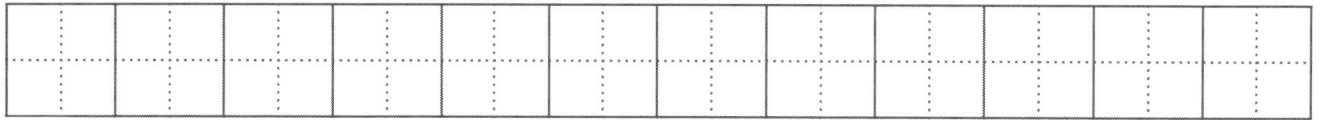

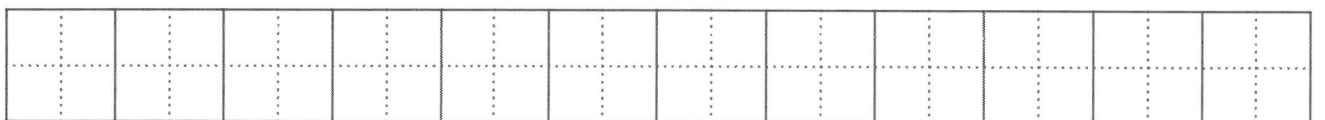

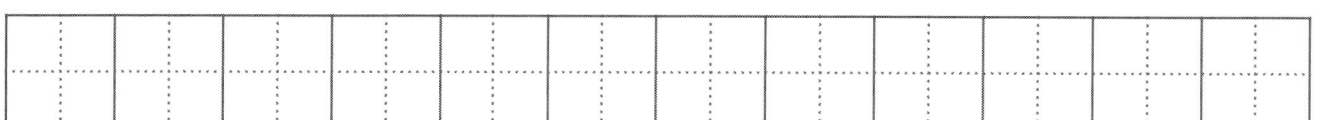

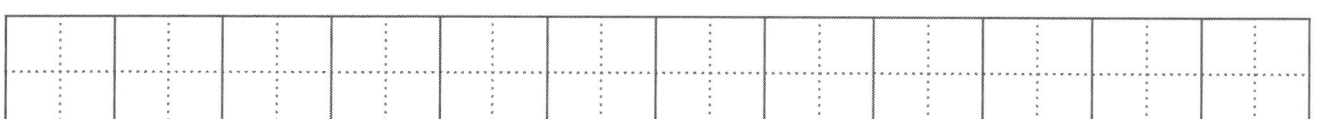

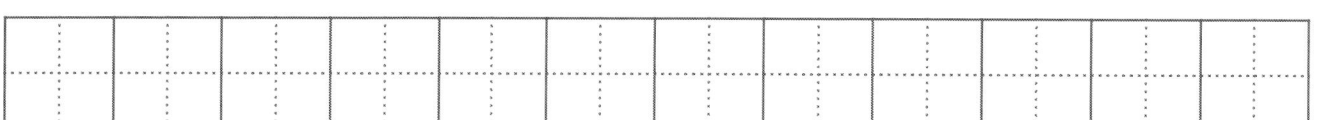

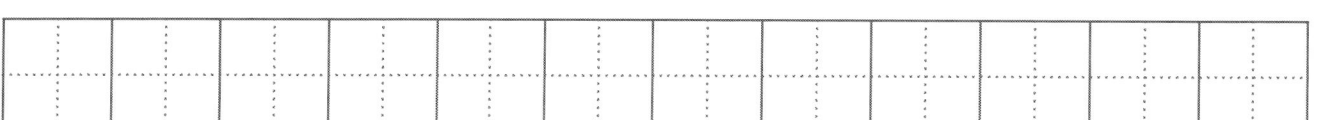

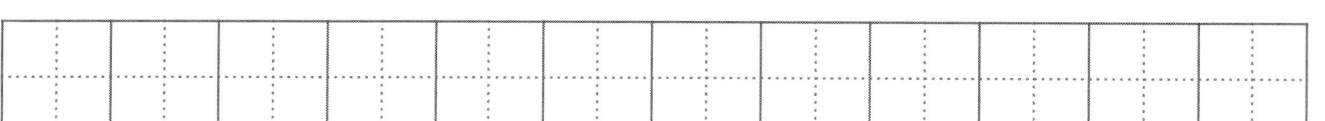

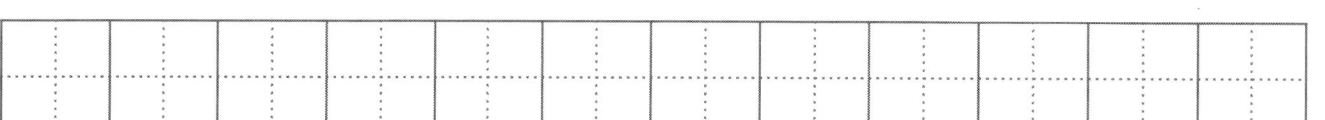

青出于蓝

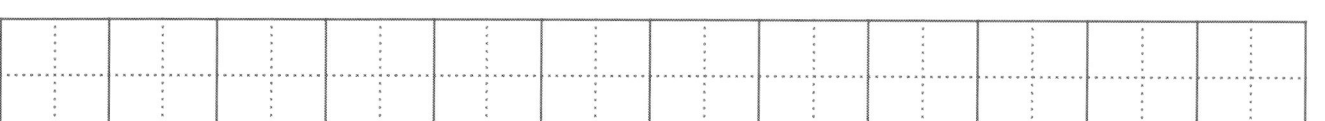

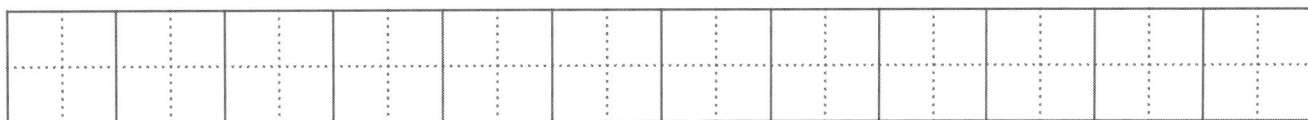
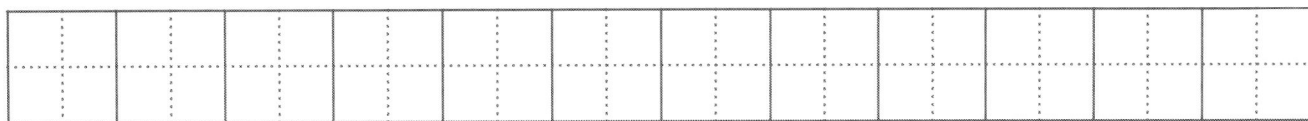
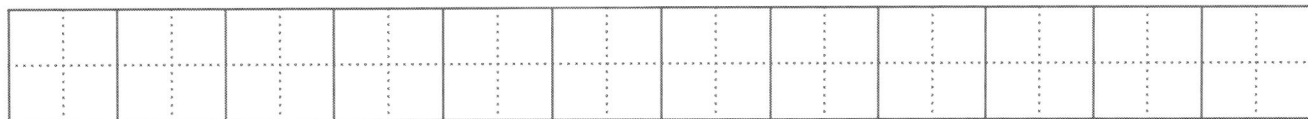
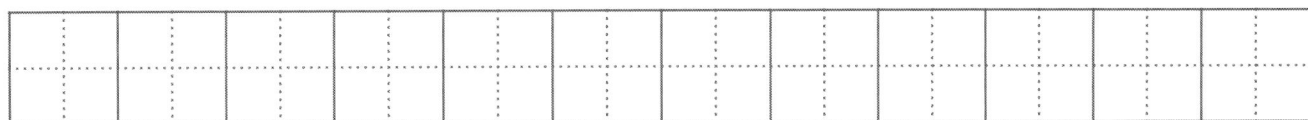
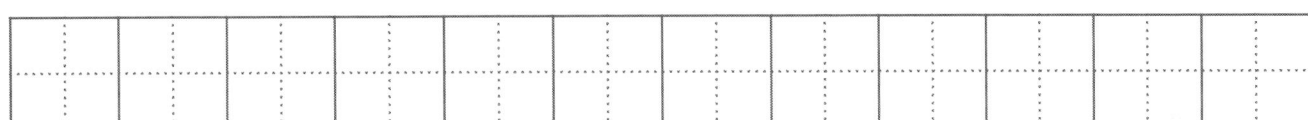
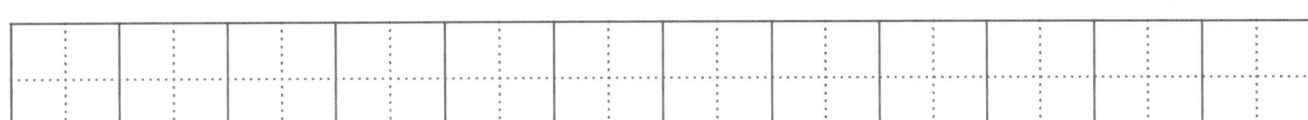
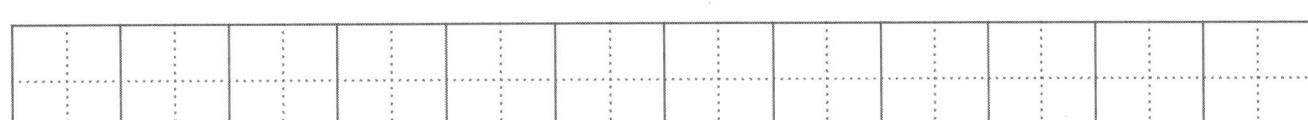

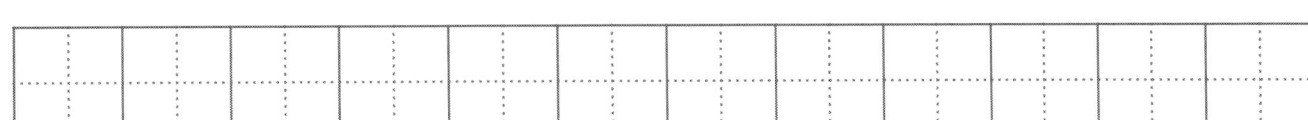

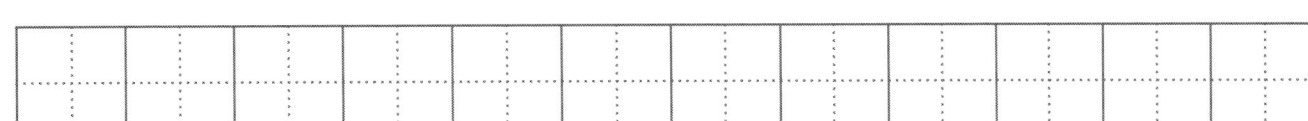

而胜于蓝

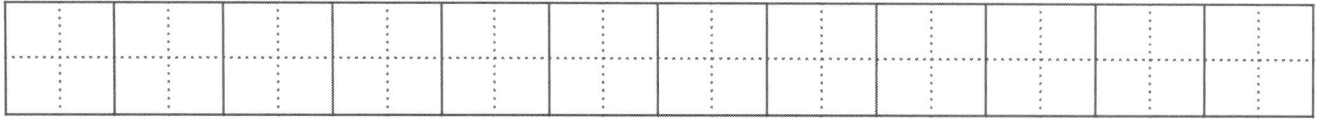
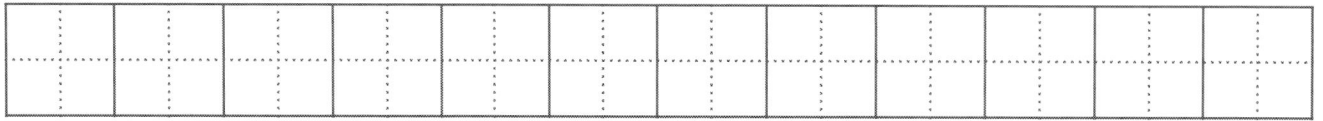
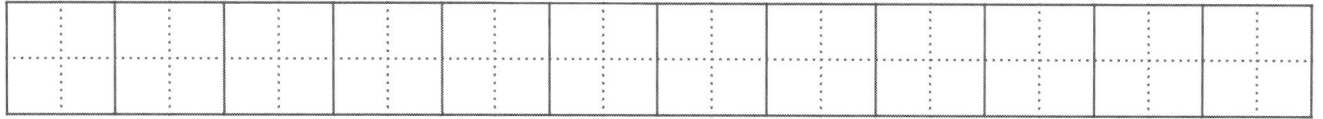
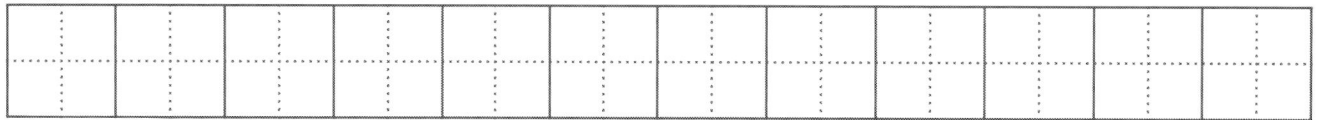
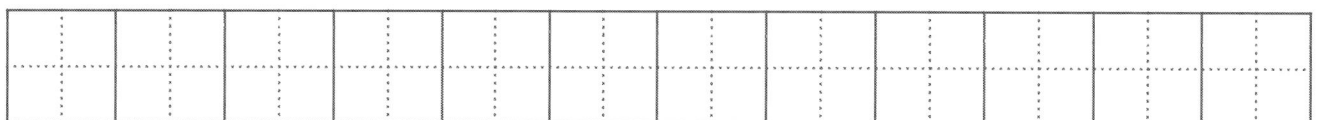
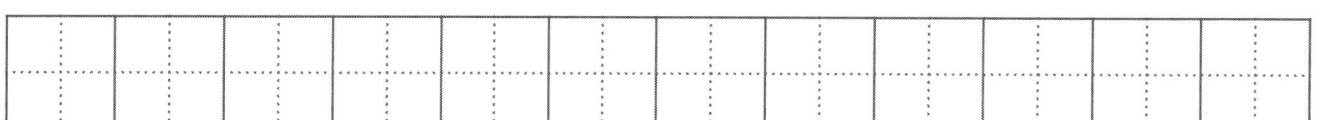
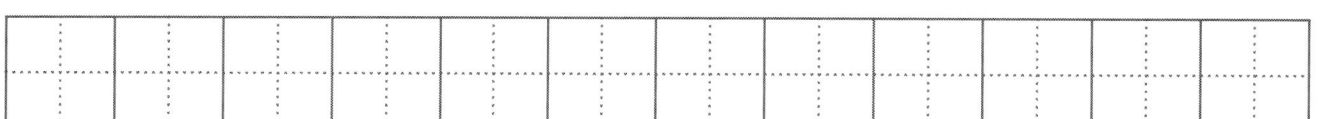
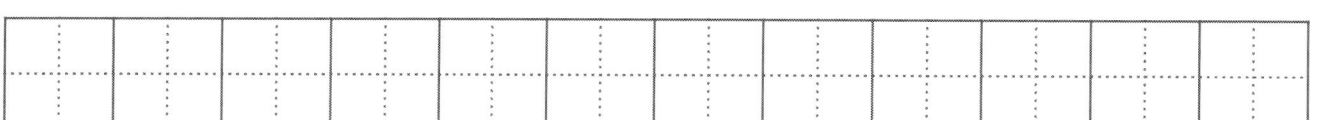
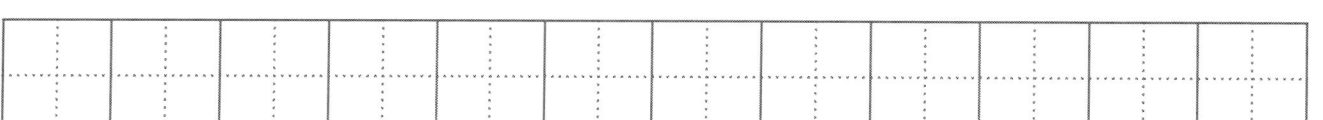
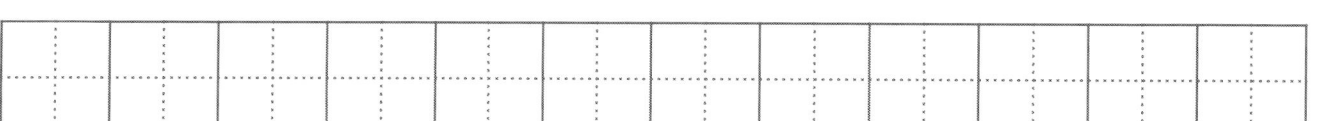
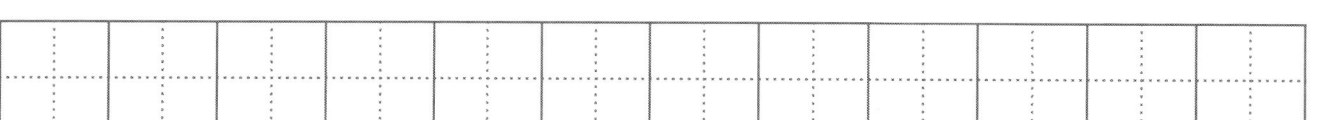
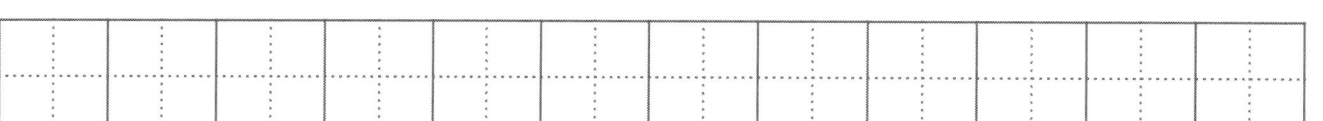

青 出 于 蓝

而胜于蓝

而胜于蓝

海 纳 百 川 ， 有 容 乃 大 。

The vastness of the ocean comes from
its accepting of thousands of rivers.
- A wise man listens to all sides.

人无远虑，必有近忧。

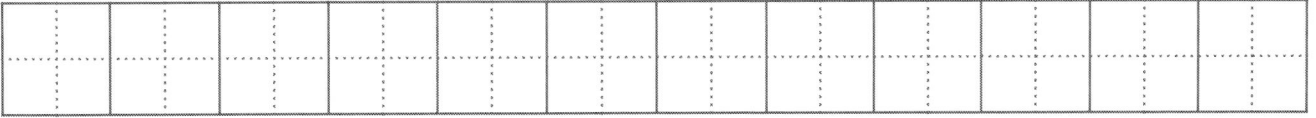

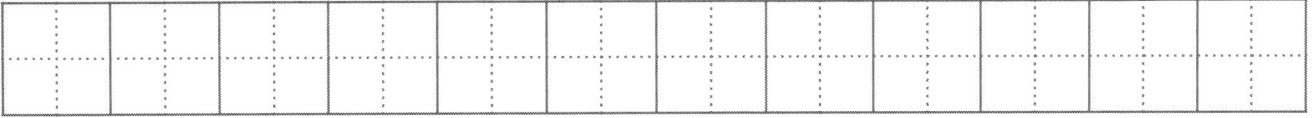

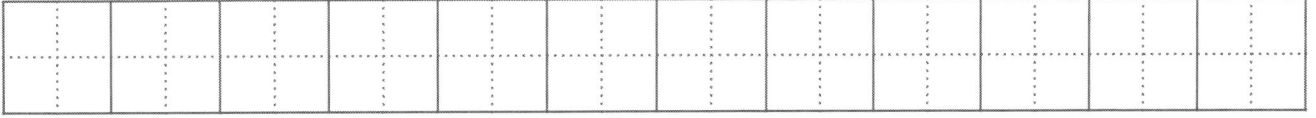

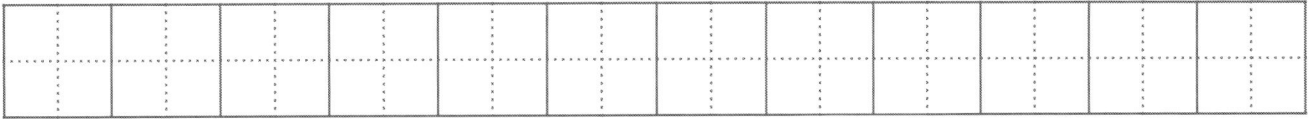

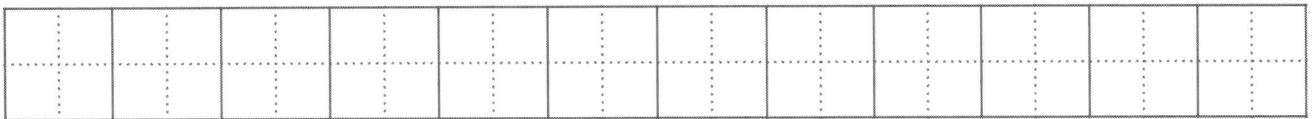

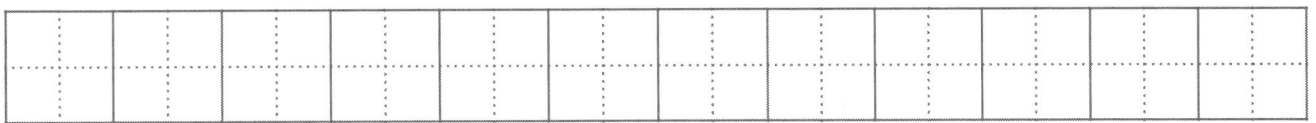

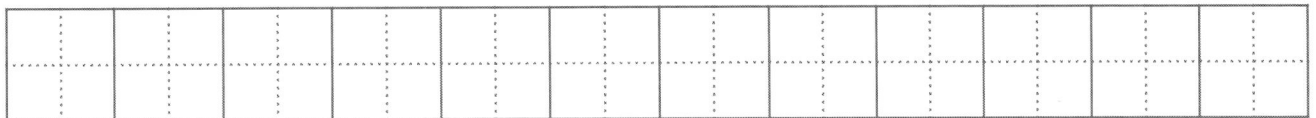

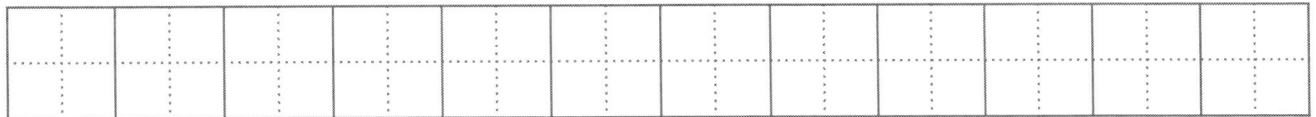

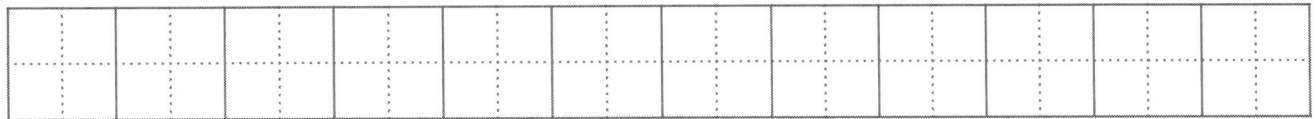

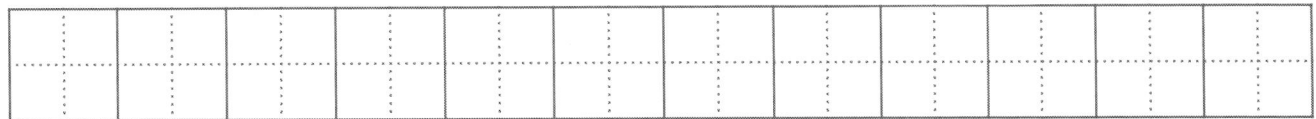

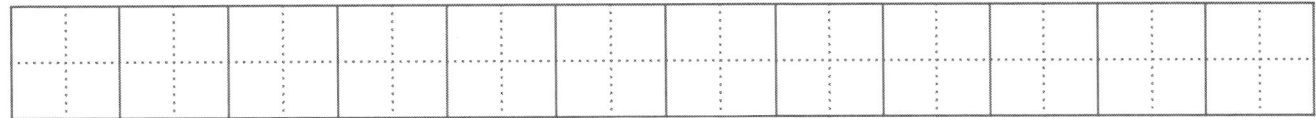

61

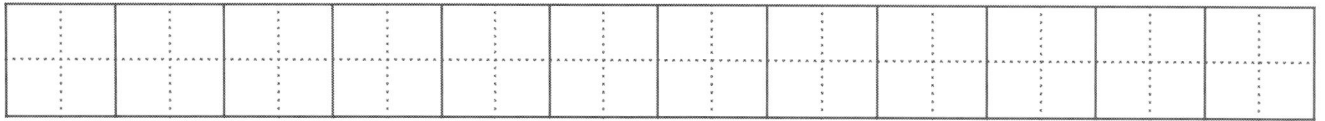
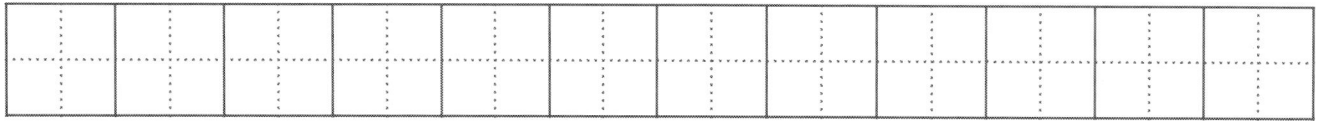
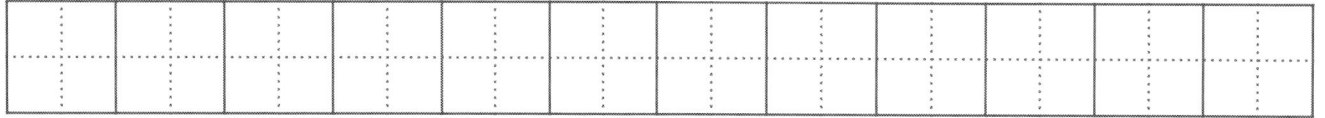
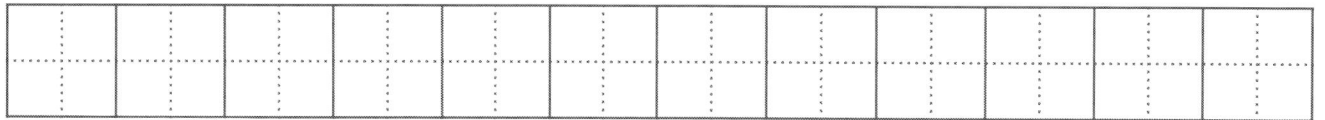
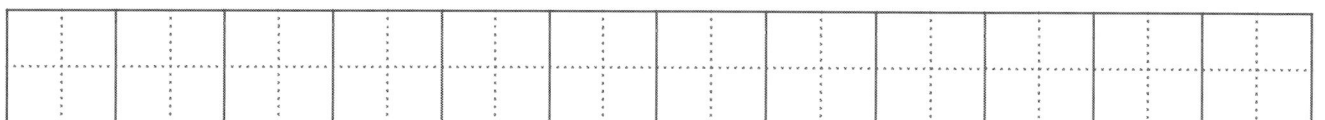
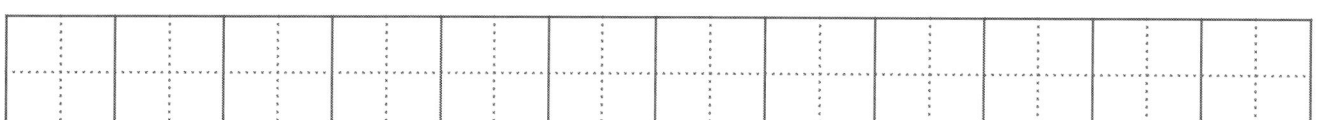

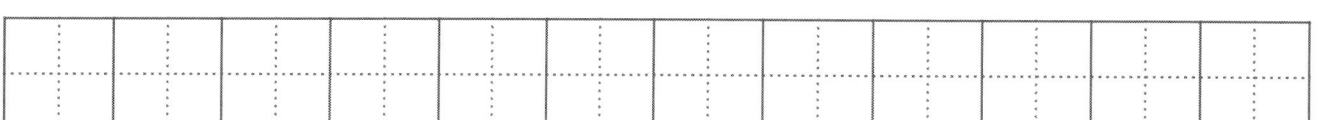
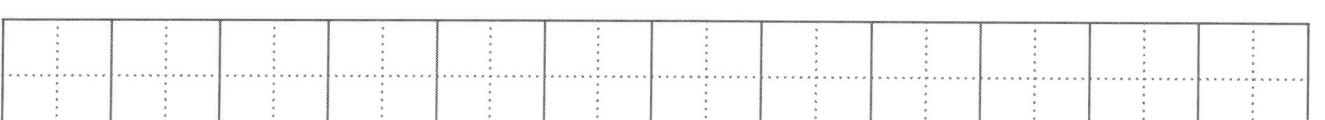
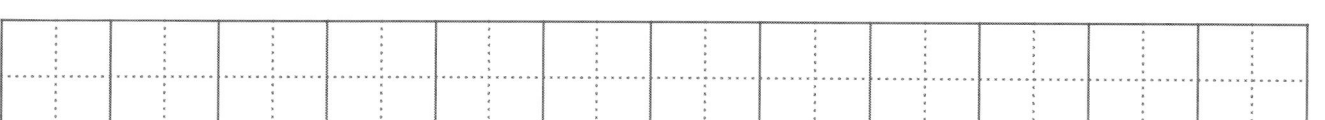
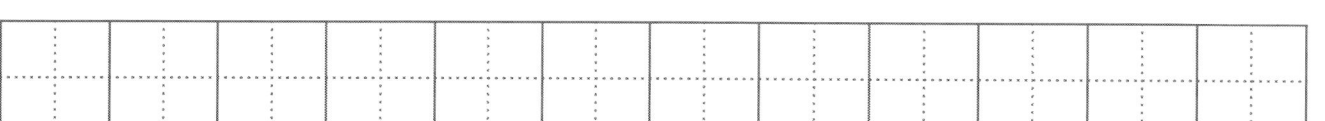
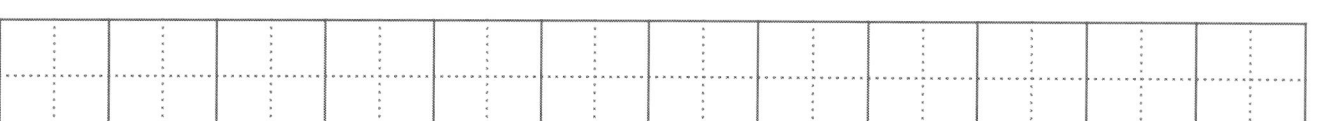

有容乃大

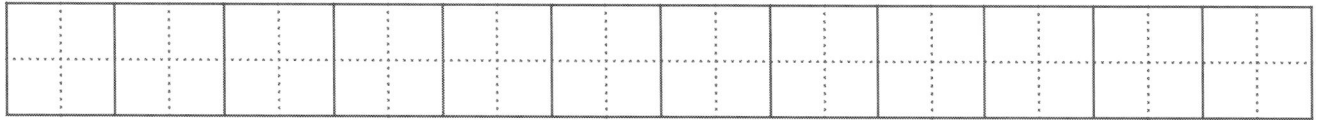

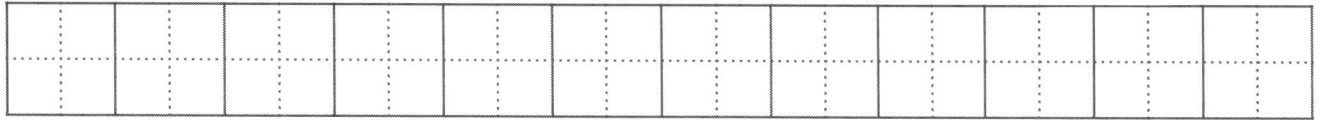

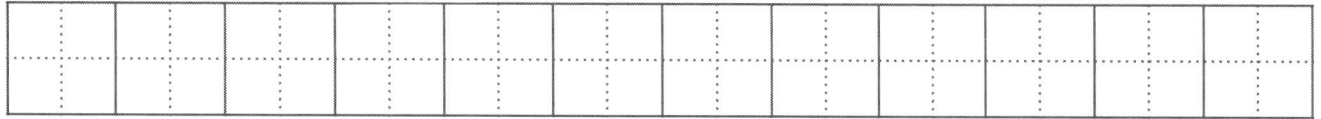

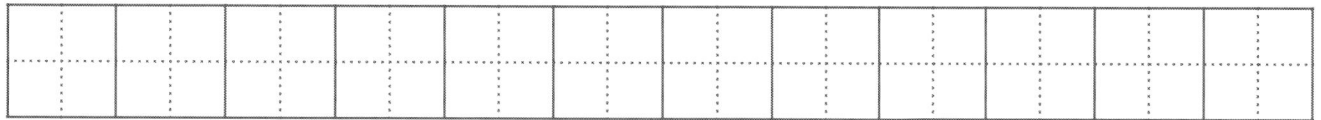

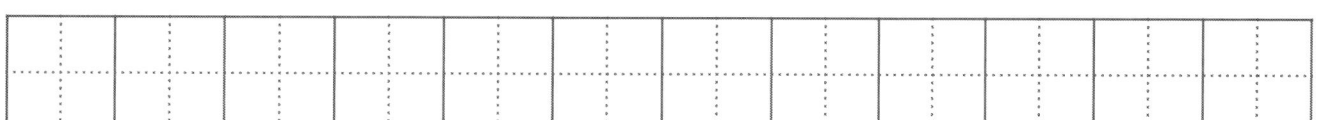

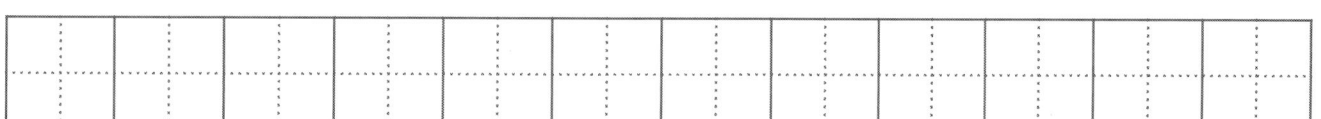

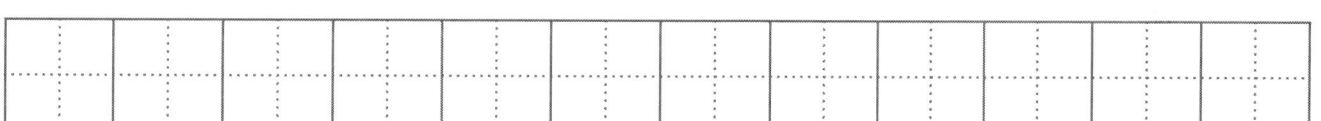

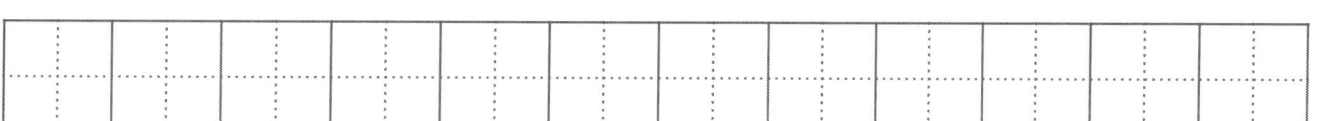

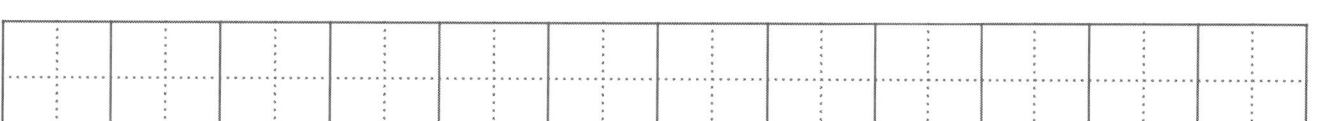

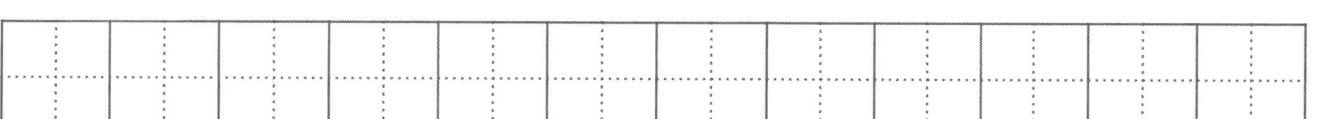

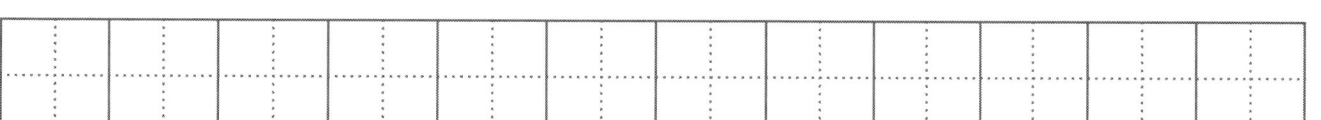

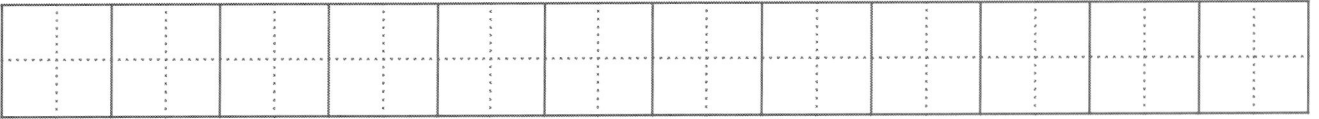
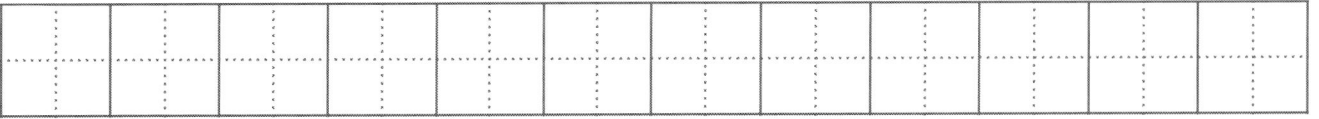
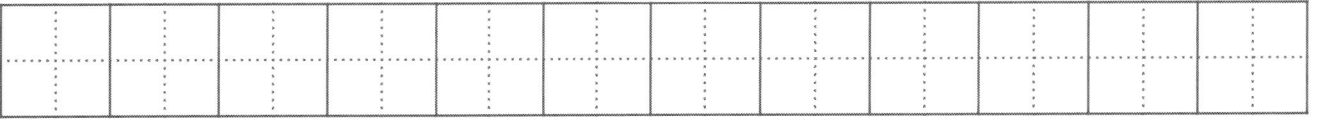
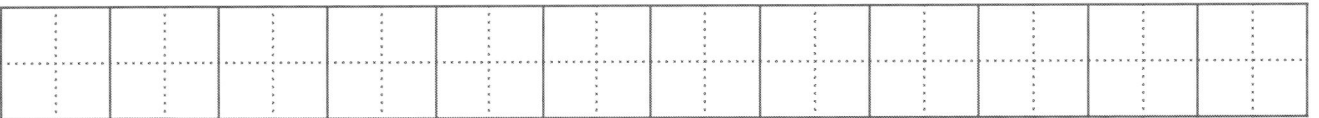
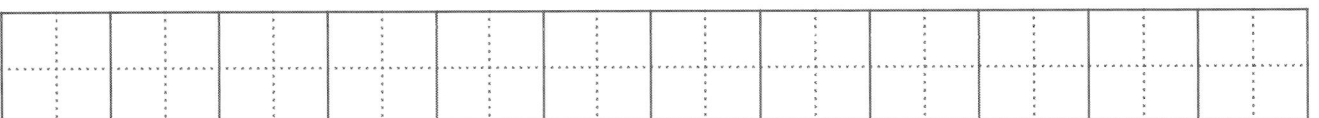
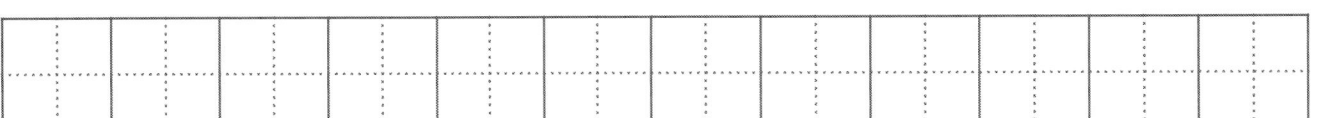
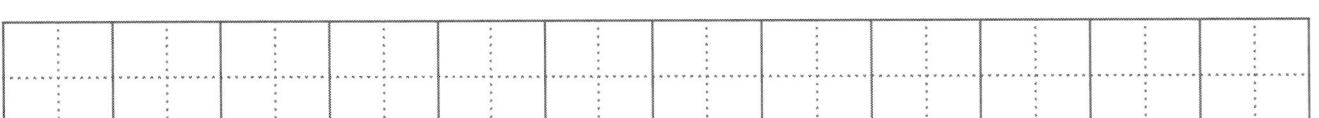
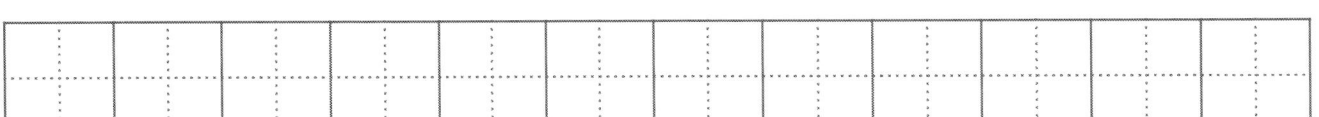
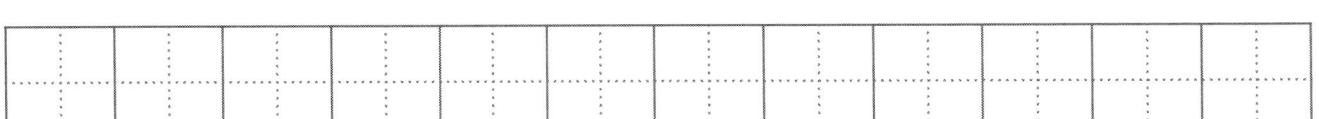
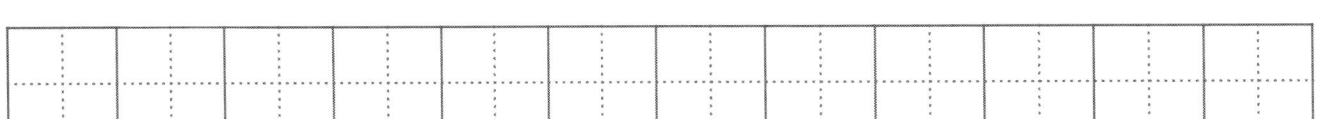
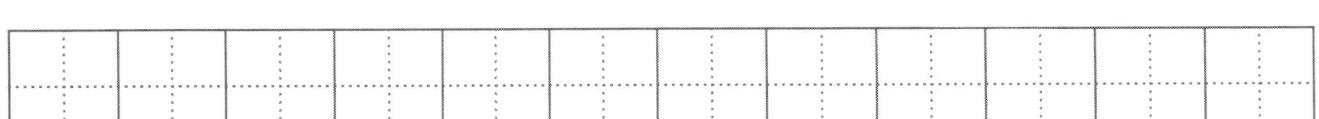
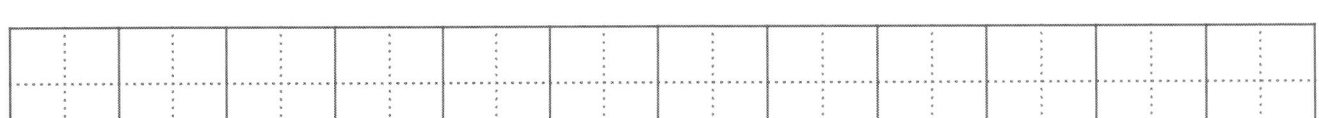

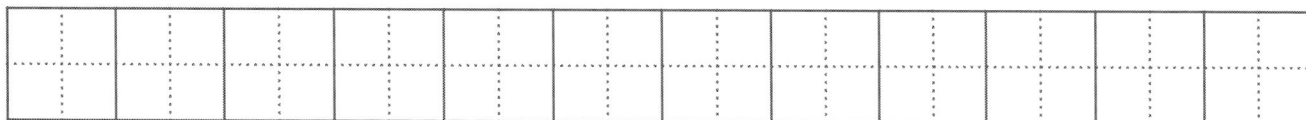

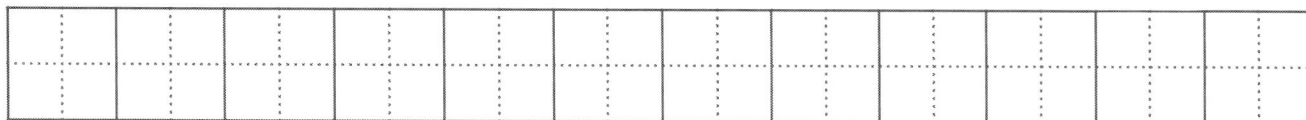

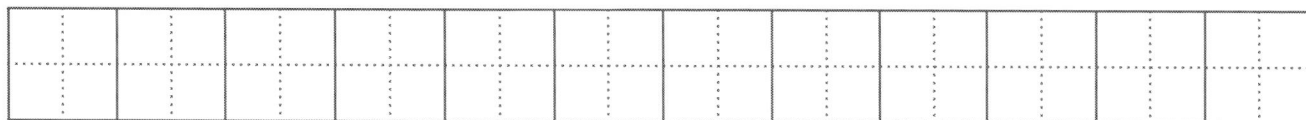

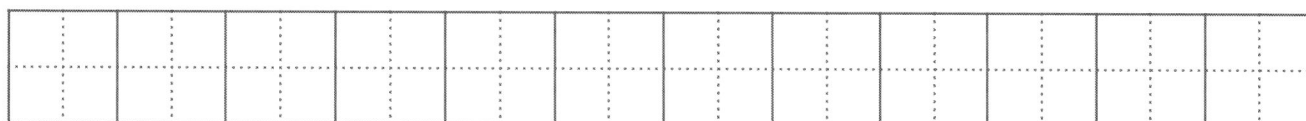

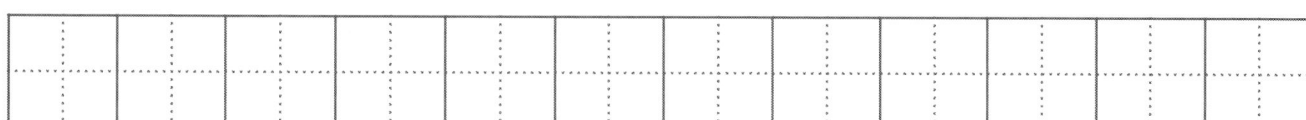

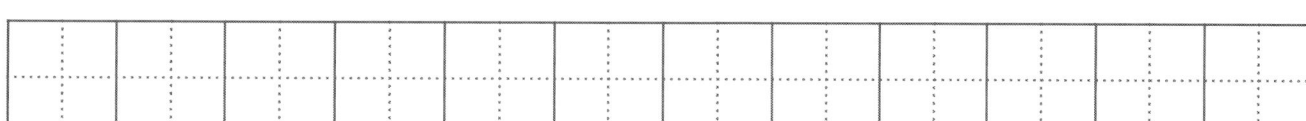

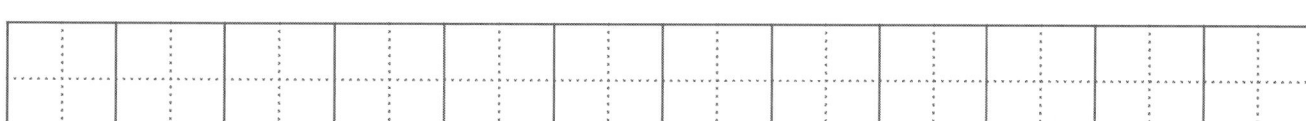

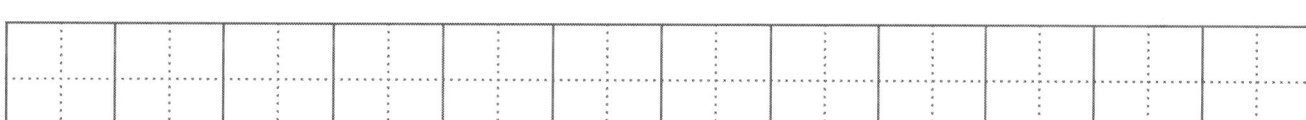

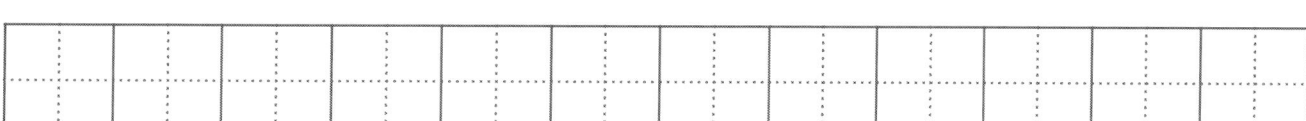

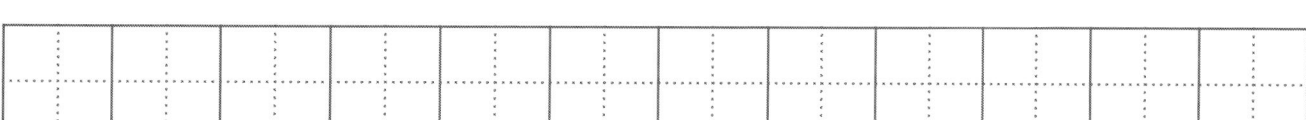

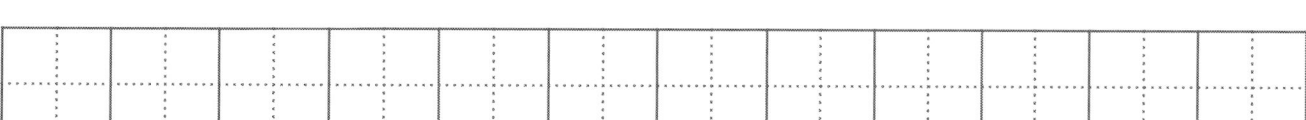

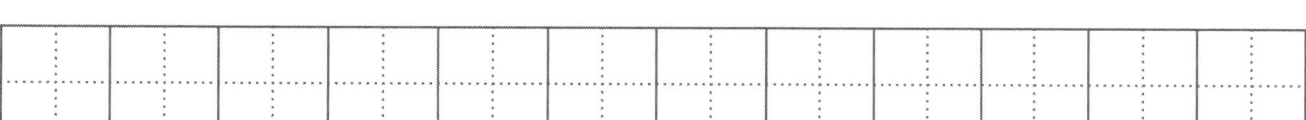

shào	zhuàng	bù	nǔ	lì		lǎo	dà	tú	shāng	bēi	
少	壮	不	努	力	，	老	大	徒	伤	悲	。

If one does not exert oneself in youth,
one will regret it in old age.

天下兴亡，匹夫有责。

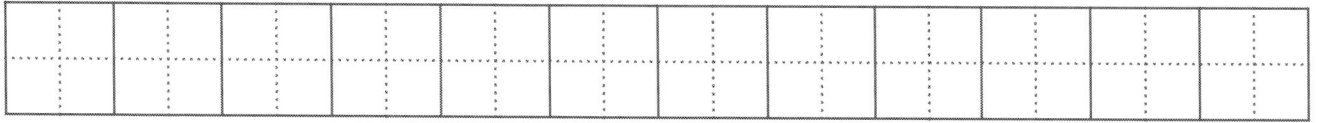

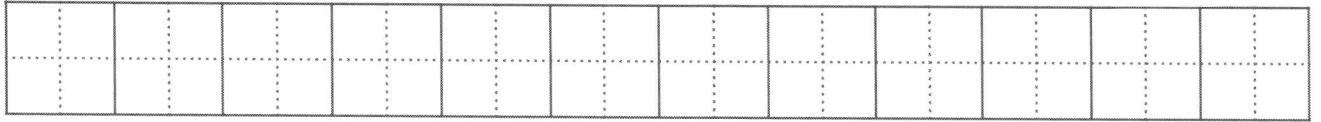

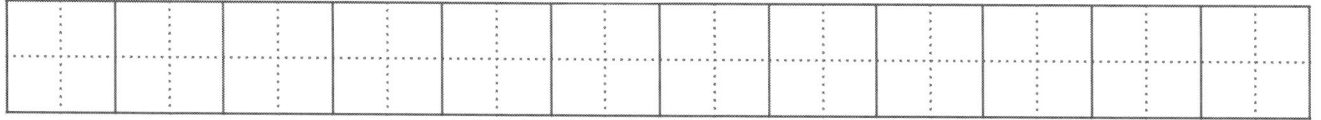

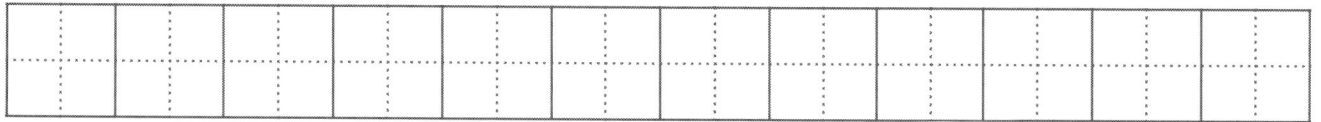

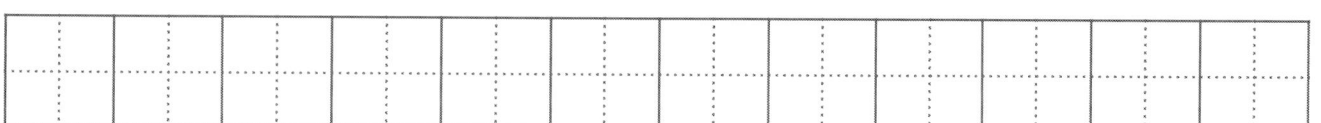

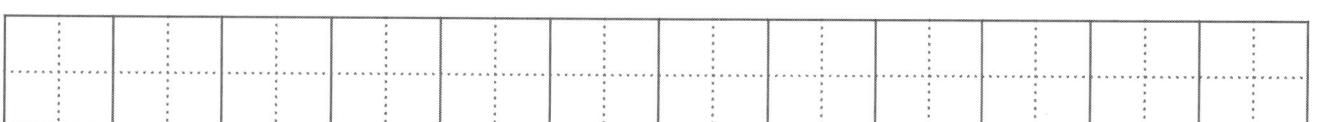

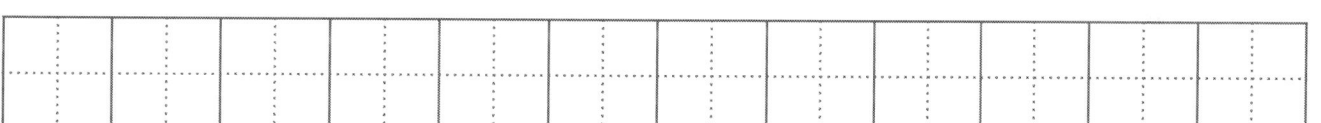

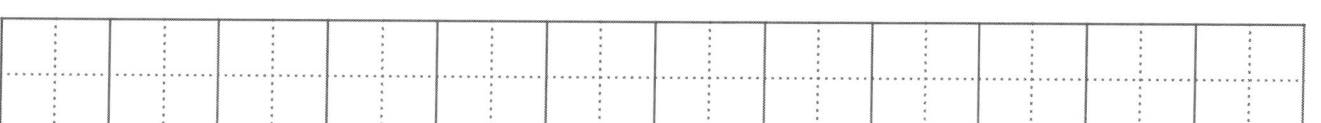

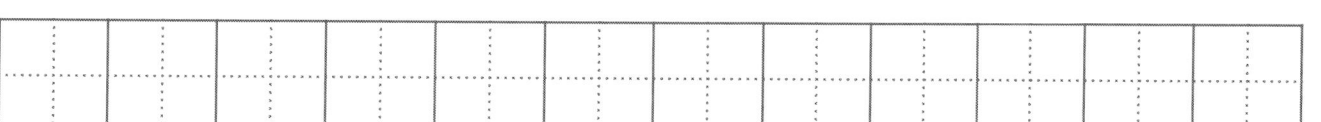

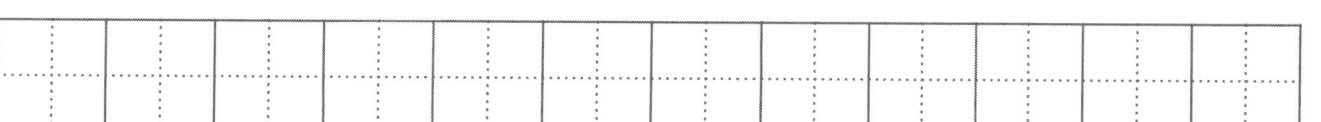

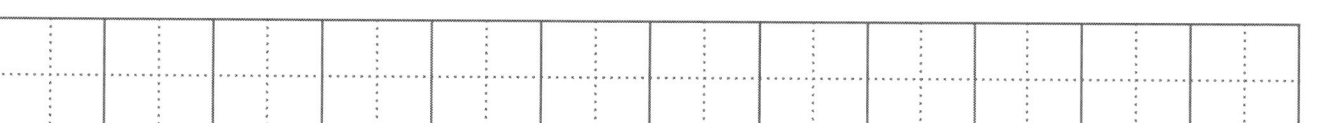

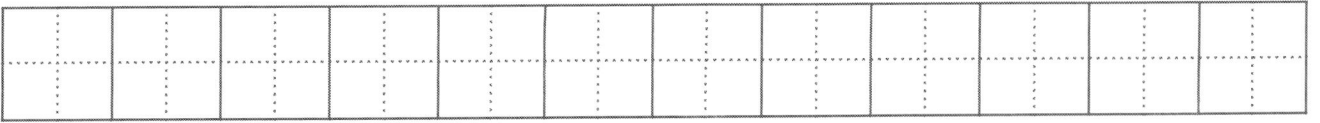

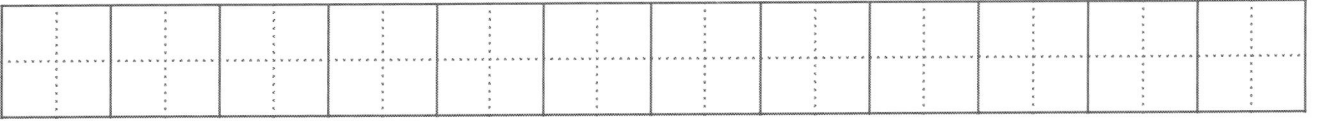

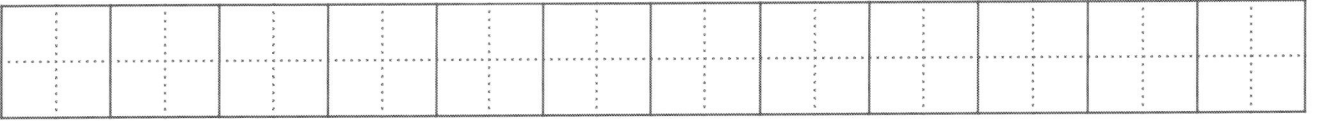

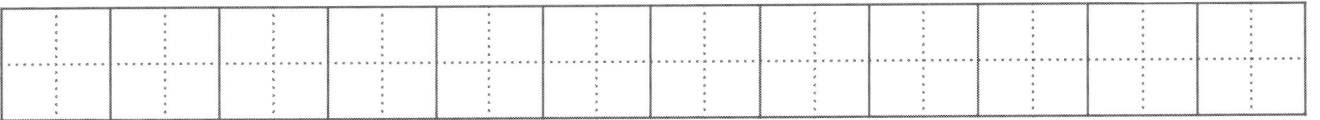

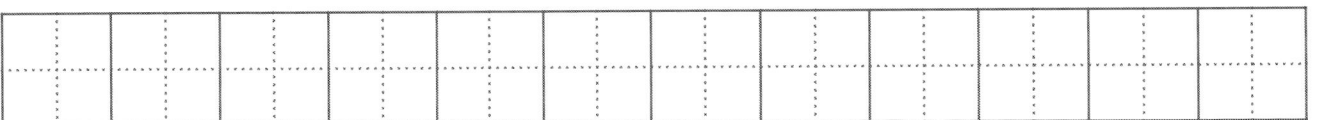

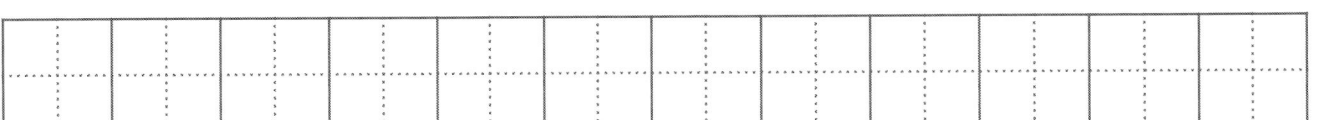

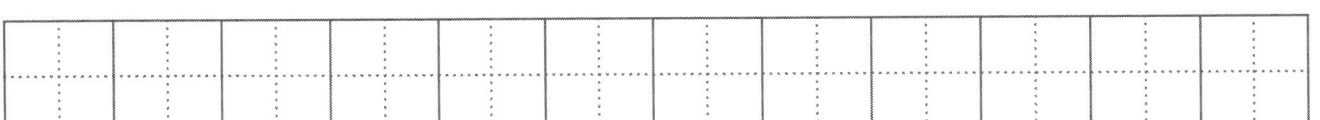

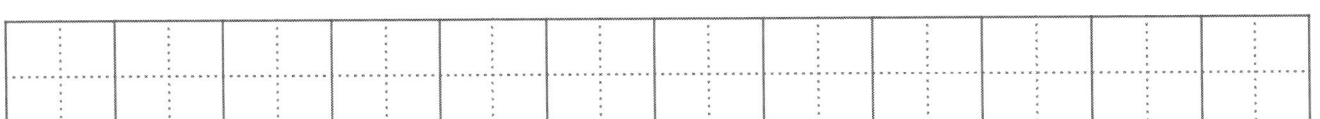

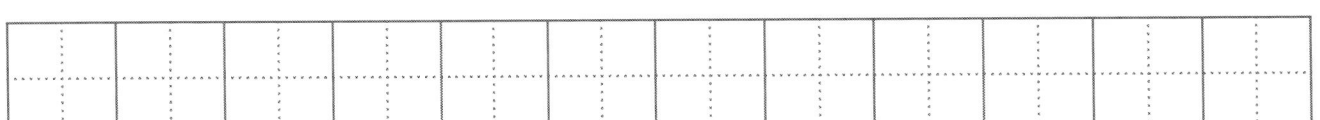

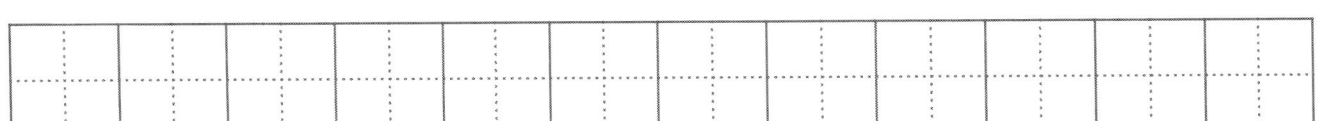

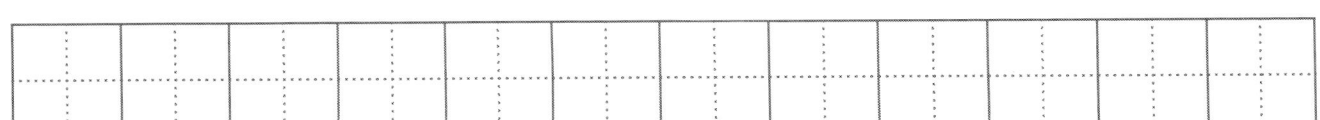

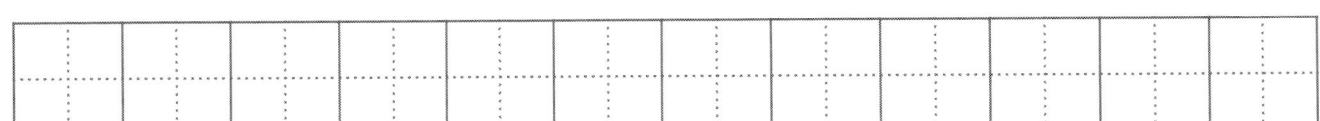

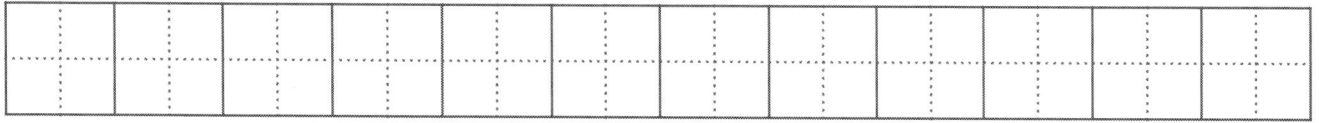

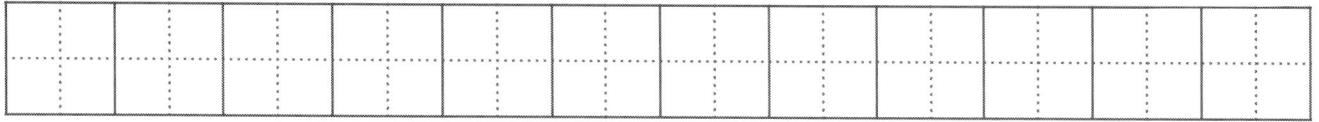

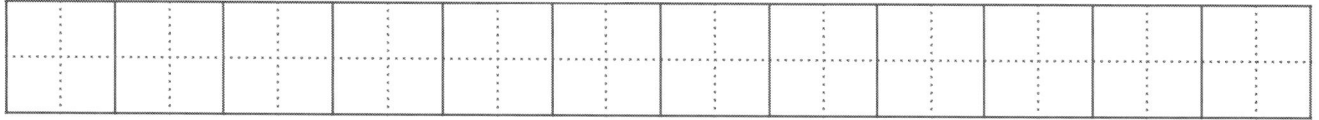

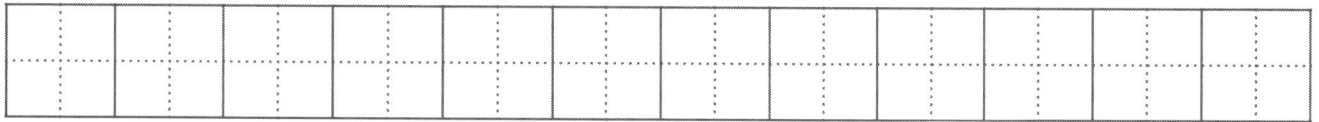

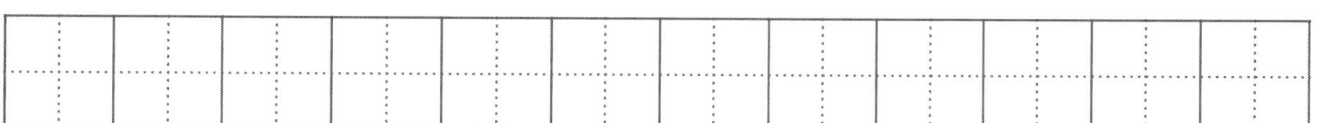

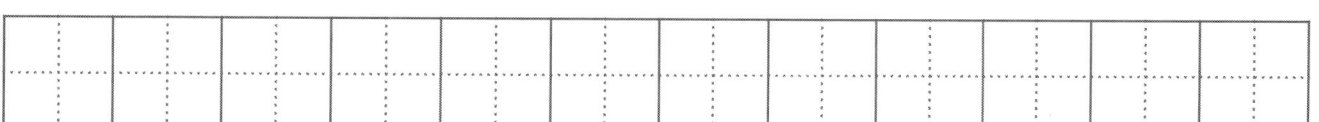

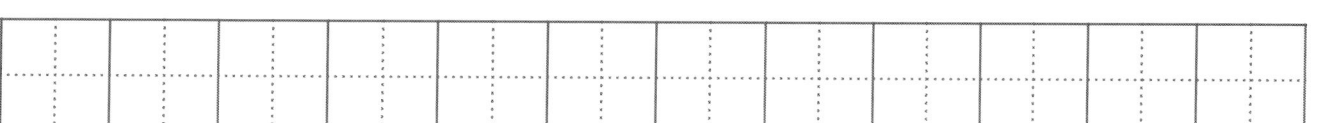

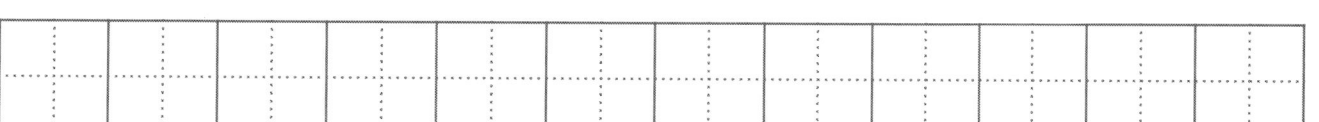

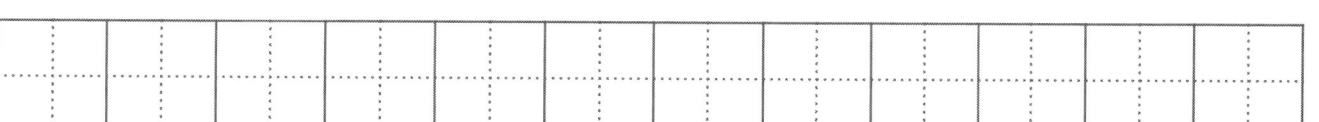

老大徒伤悲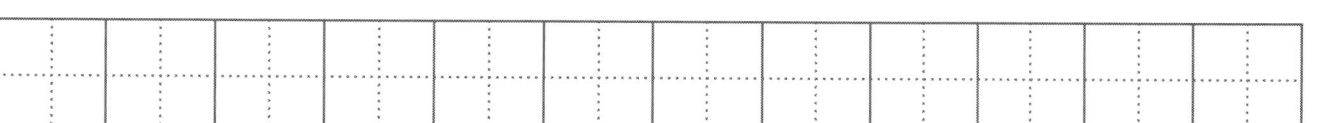

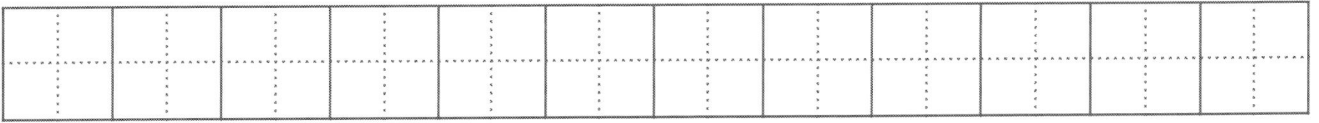
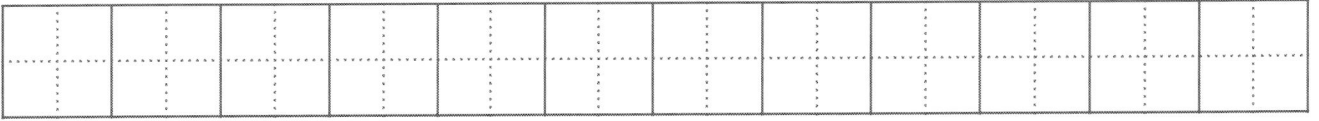
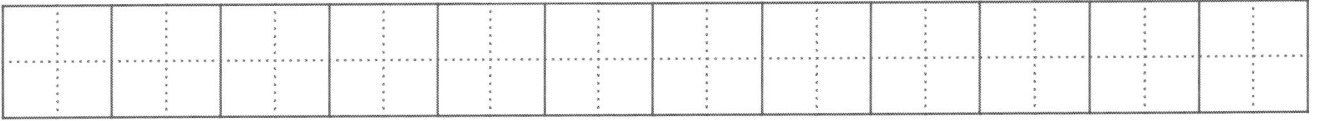
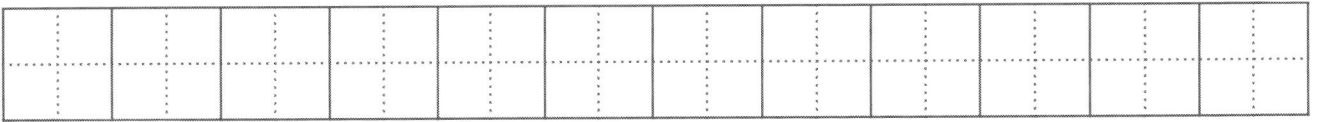
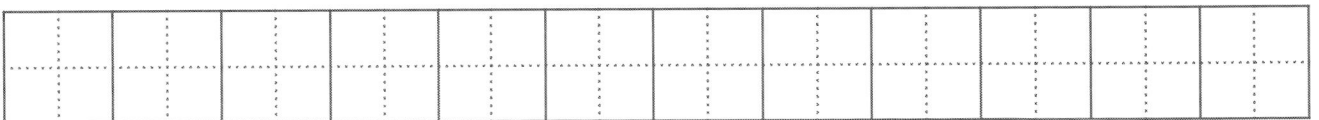
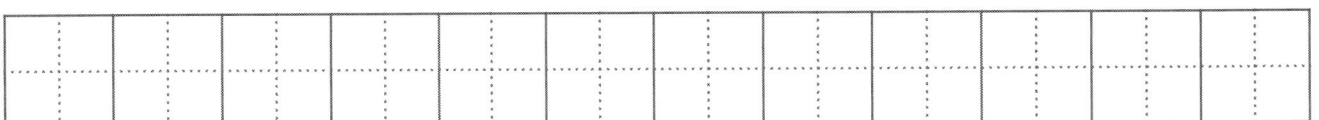
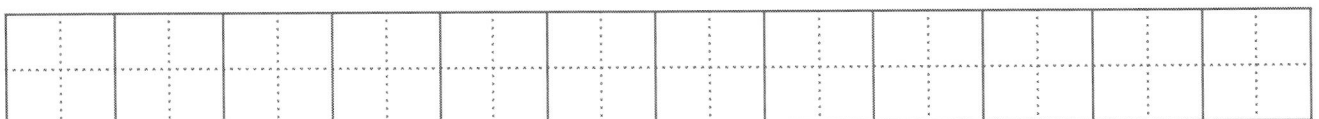
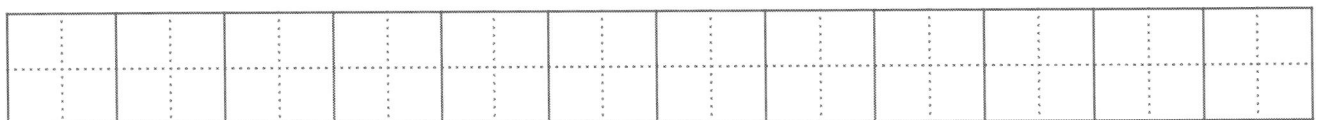
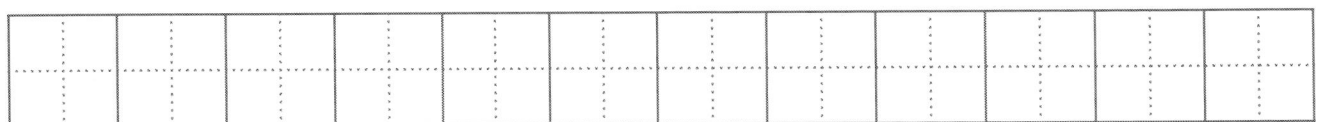

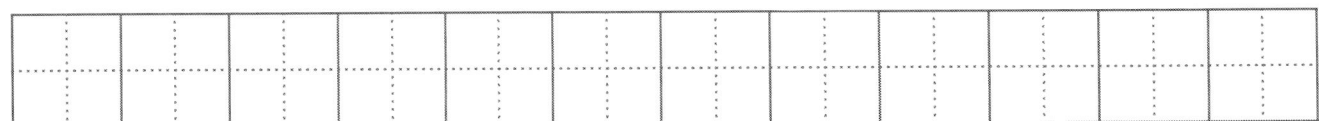
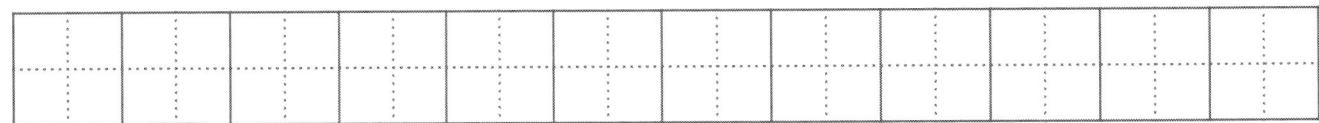

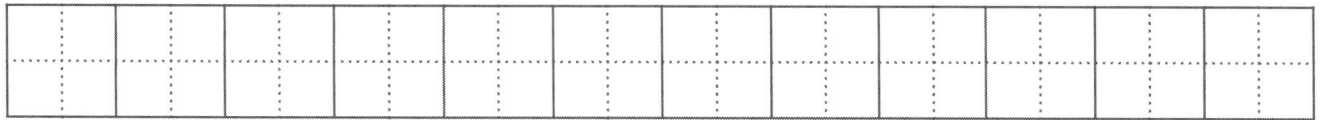
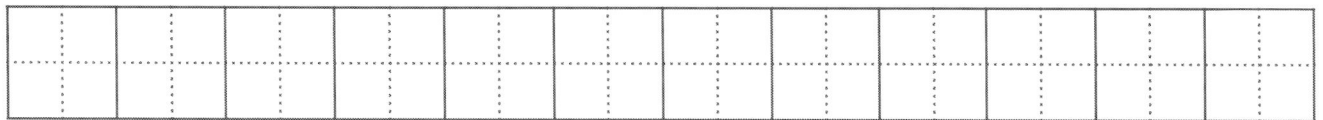
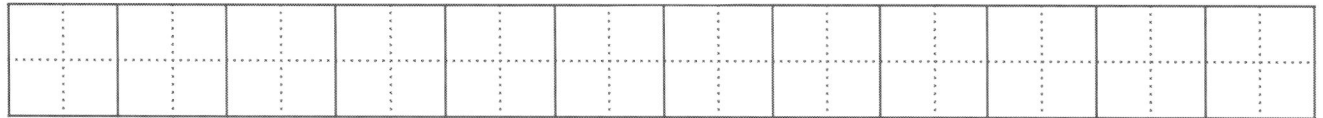
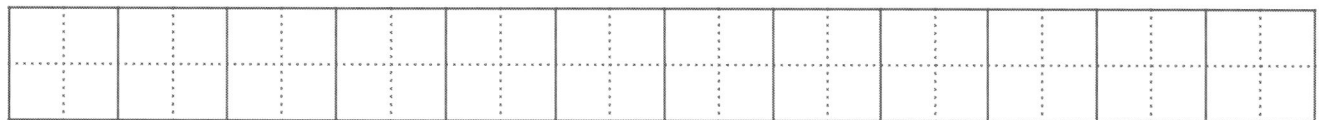
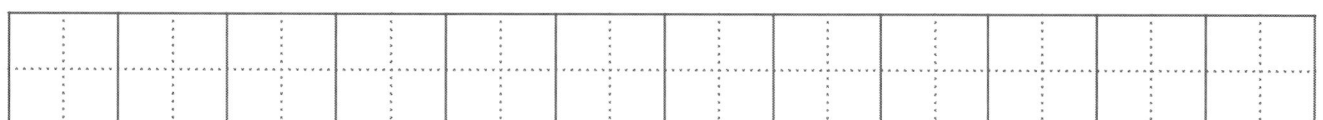
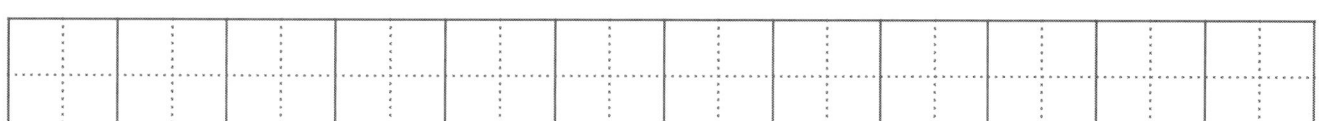
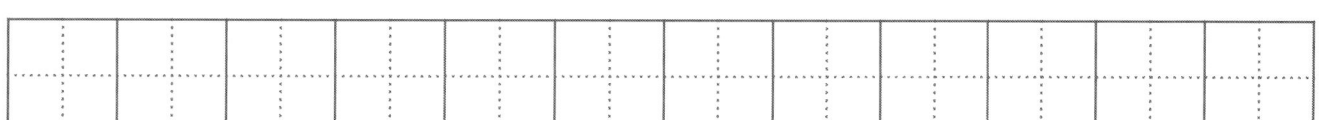
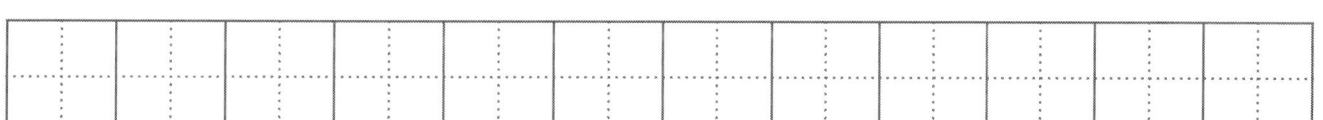
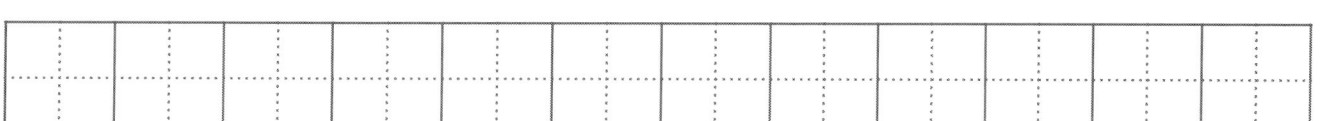
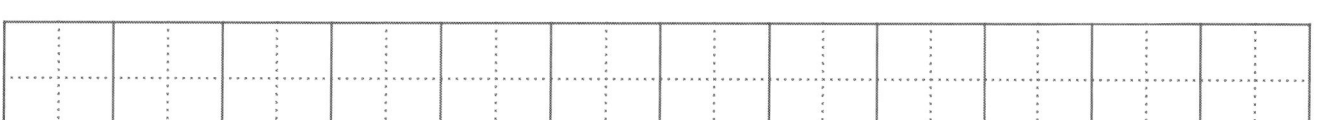
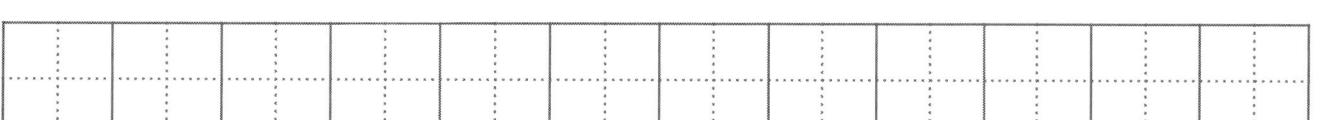

老大徒伤悲

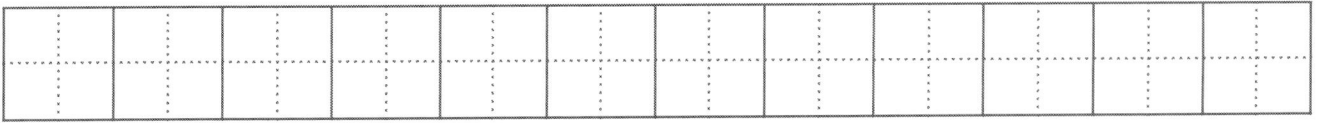
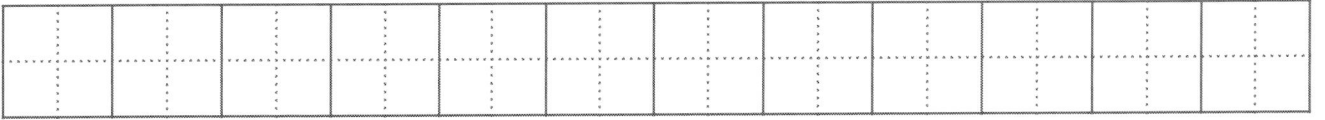
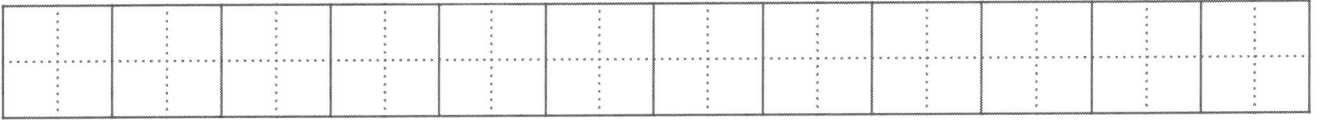
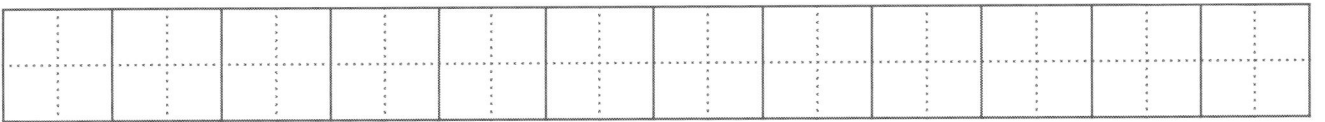
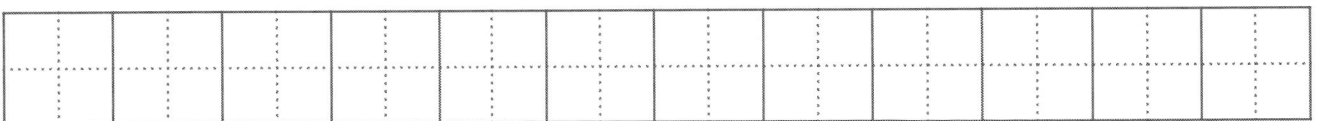
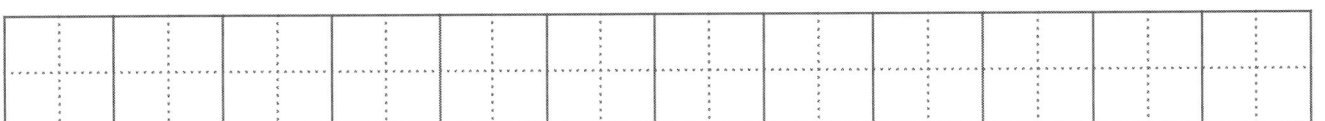
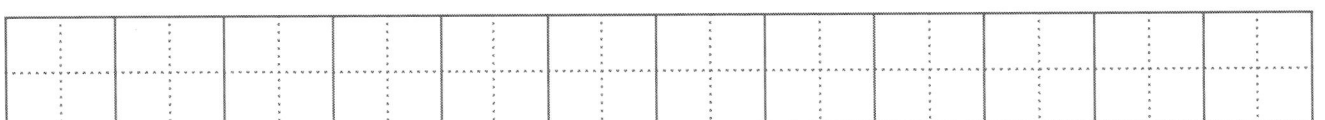
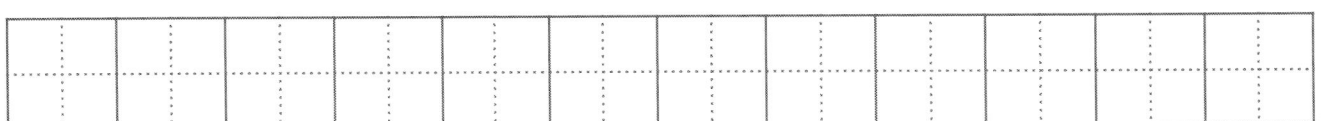
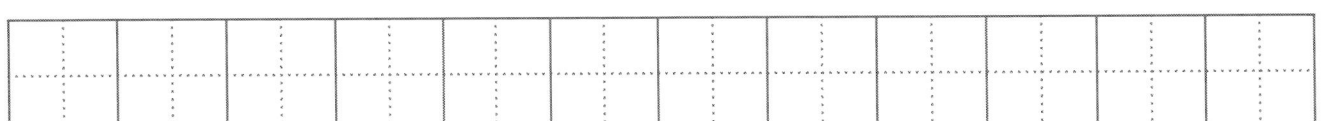
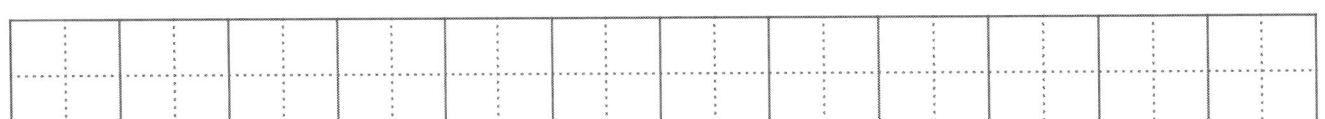
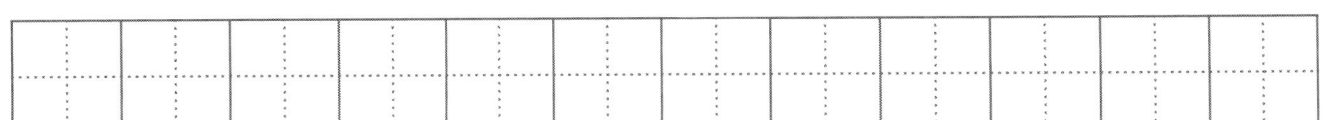
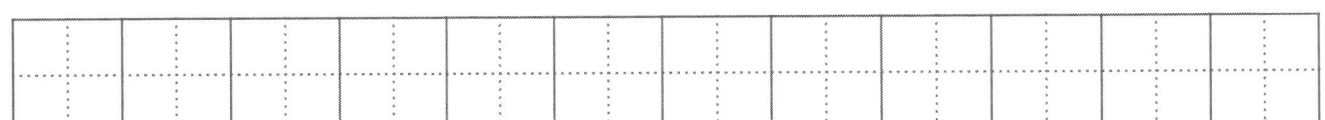

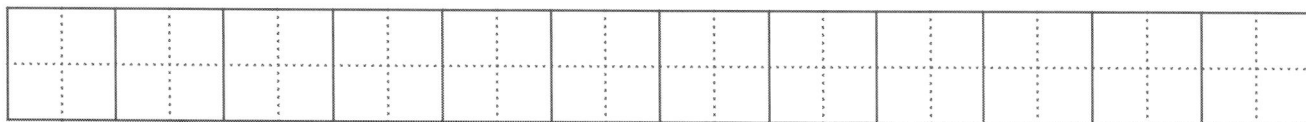

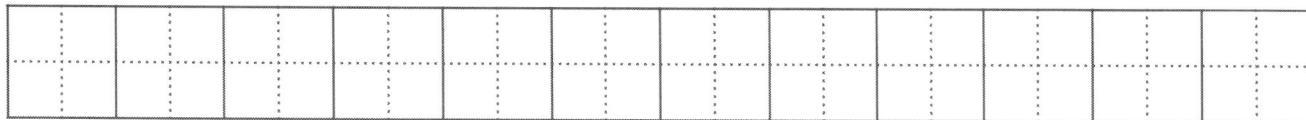

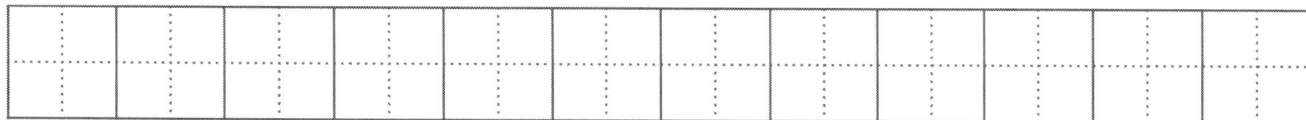

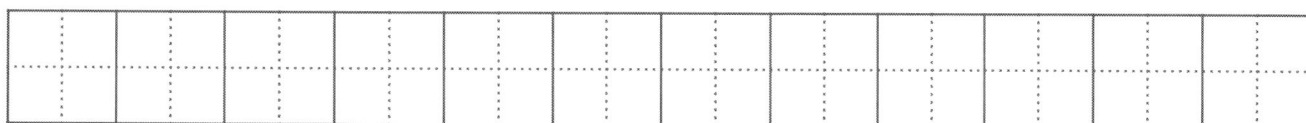

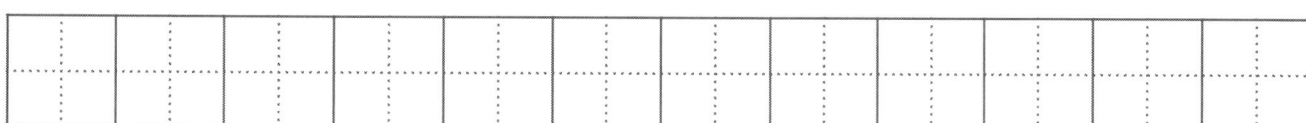

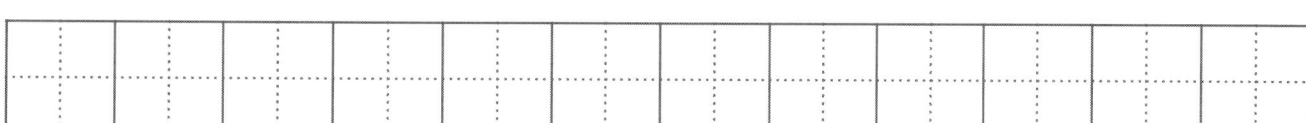

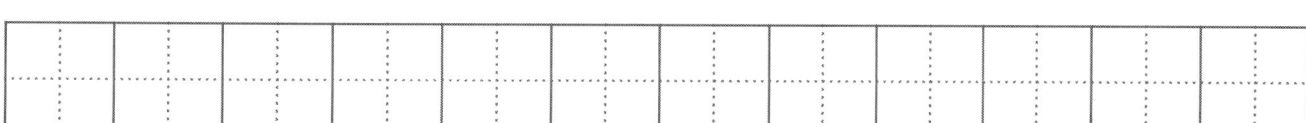

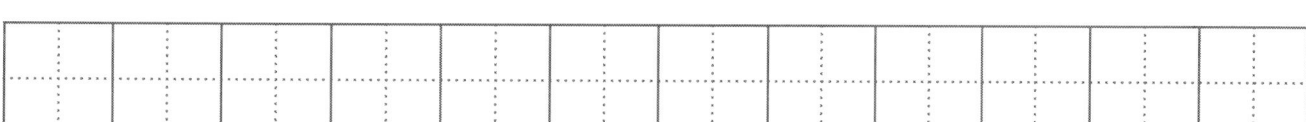

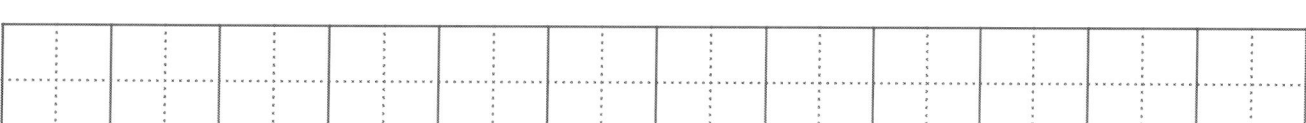

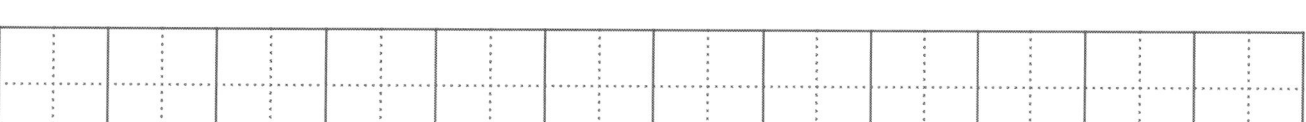

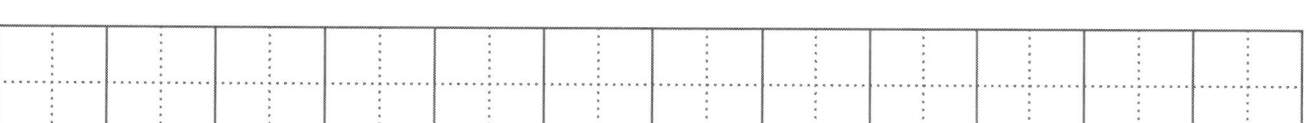

chǐ yǒu suǒ duǎn　　cùn yǒu suǒ cháng

尺 有 所 短 ， 寸 有 所 长 。

Sometimes a foot may prove short

while an inch may prove long.

- Every man has his strong and weak points.

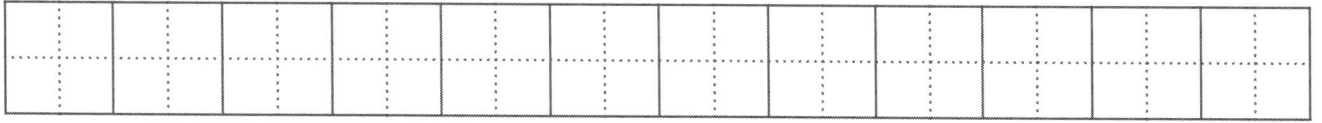

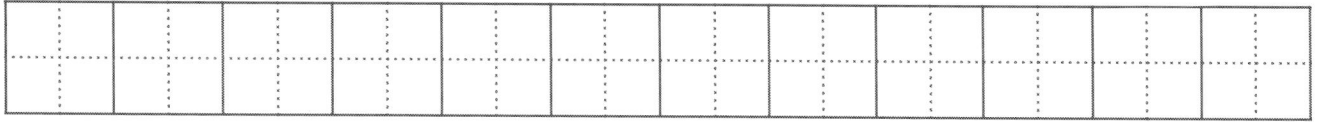

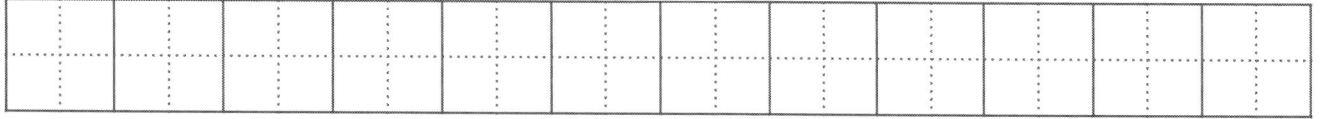

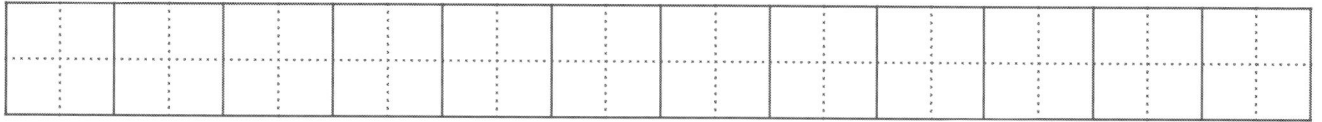

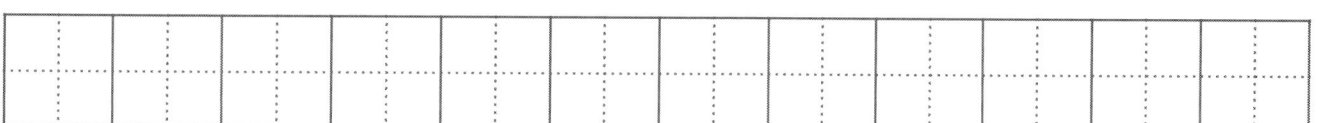

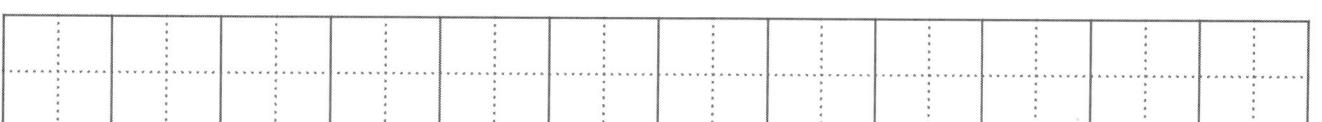

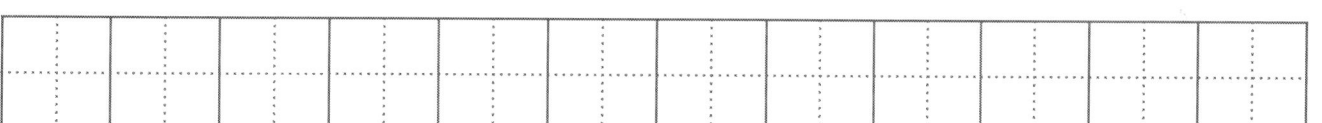

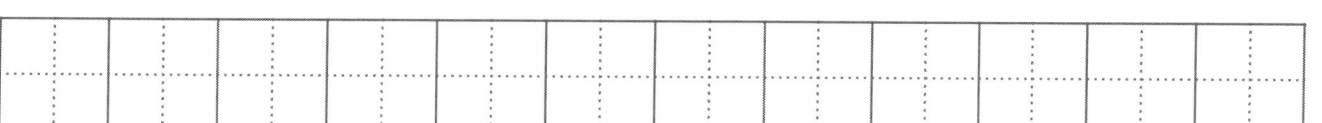

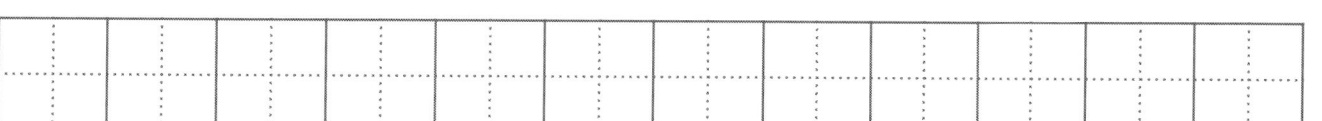

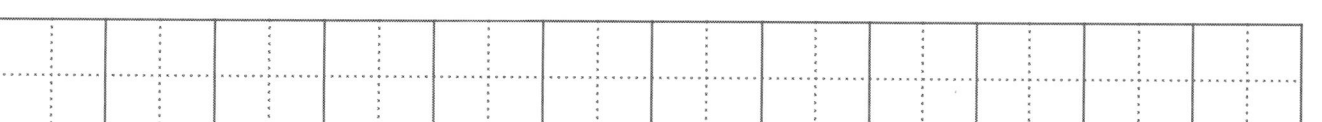

熟能生巧

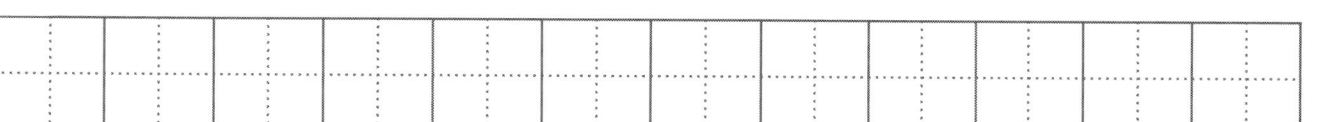

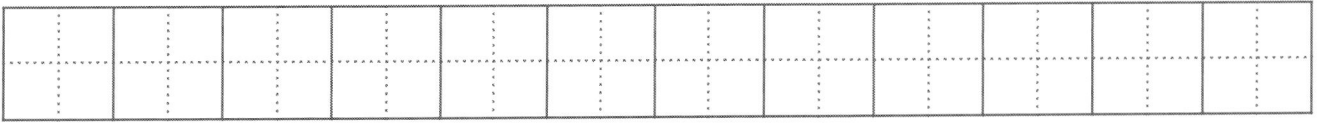
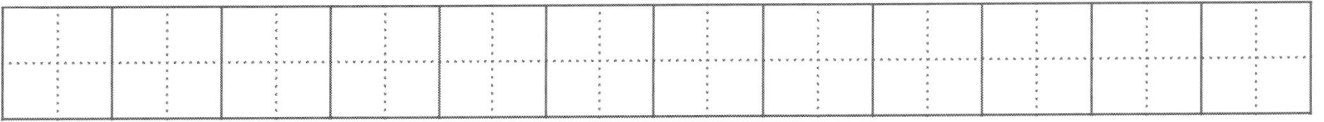
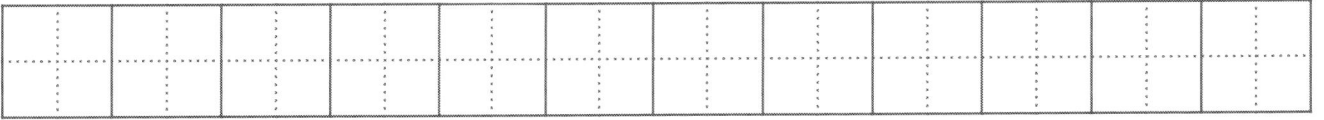
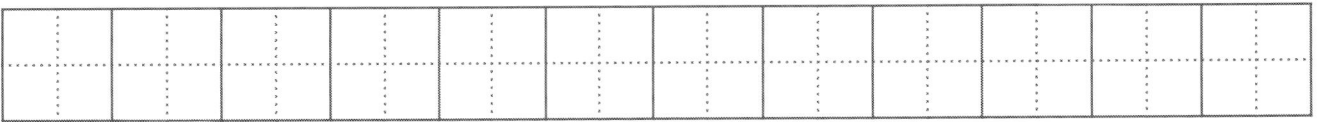
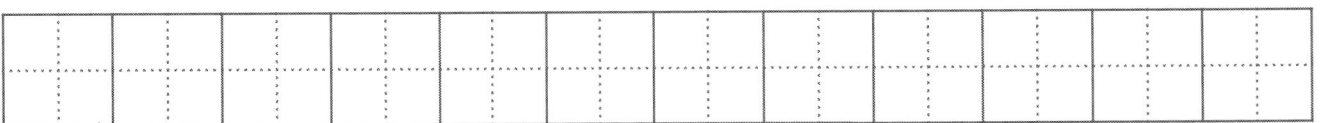
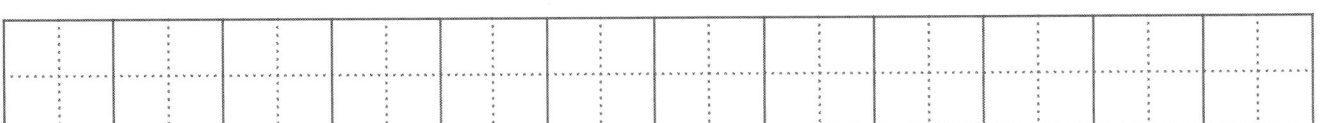
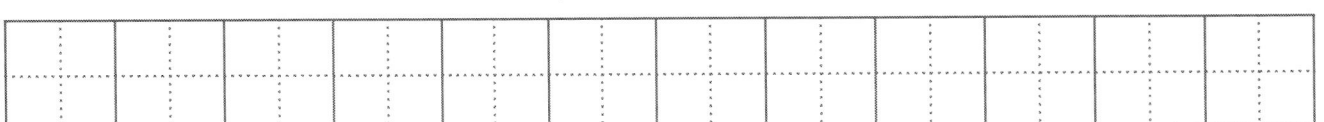
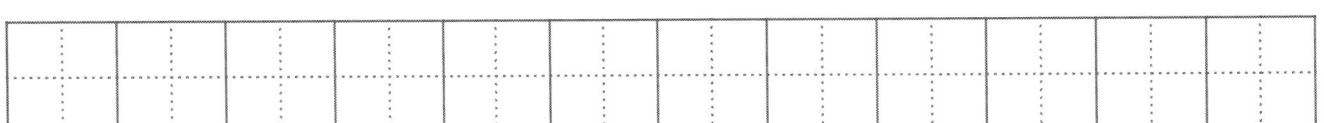
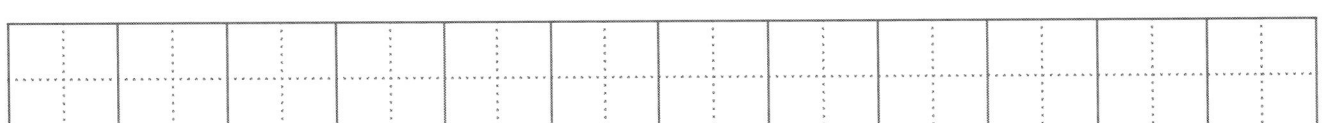
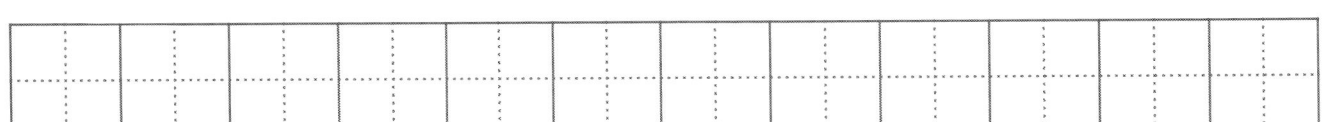

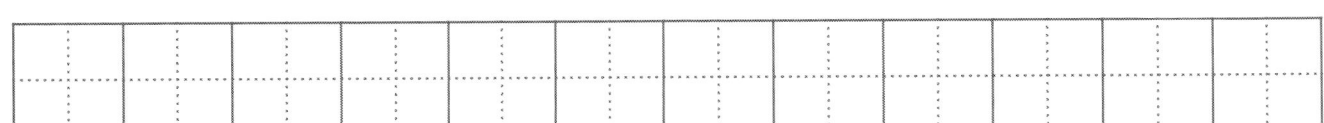

	jǐ	suǒ	bù	yù		wù	shī	yú	rén		
	己	所	不	欲	，	勿	施	于	人	。	

Treat others as you would like to be treated.

读万卷书，行万里路。

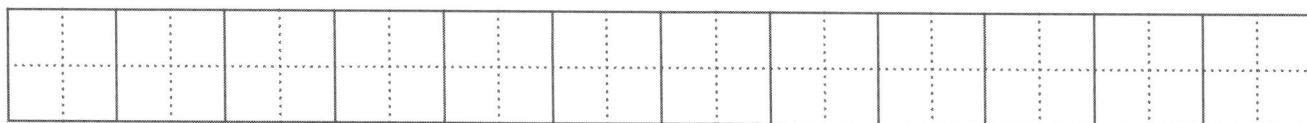

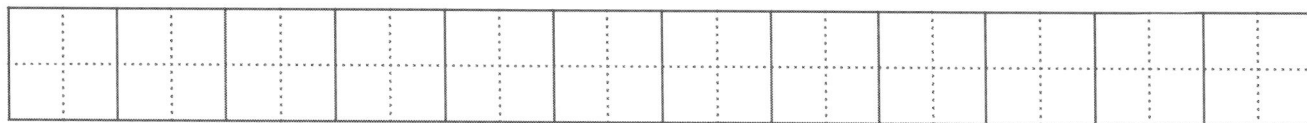

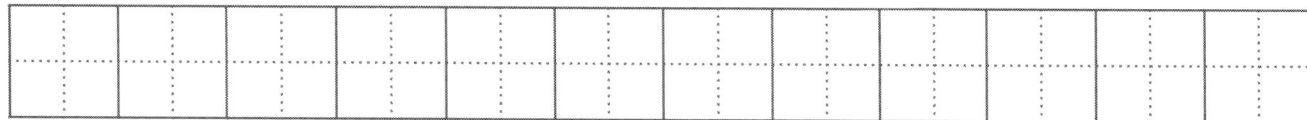

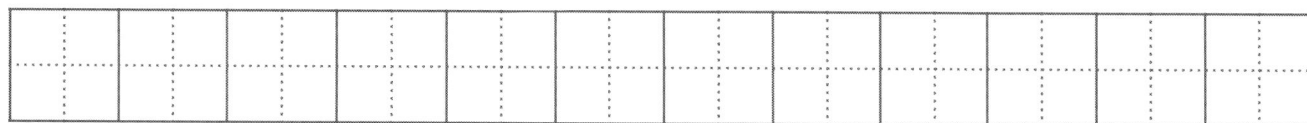

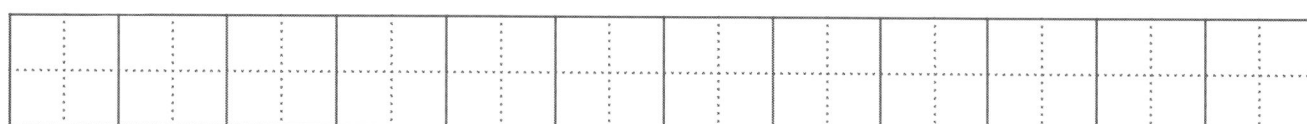

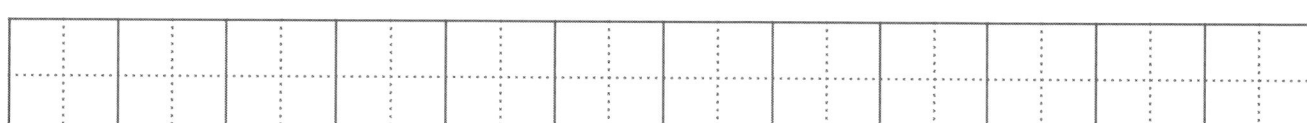

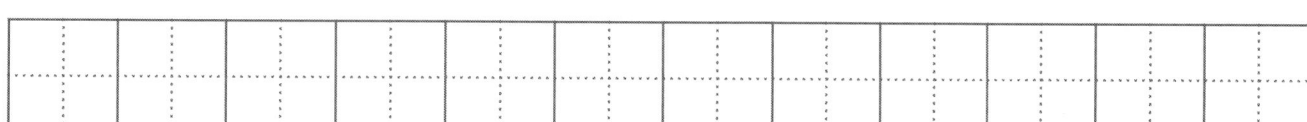

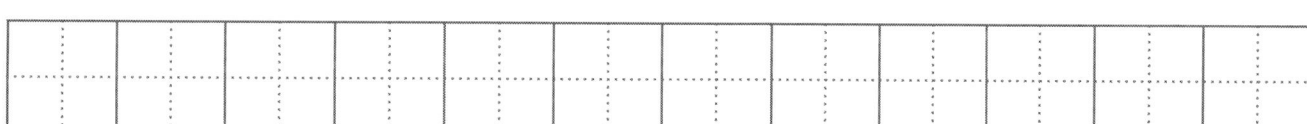

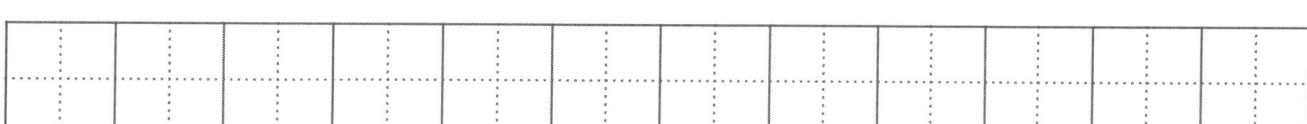

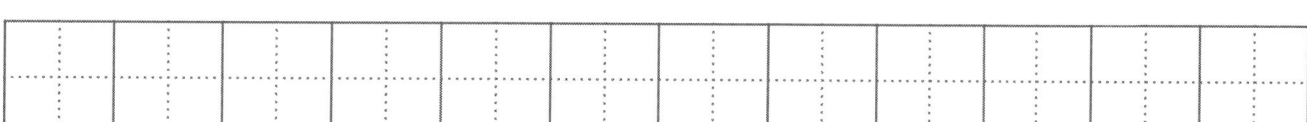

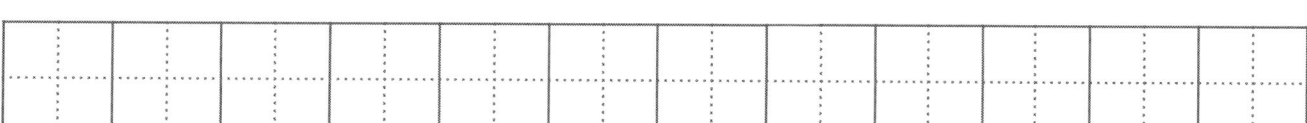

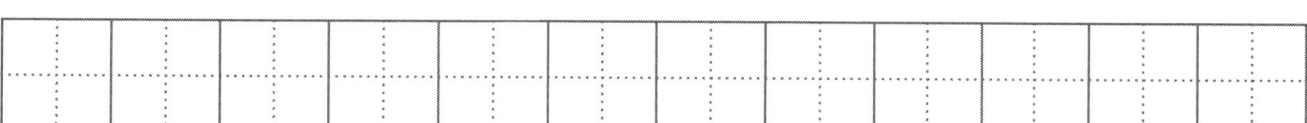

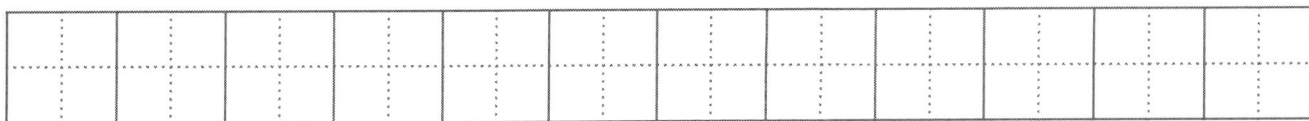

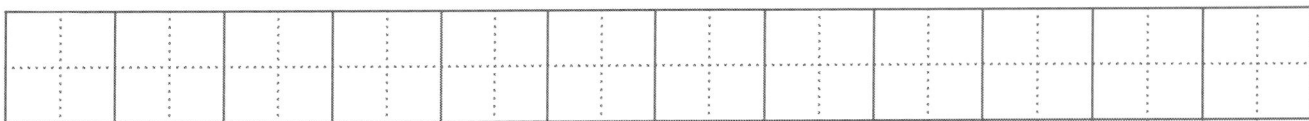

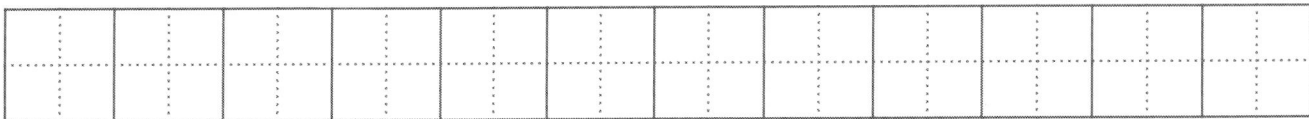

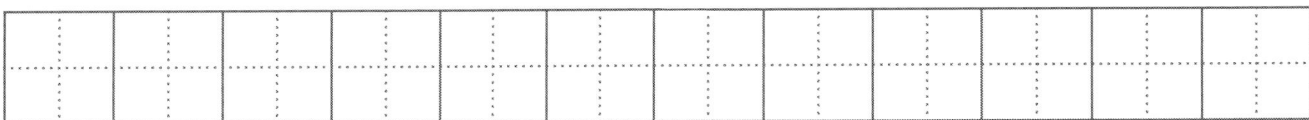

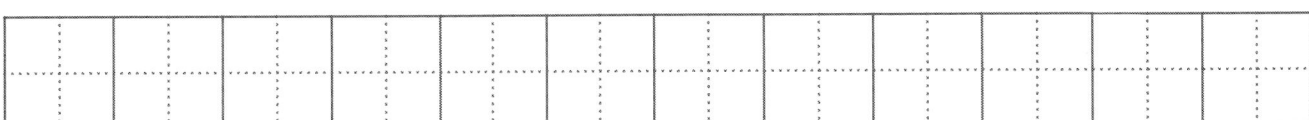

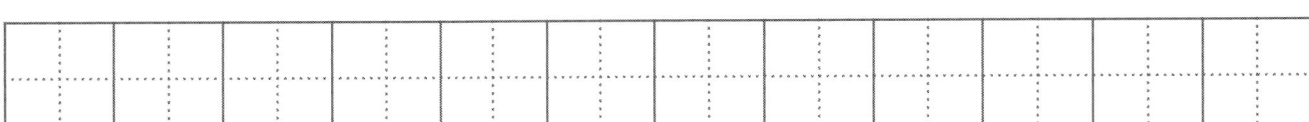

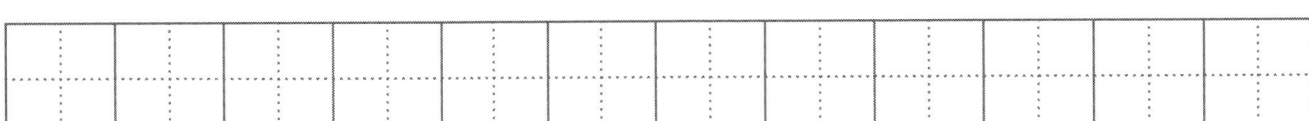

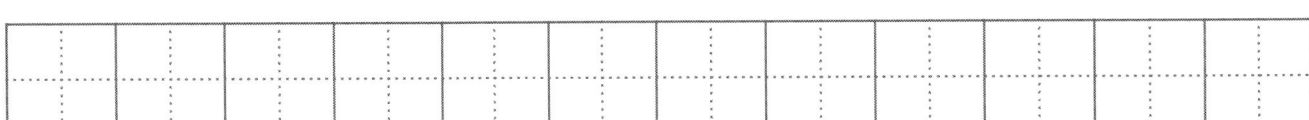

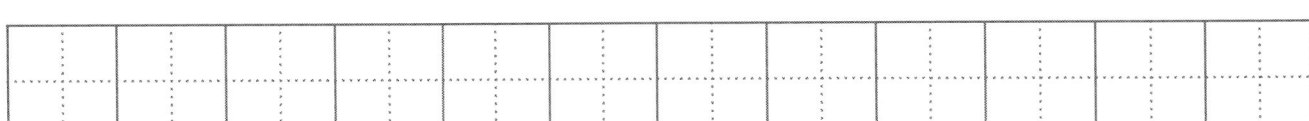

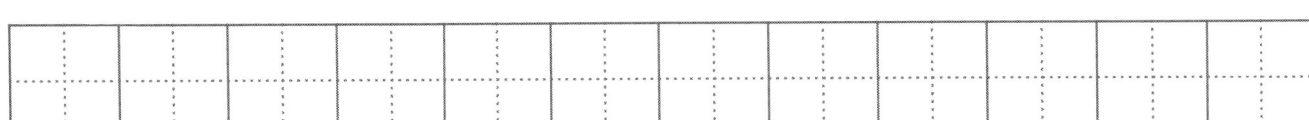

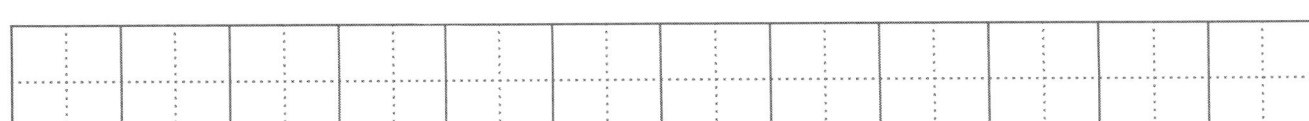

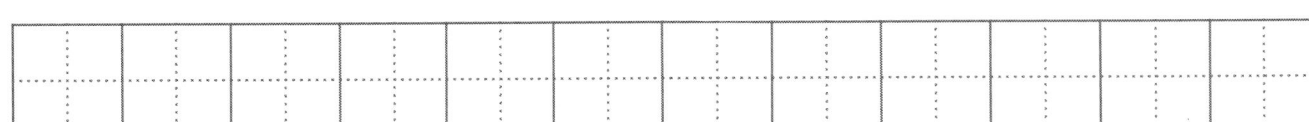

勿施于人

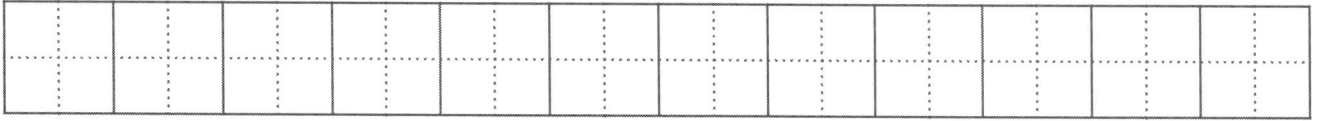
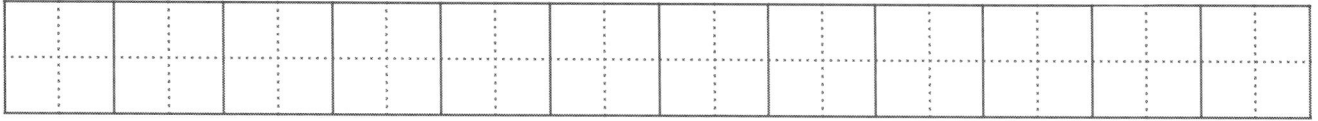
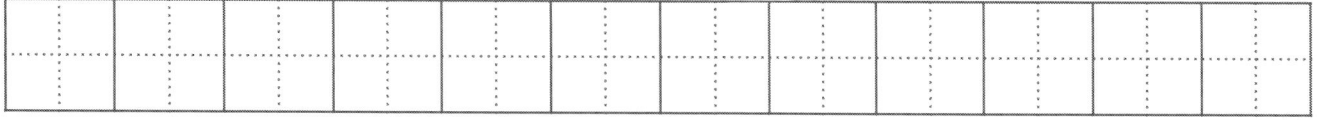
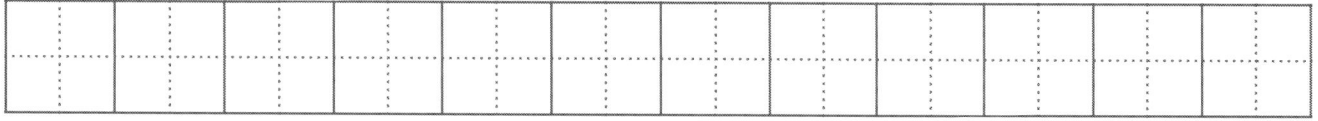
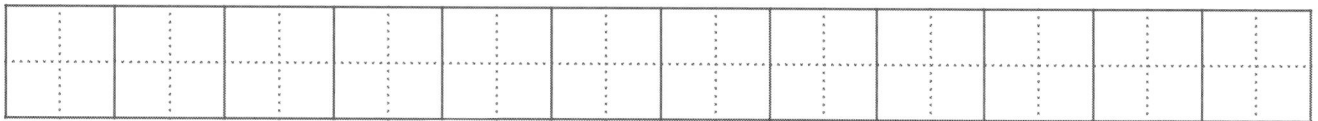
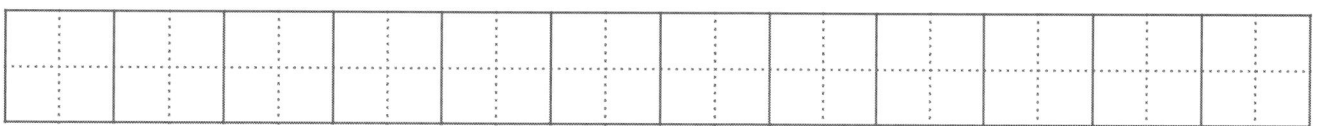
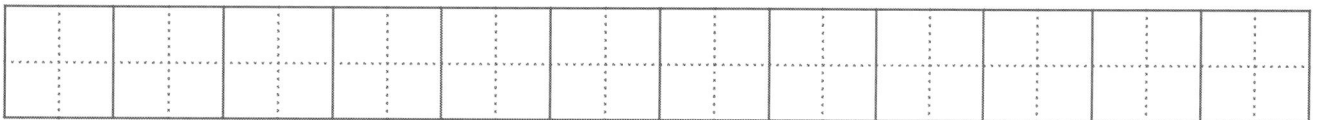
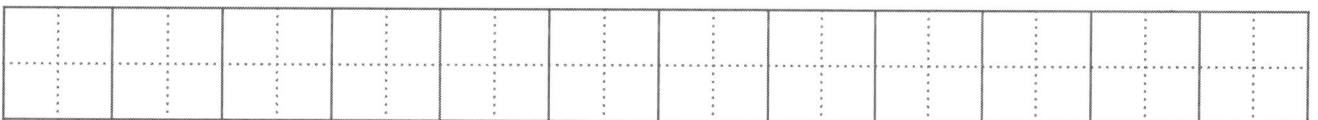
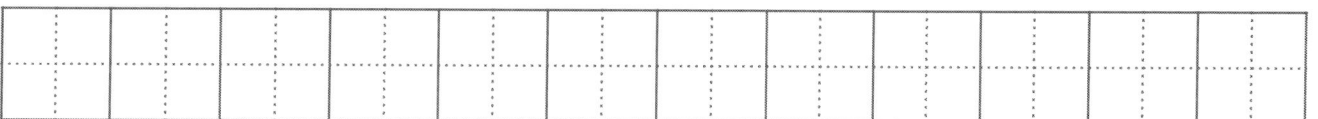
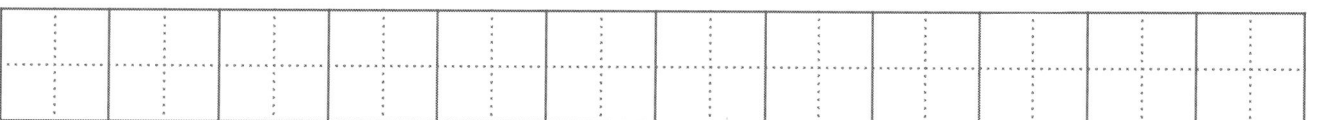
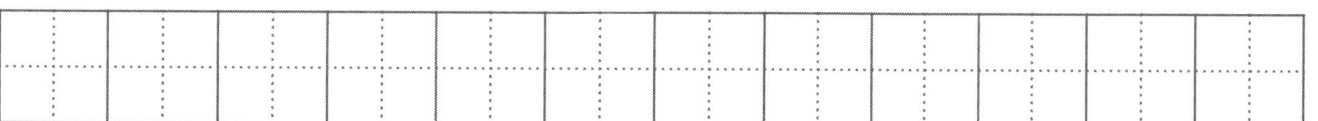

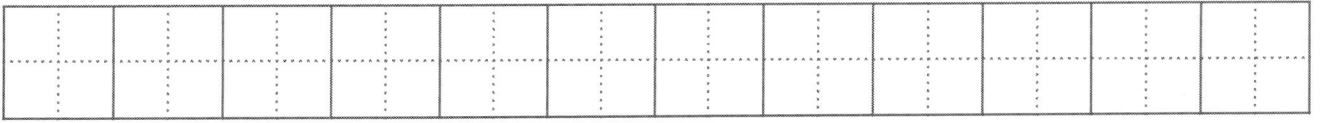
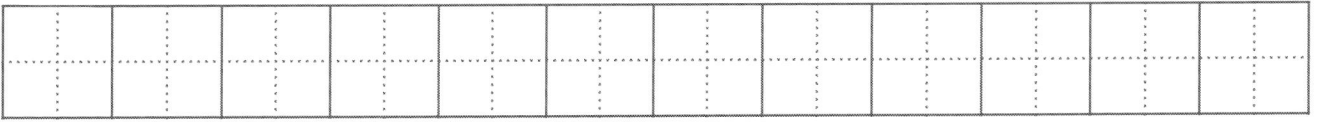
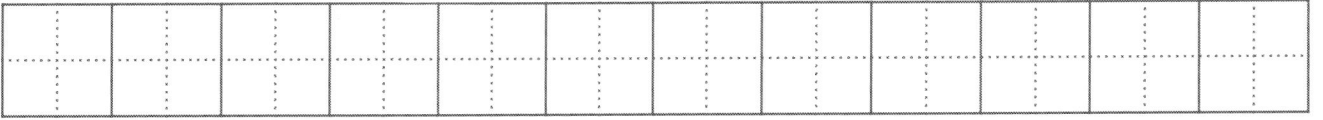
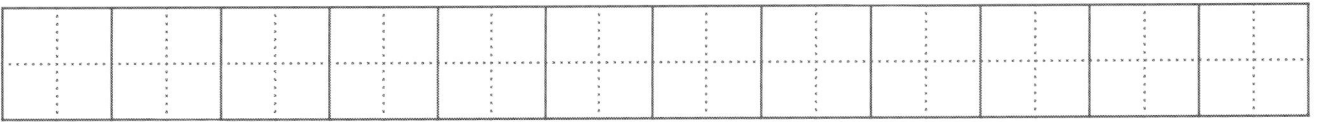
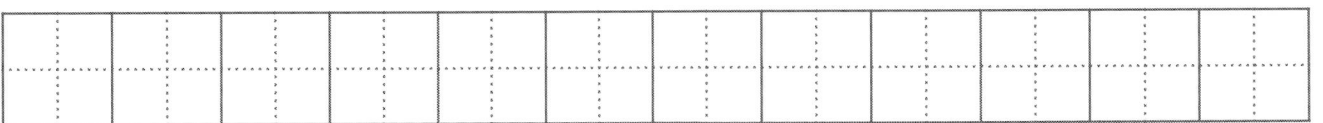
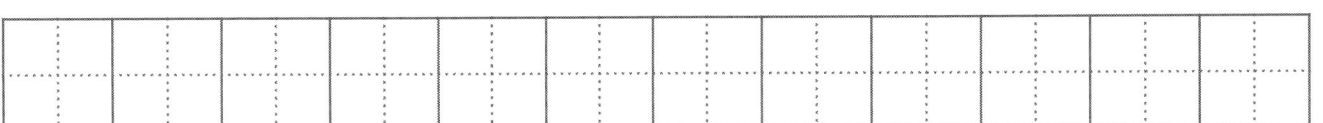
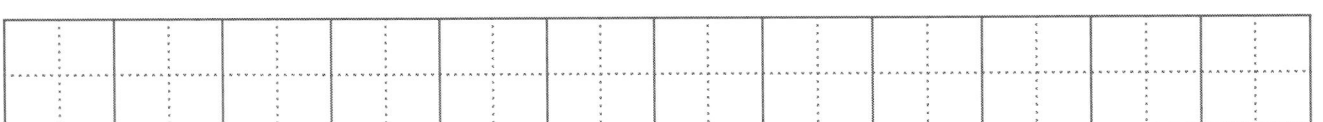
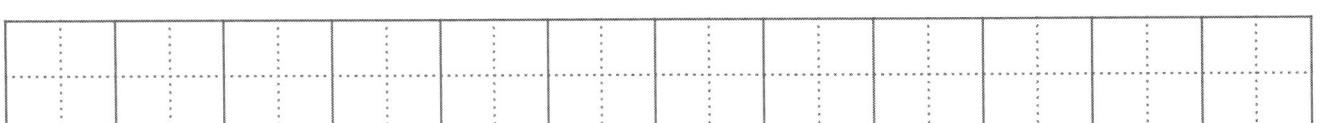
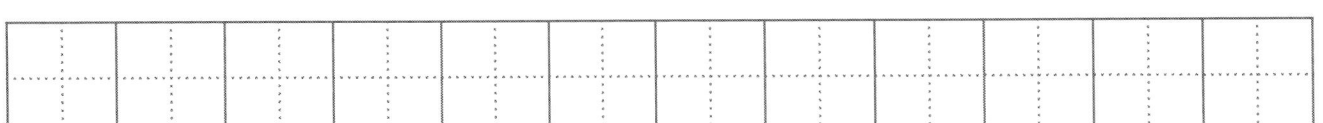
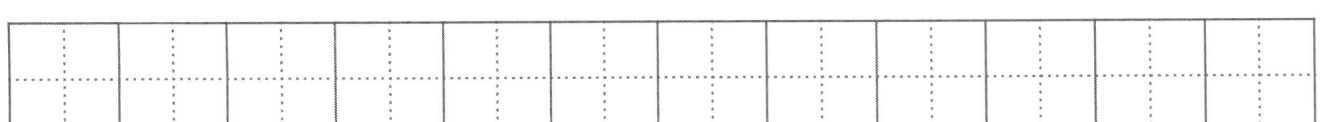
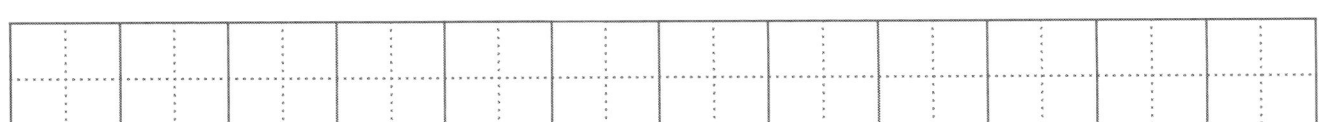
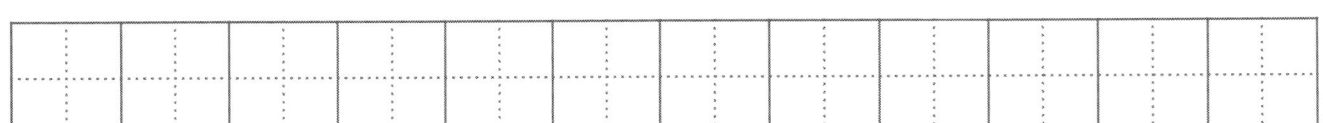

勿施于人

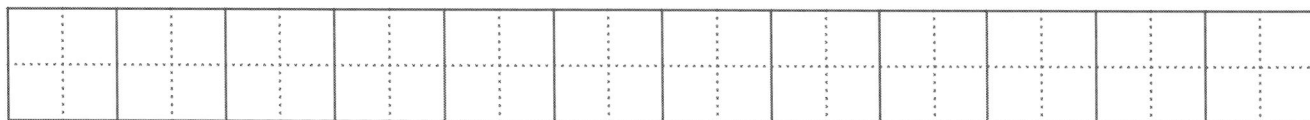

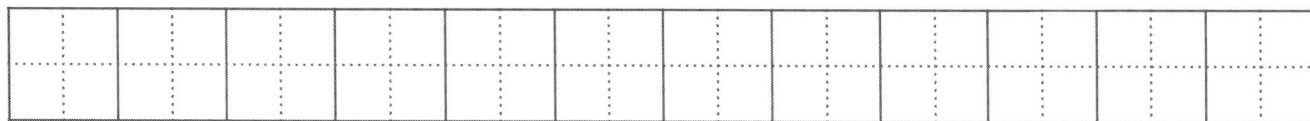

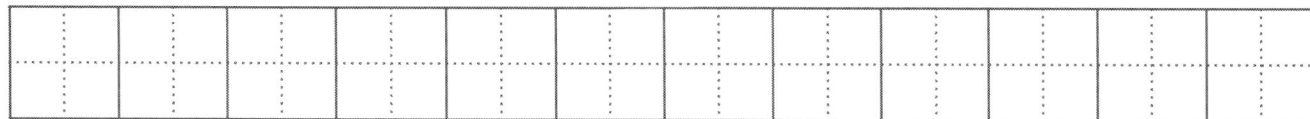

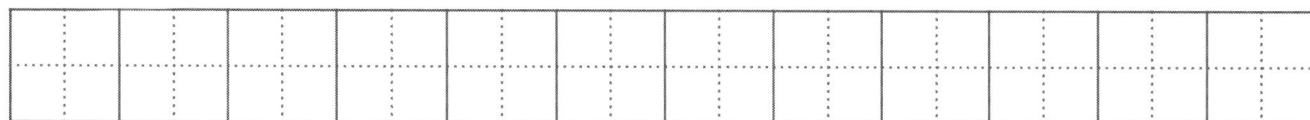

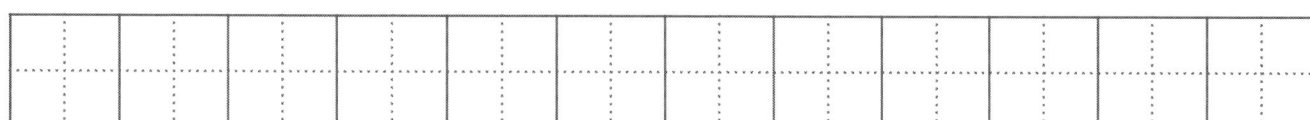

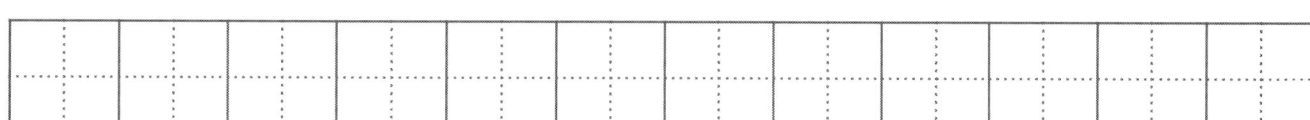

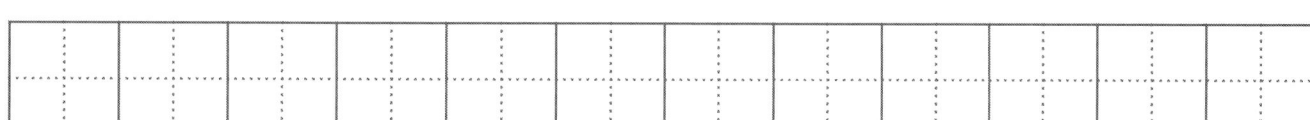

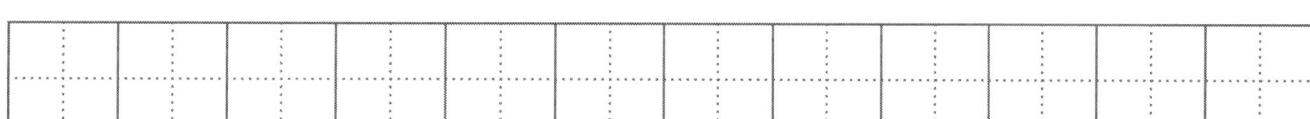

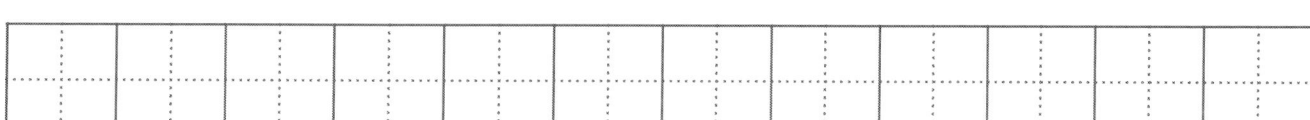

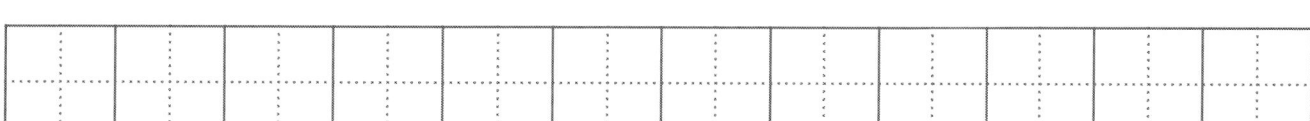

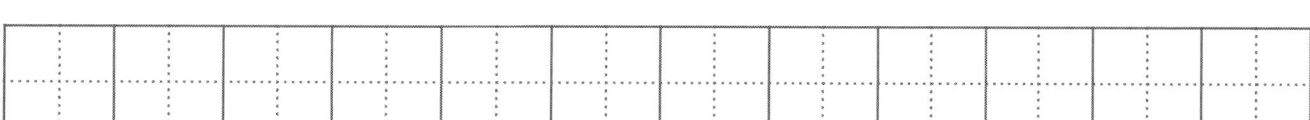

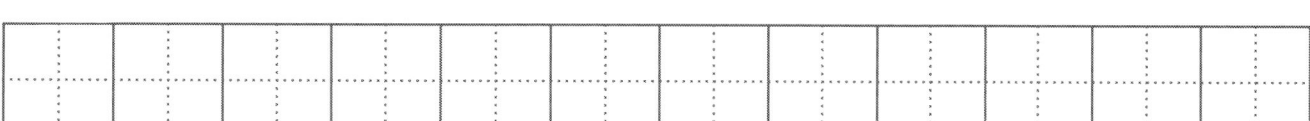

生 当 作 人 杰 ， 死 亦 为 鬼 雄 。

Alive, thrive to be a man of men;
Be soul of souls, even if I am dead.

海纳百川，有容乃大。

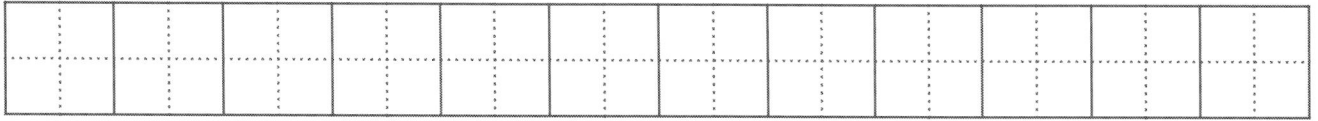

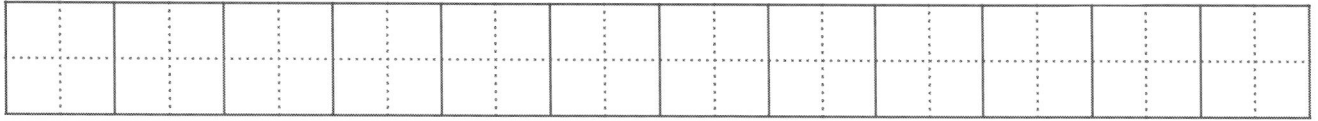

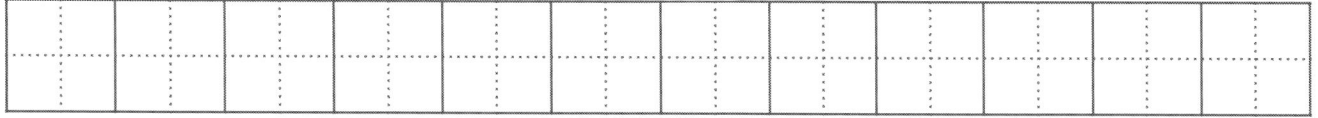

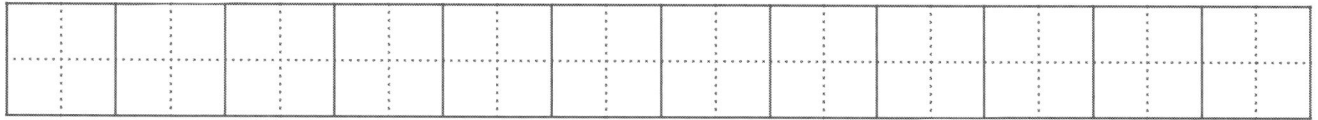

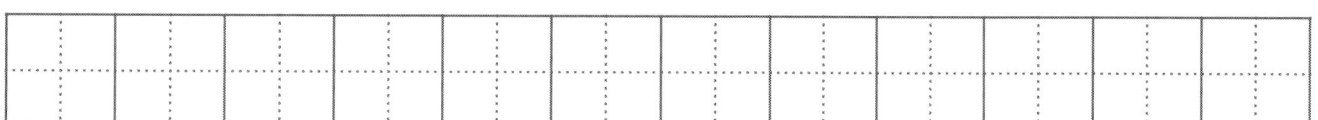

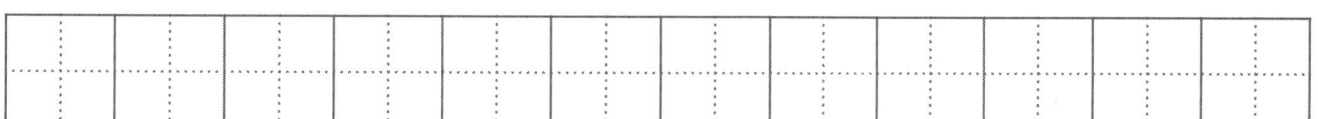

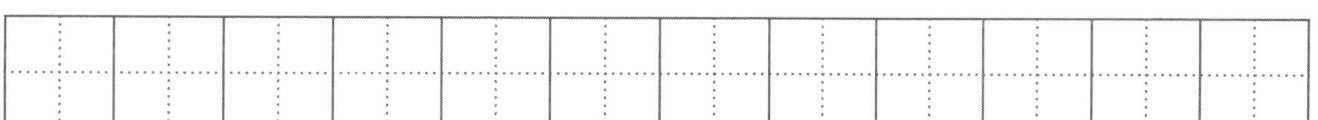

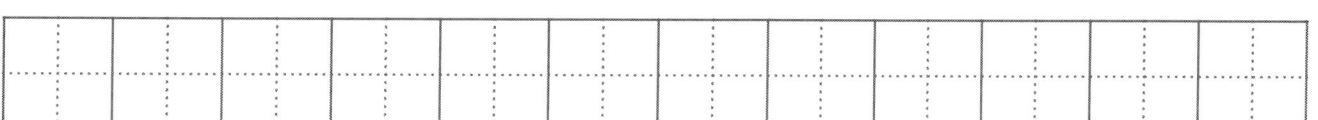

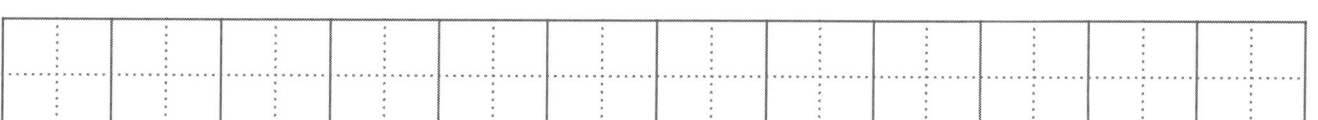

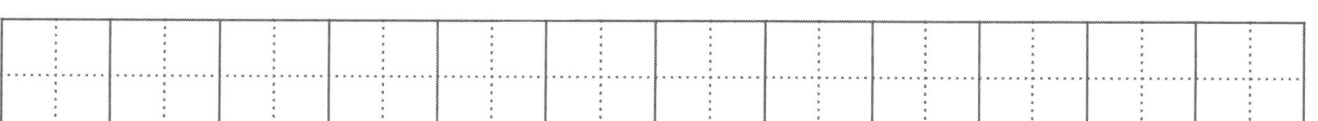

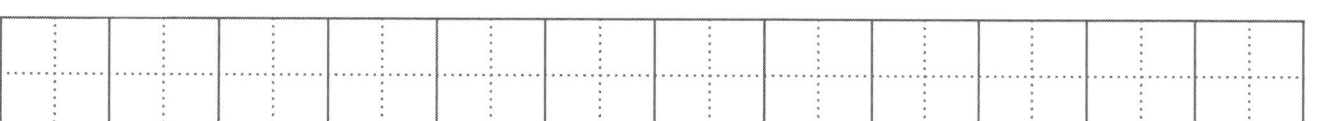

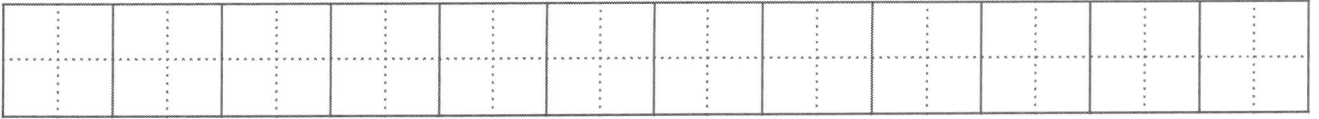
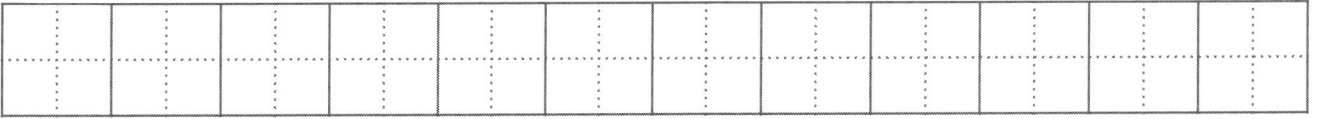
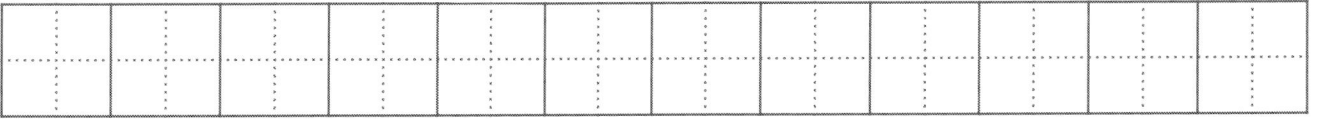
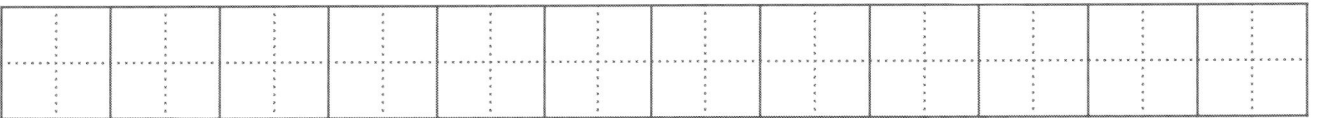
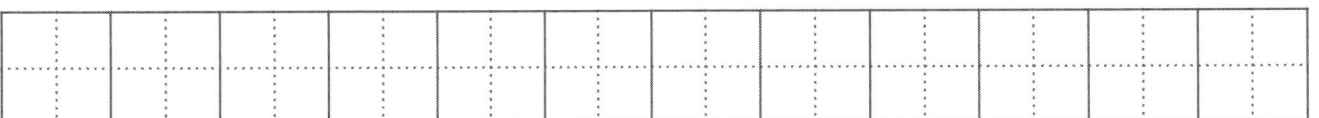
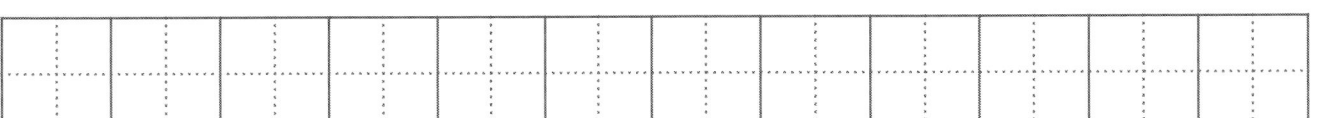

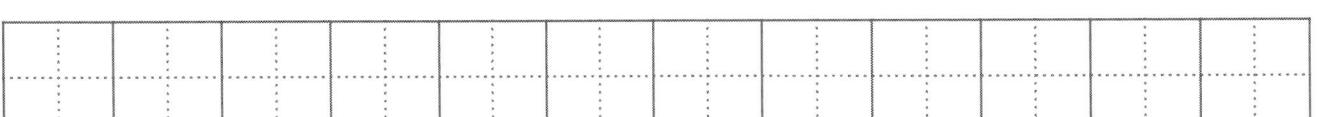
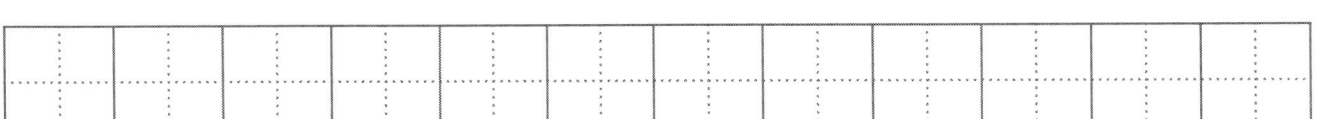
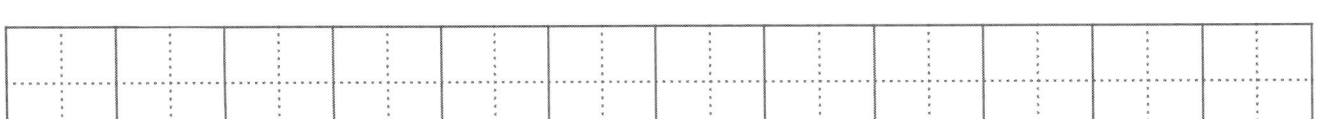
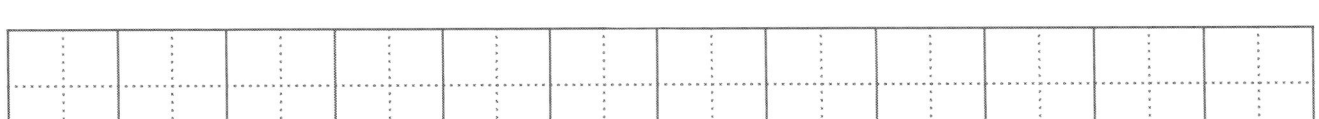
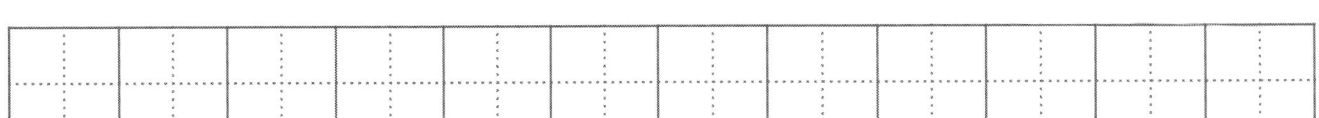

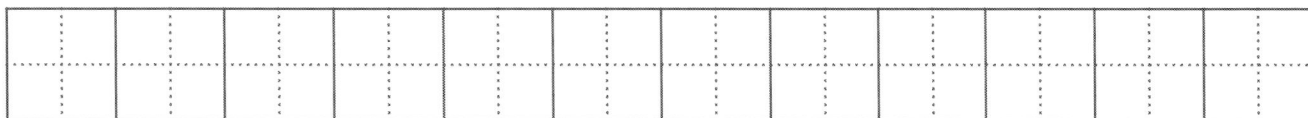

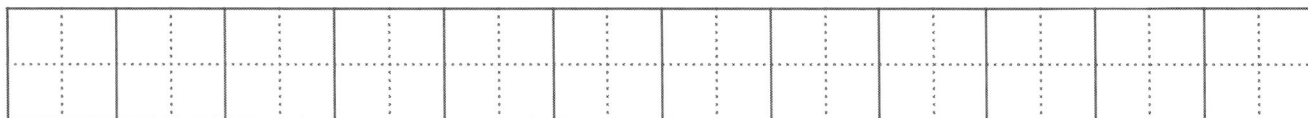

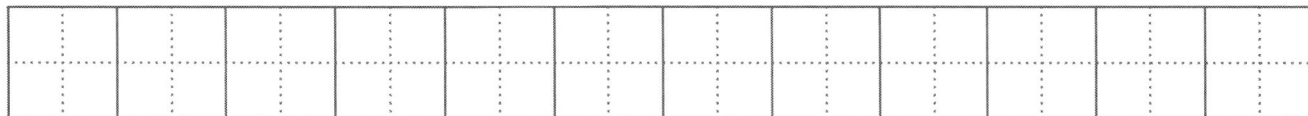

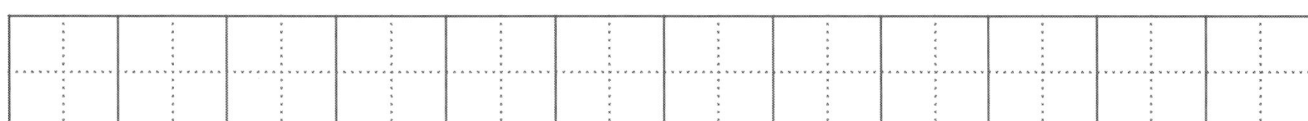

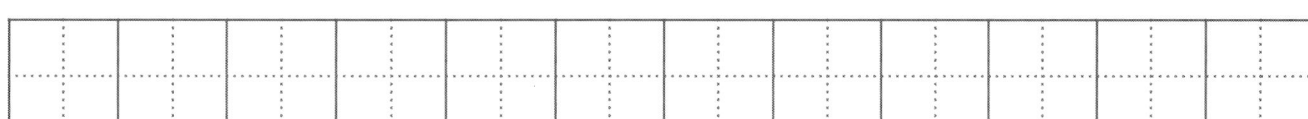

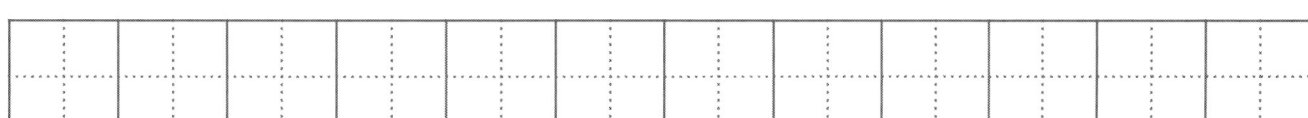

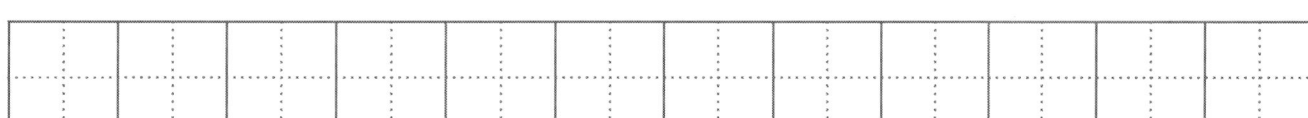

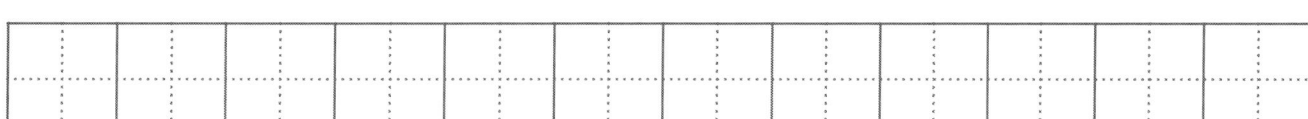

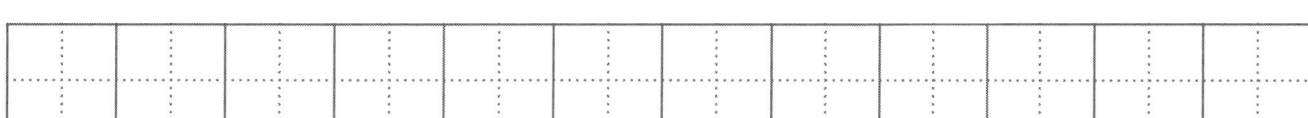

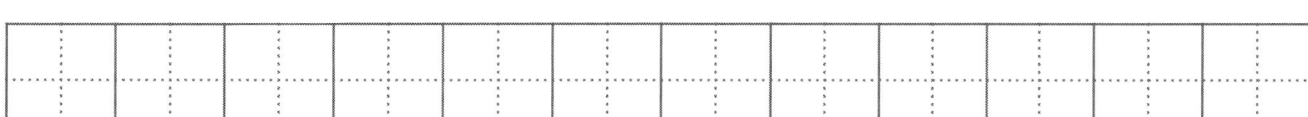

死亦为鬼雄

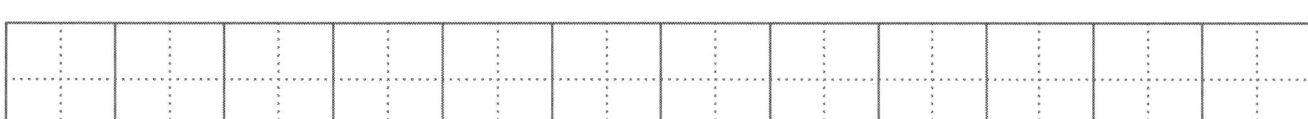

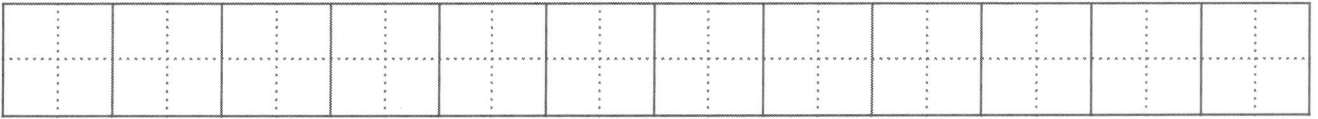
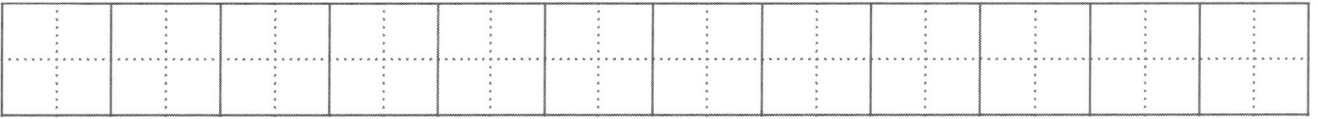
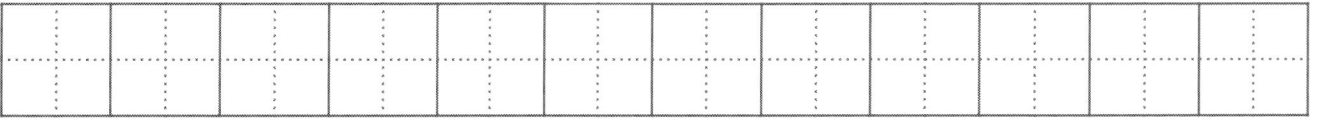
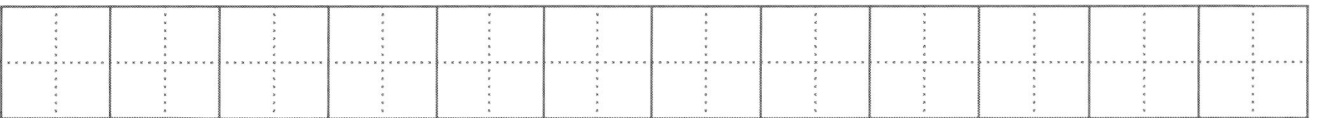
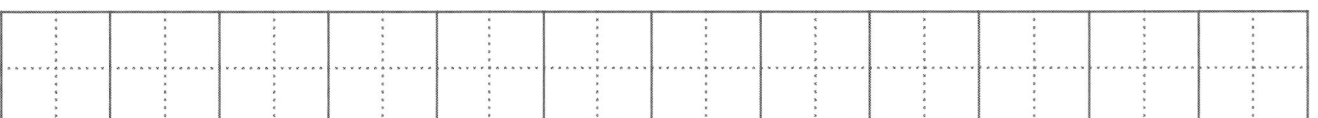

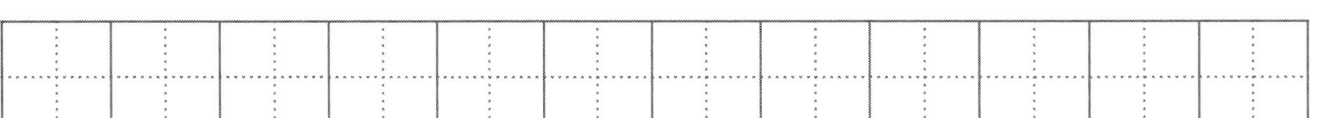
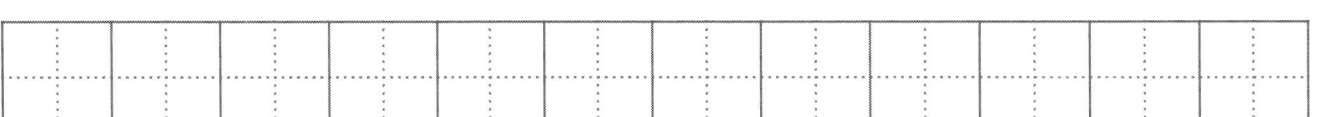
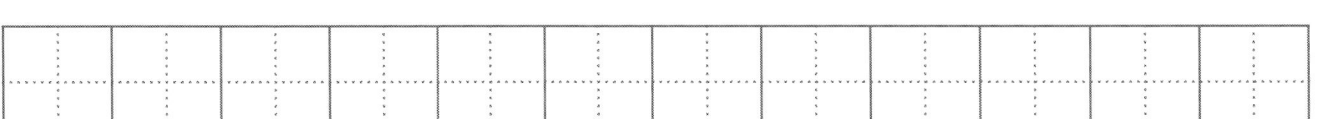
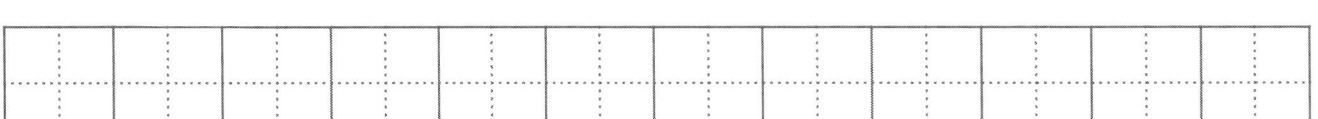
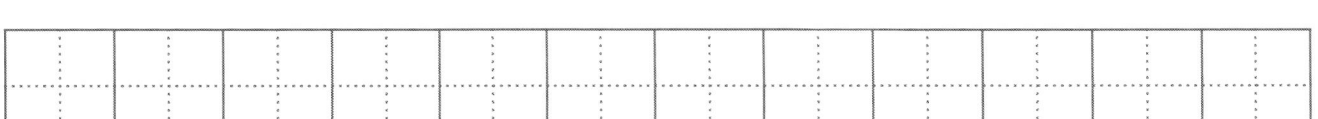
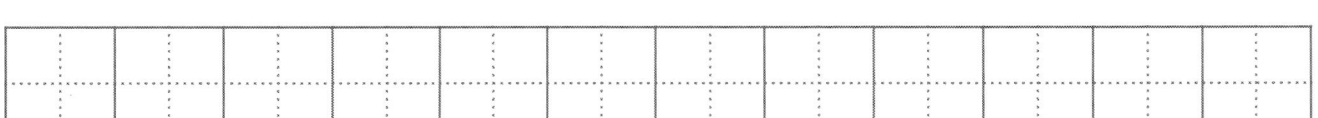

死亦为鬼雄

兼 听 则 明 ， 偏 信 则 暗 。

Listen to both sides, you will be enlightened;
heed only one side, you will be benighted.

千里之行，始于足下。

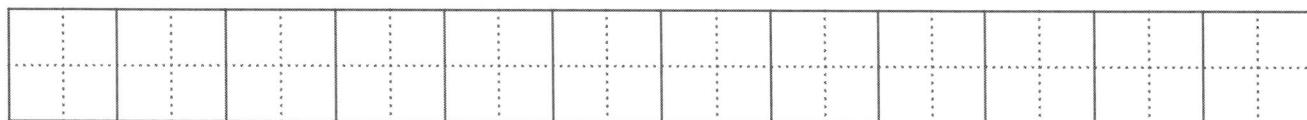

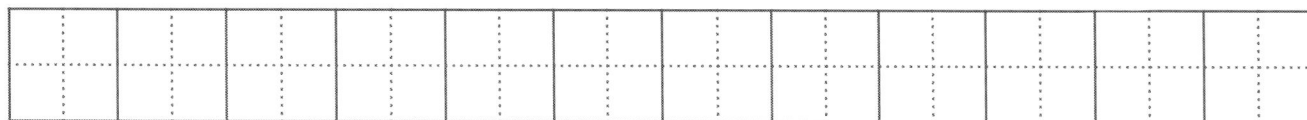

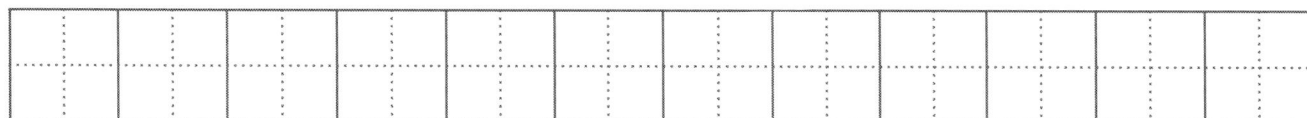

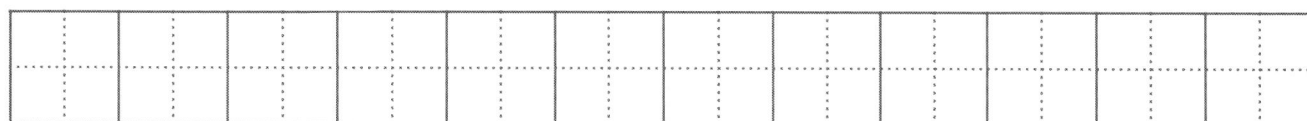

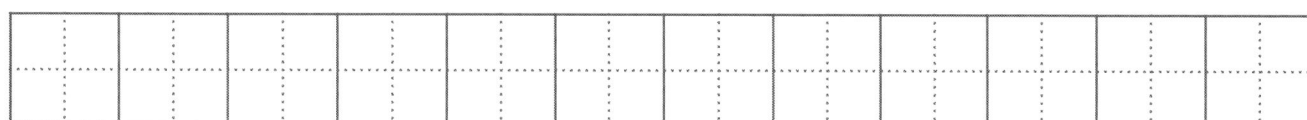

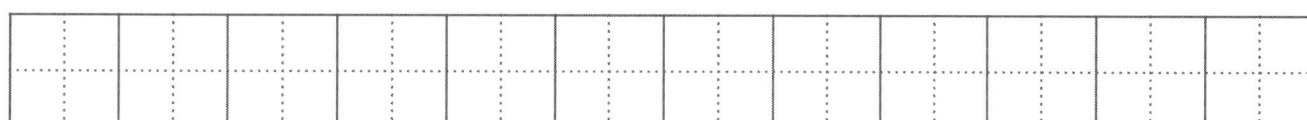

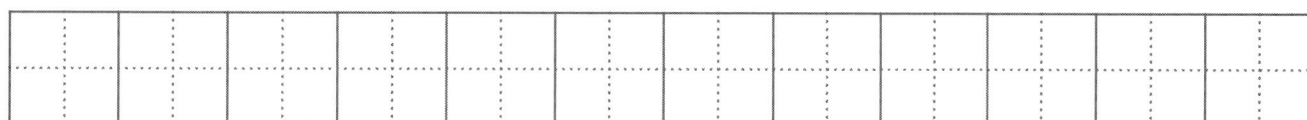

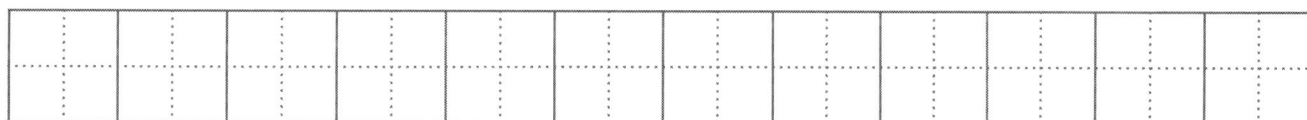

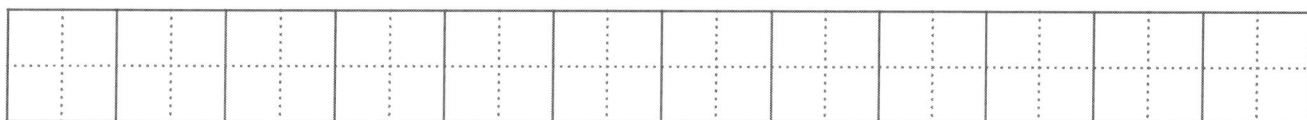

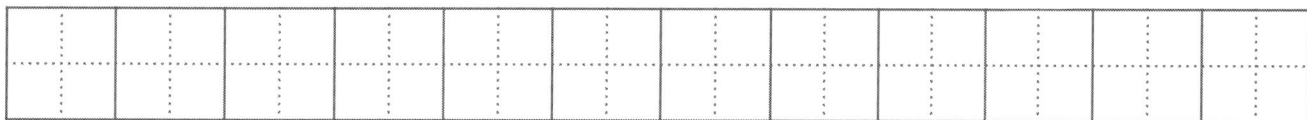

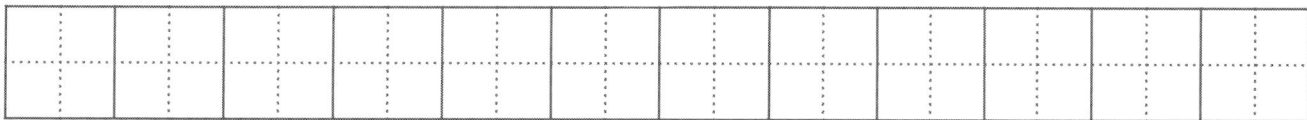

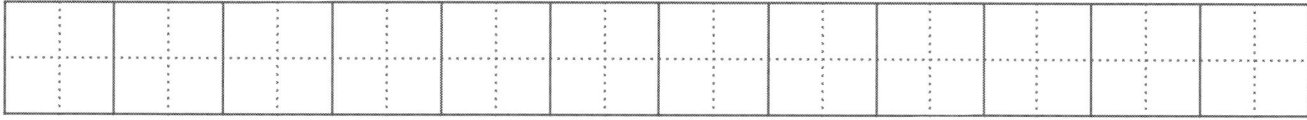

91

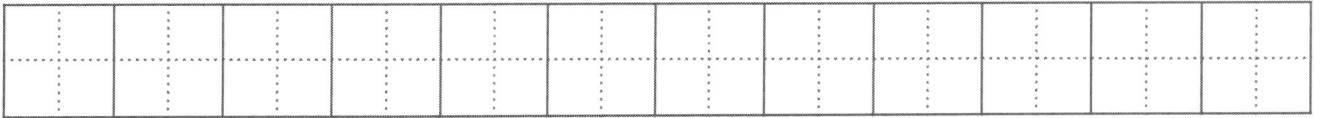
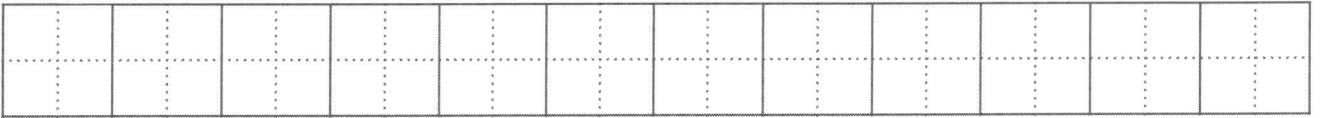
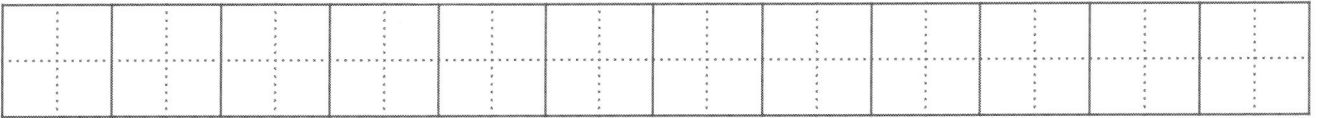

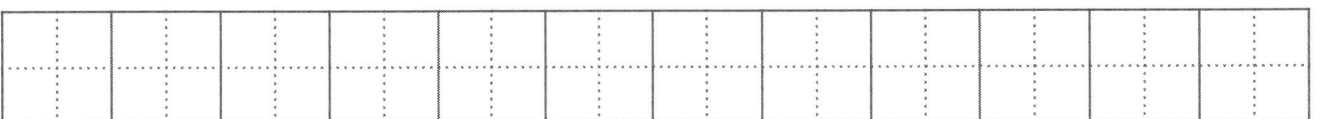
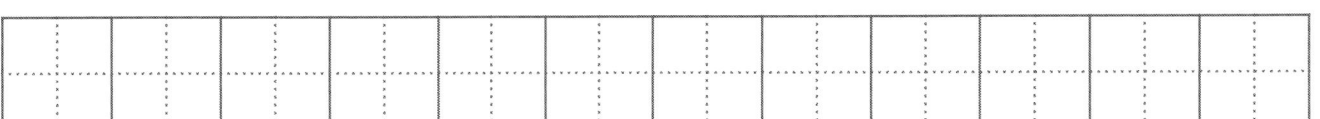
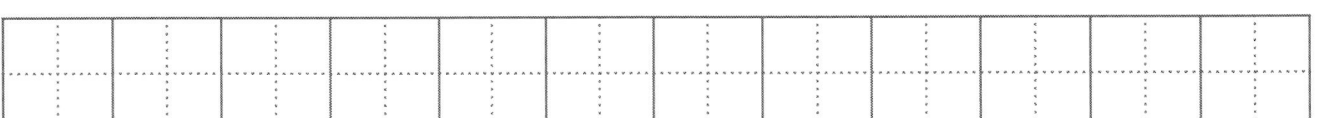

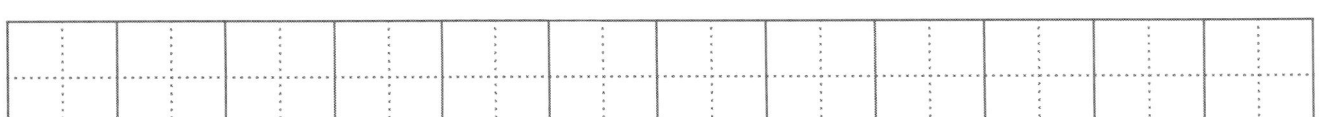
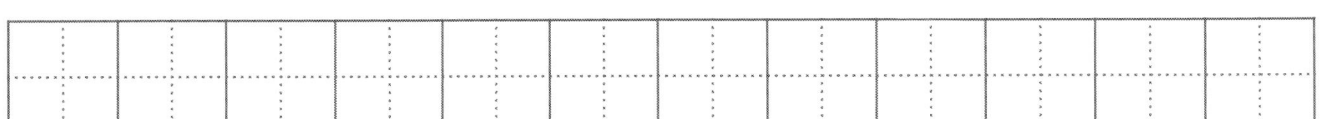

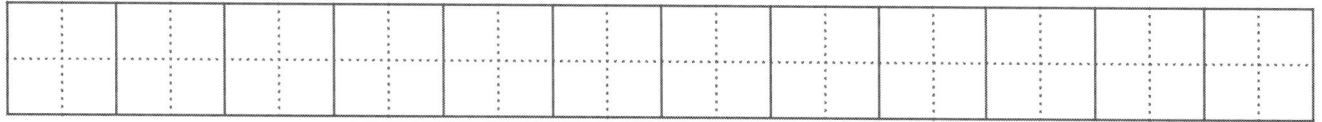

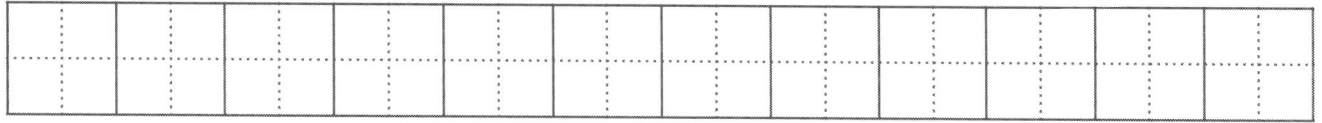

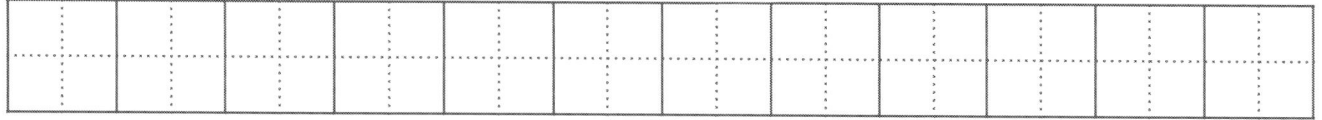

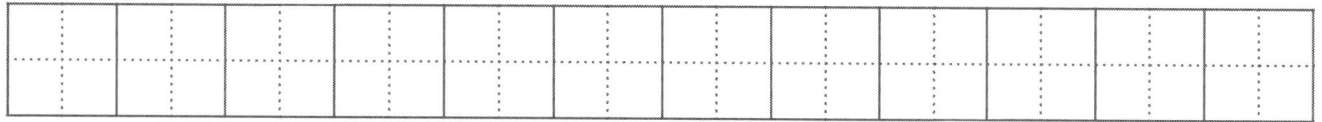

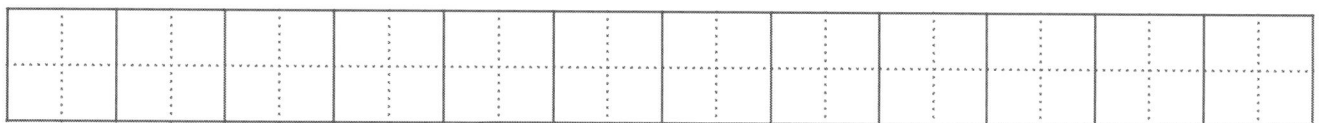

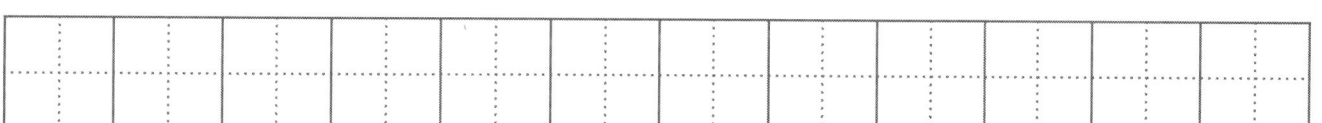

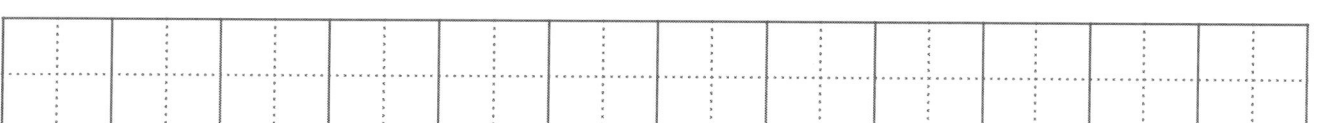

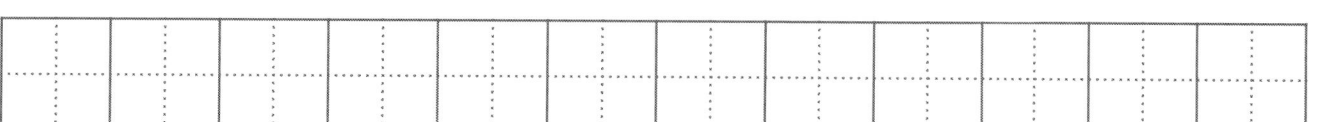

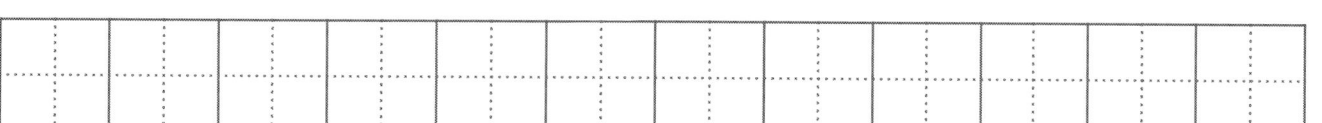

偏信则暗

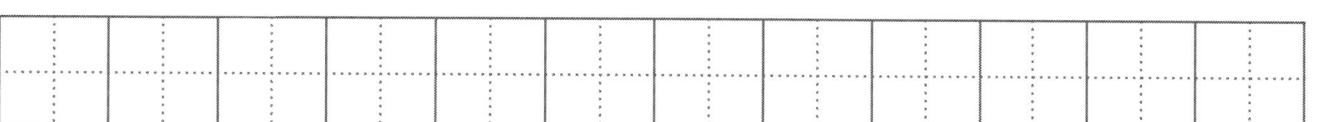

偏信则暗

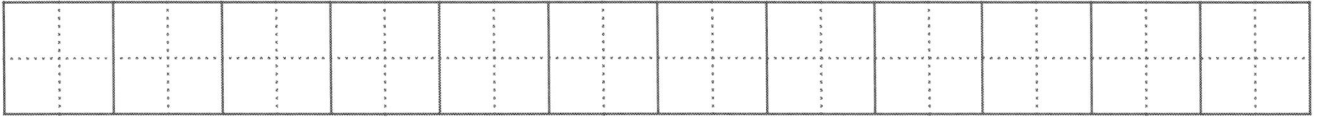
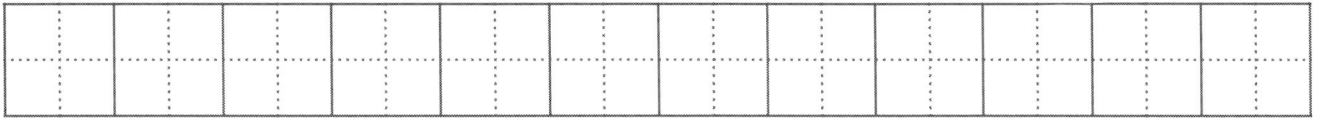
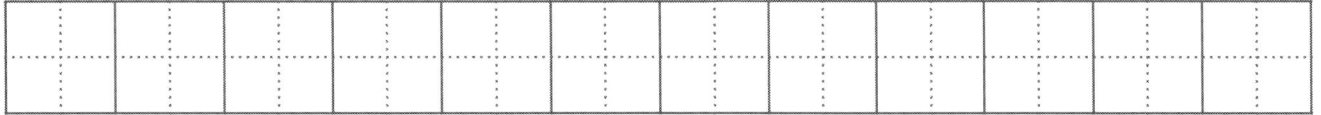
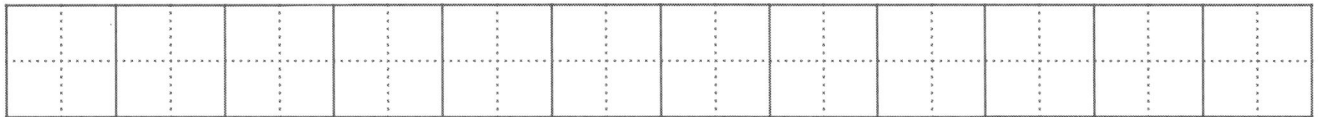
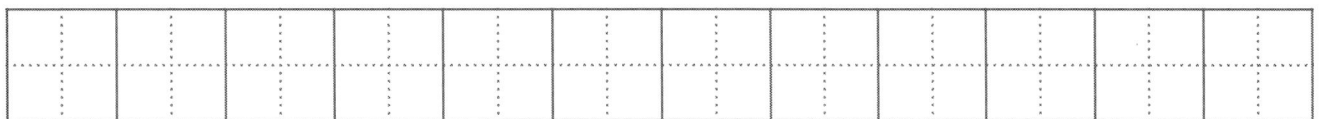
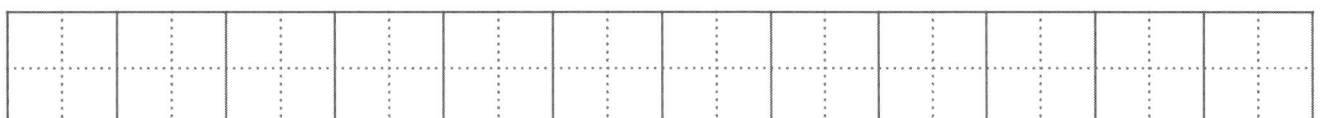

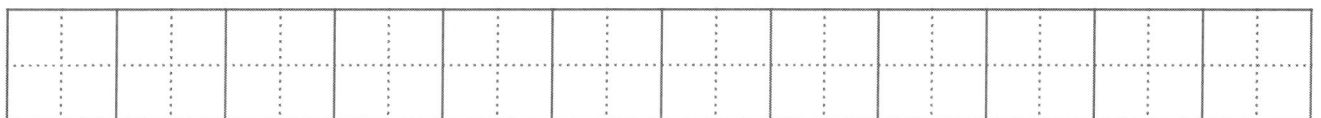
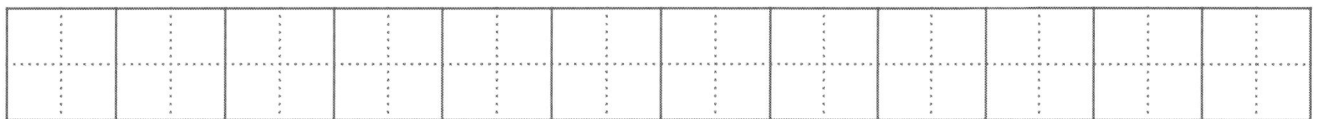
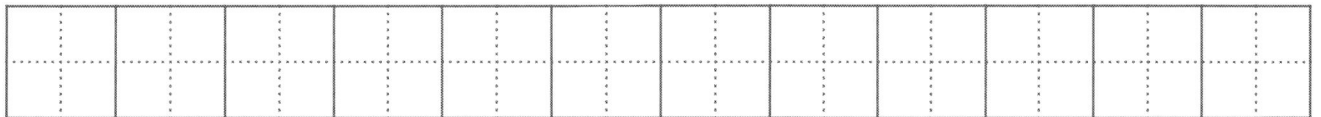
偏信则暗
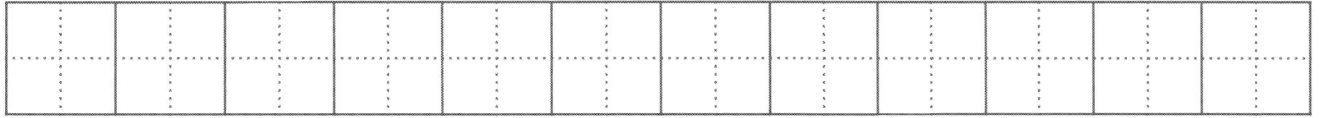

huì	dāng	líng	jué	dǐng		yì	lǎn	zhòng	shān	xiǎo	
会	当	凌	绝	顶	，	一	览	众	山	小	。

I must ascend the mountain's crest.
It dwarfs all peaks under my feet.

水 滴 石 穿

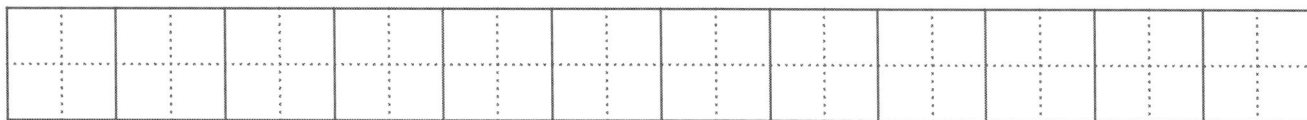
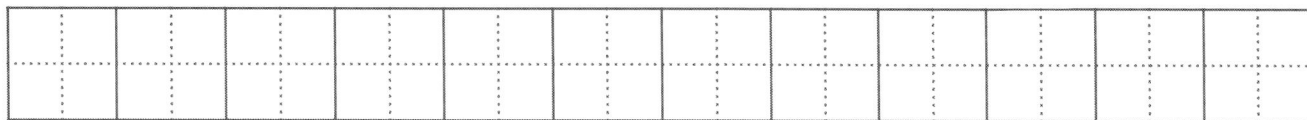
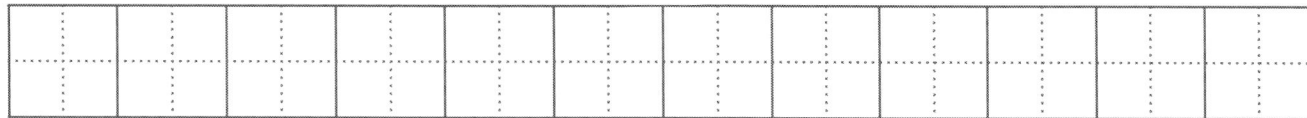
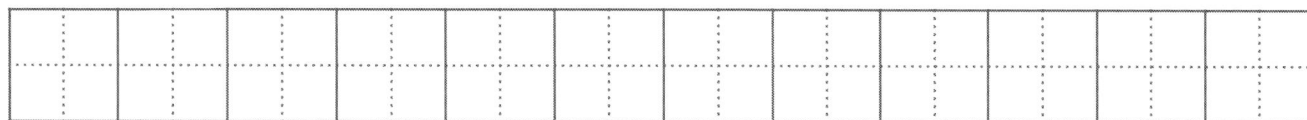
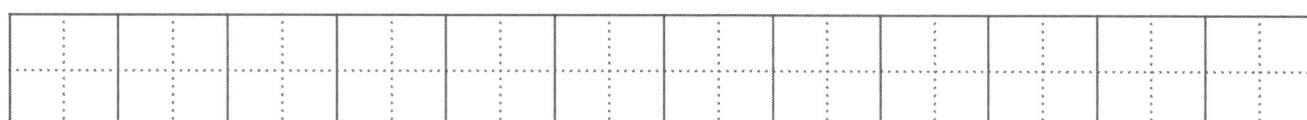
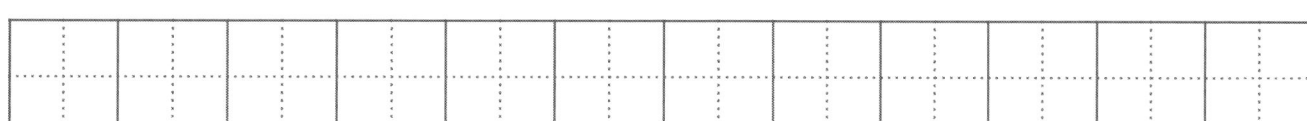
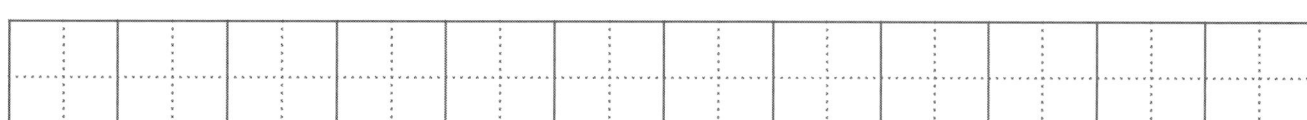
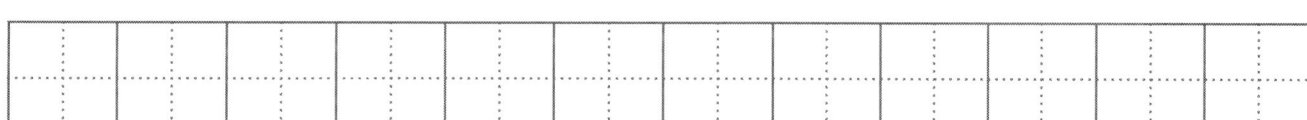
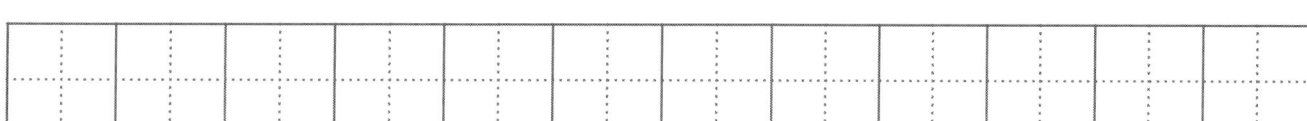
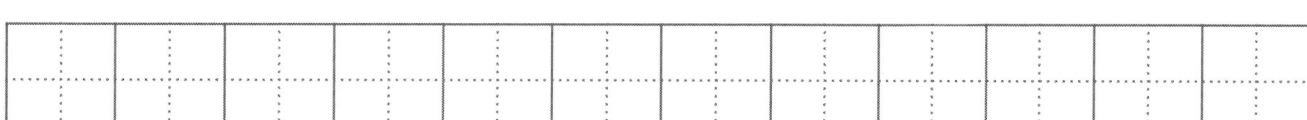
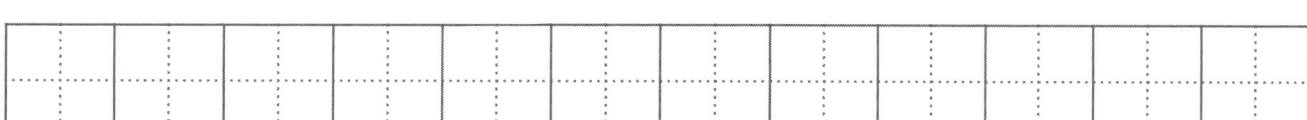
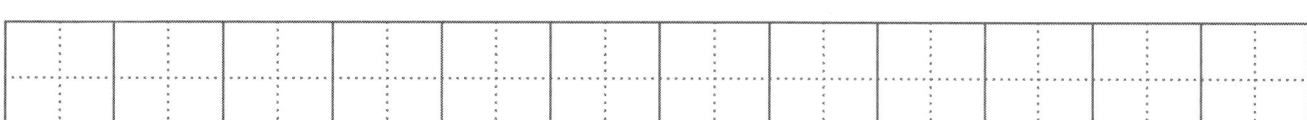

水 滴 石 穿

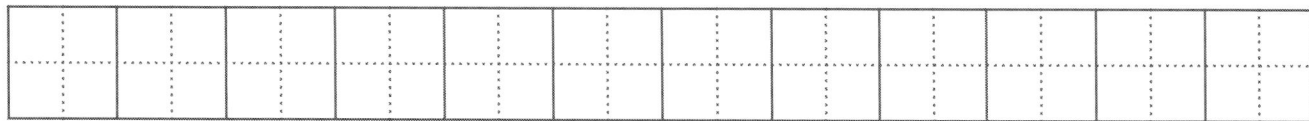

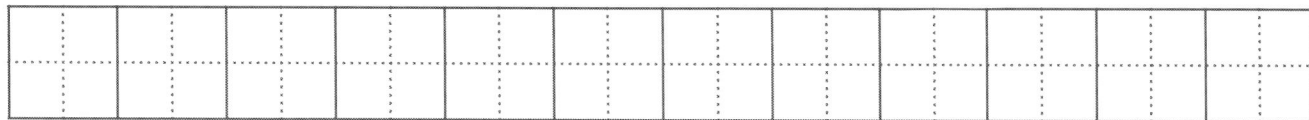

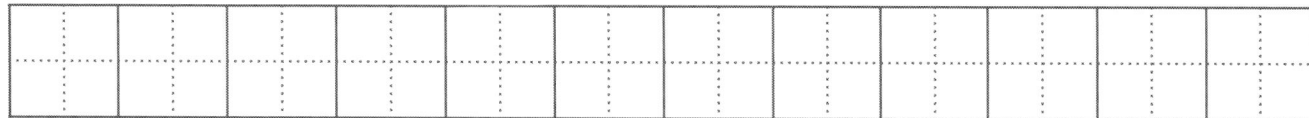

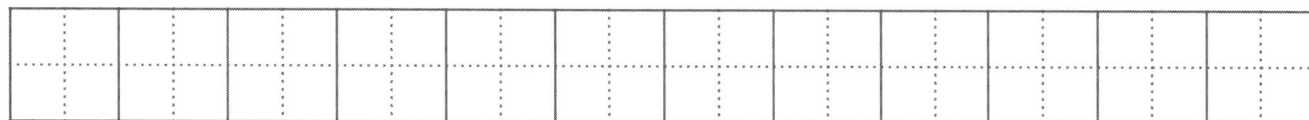

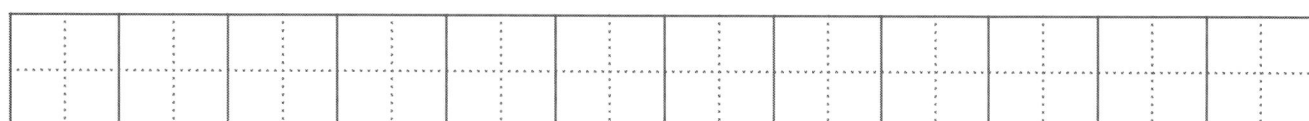

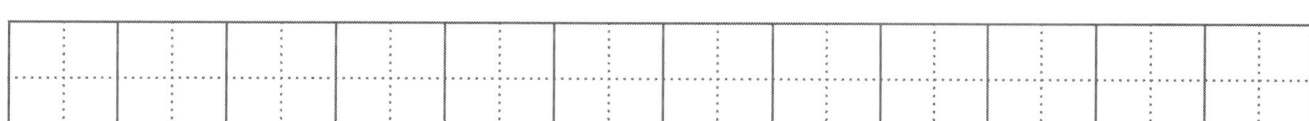

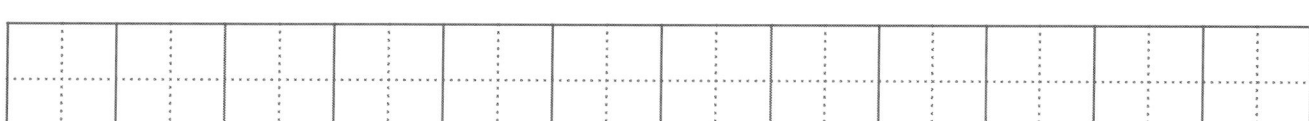

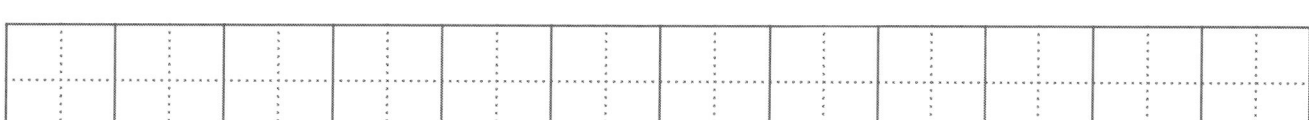

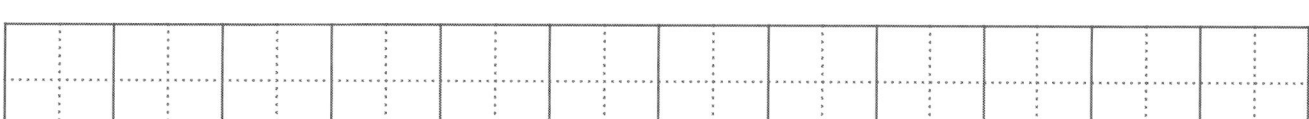

一览众山小

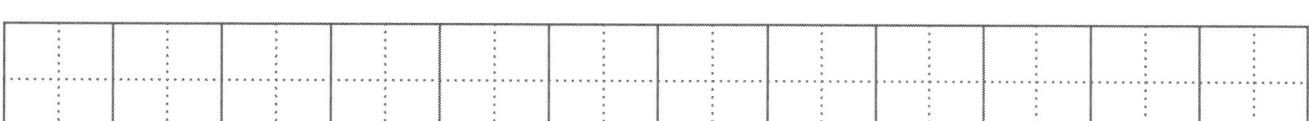

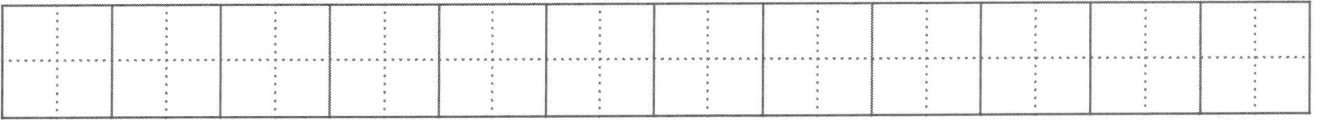
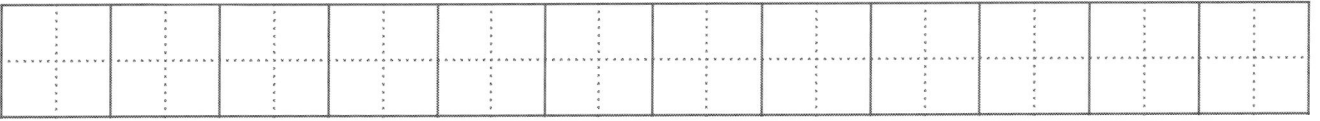
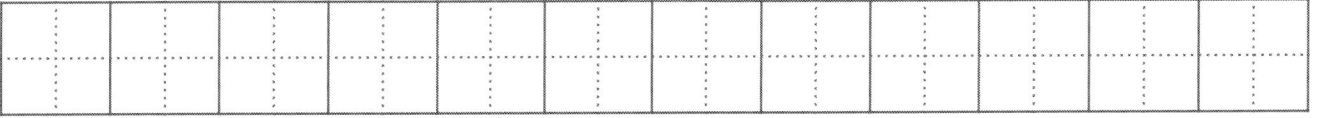
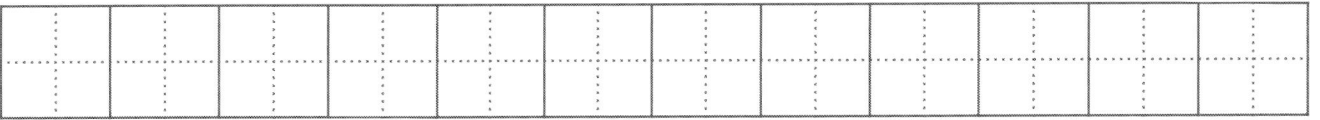
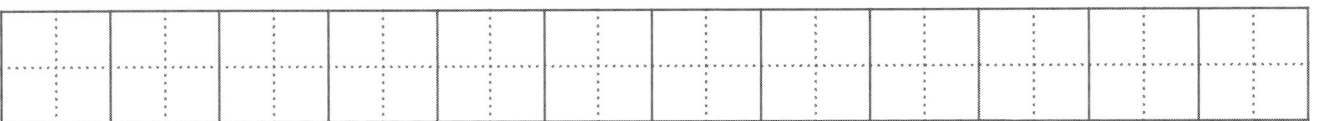
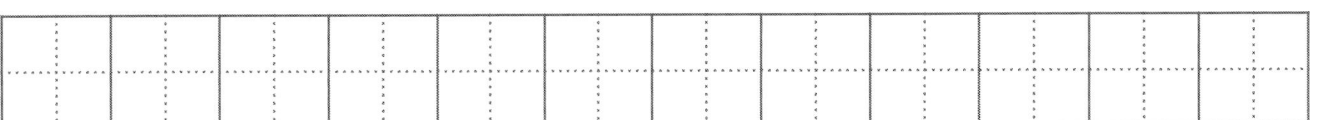
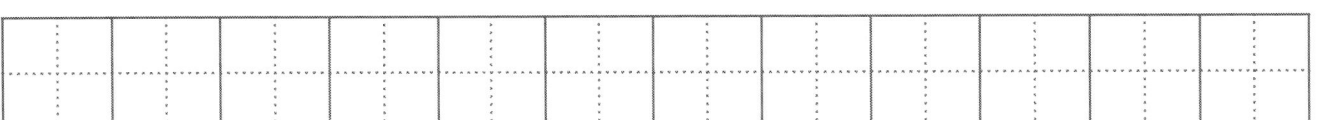
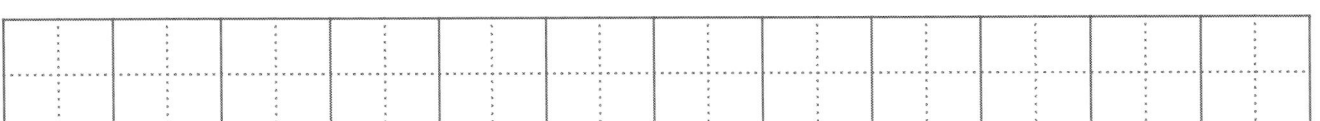
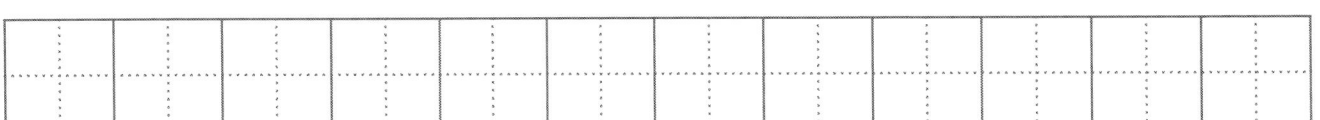
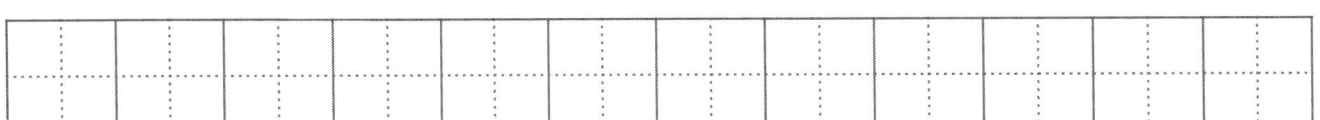

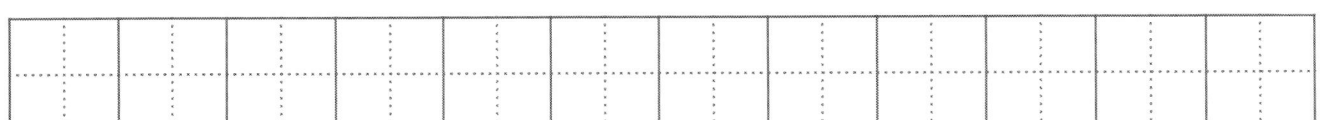

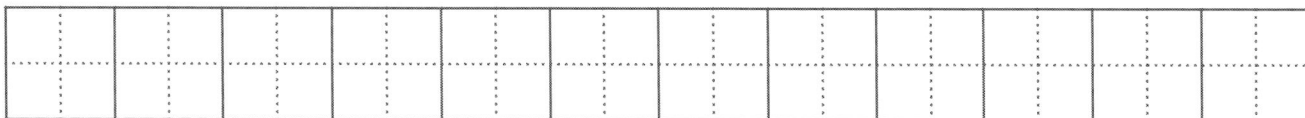
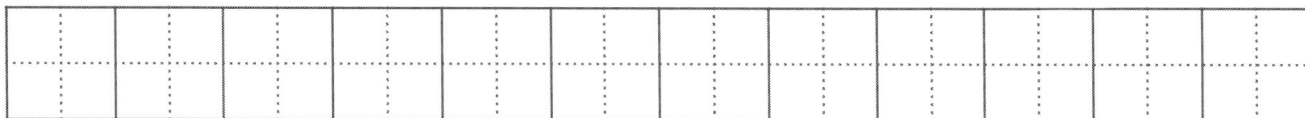
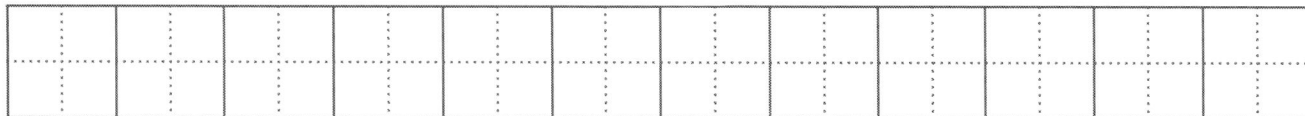
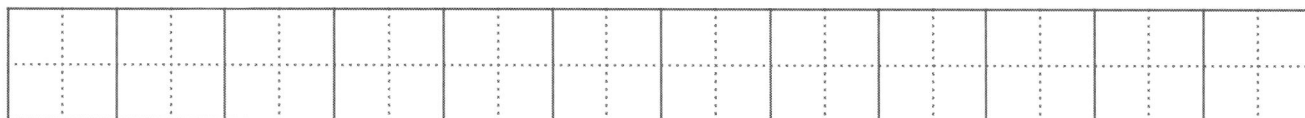
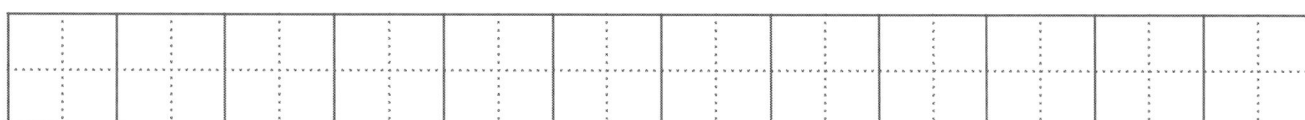

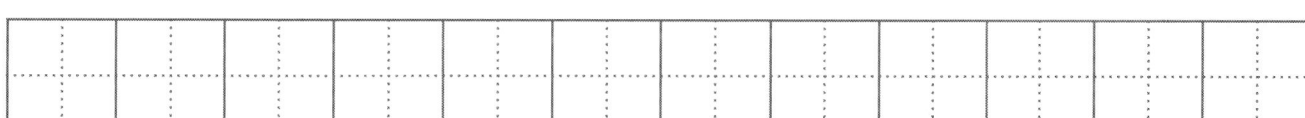
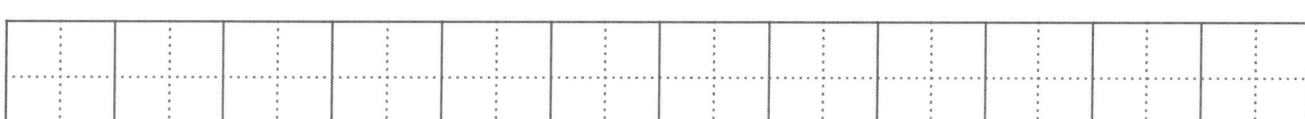
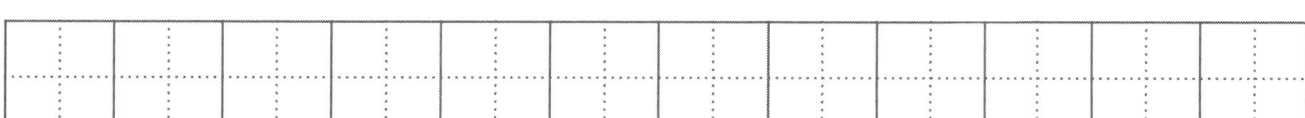
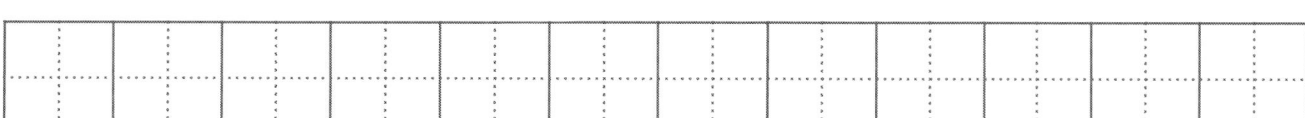
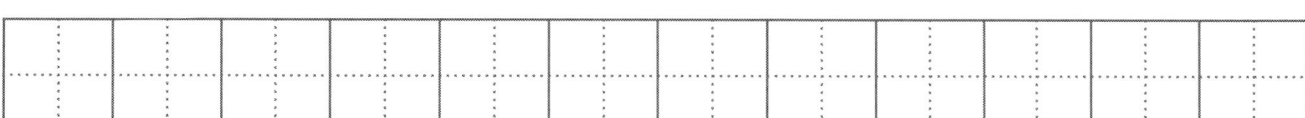

qián shì bù wàng hòu shì zhī shī

前 事 不 忘 ， 后 事 之 师 。

Don't forget past events,
as they can guide you in the future.

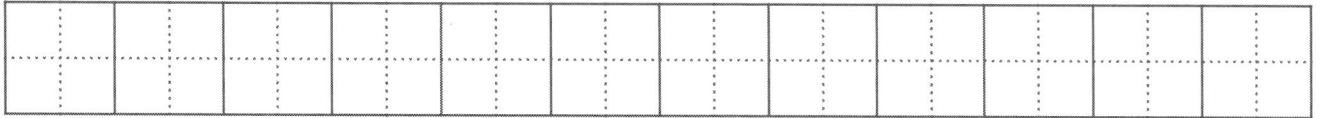
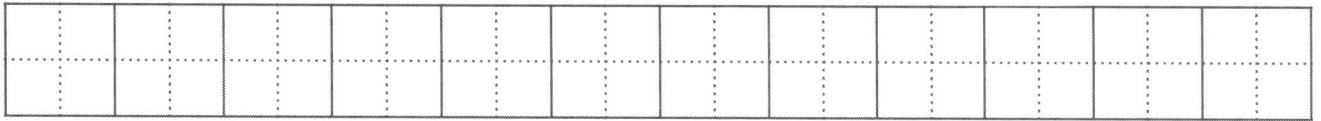
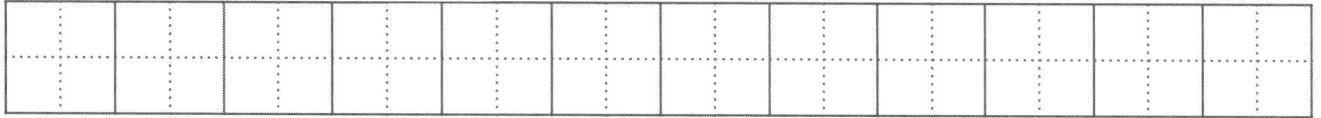
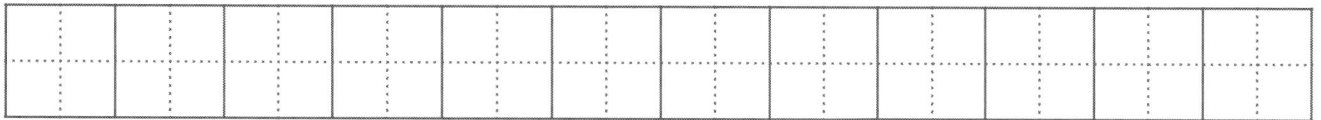
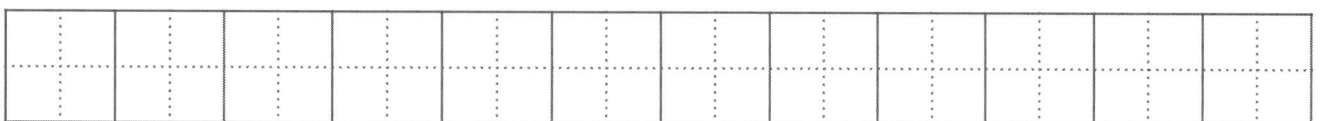
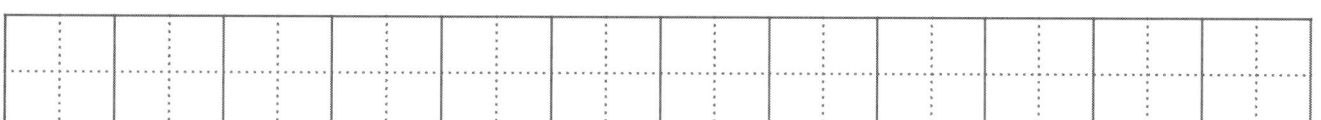
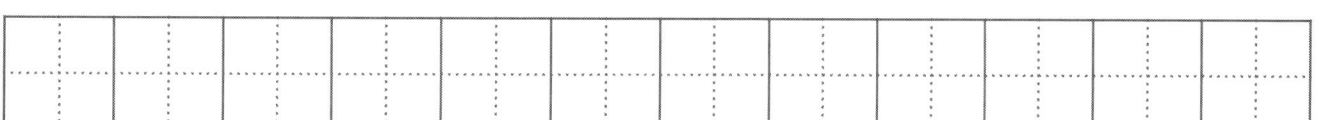
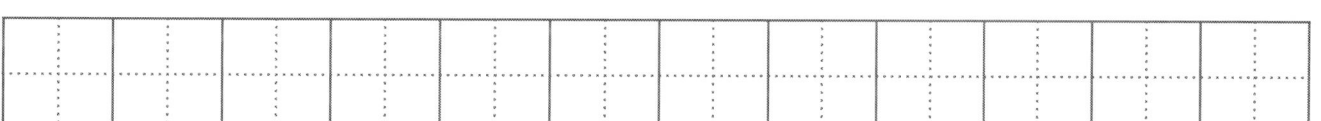

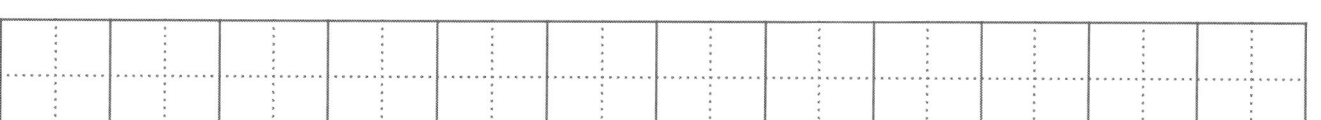
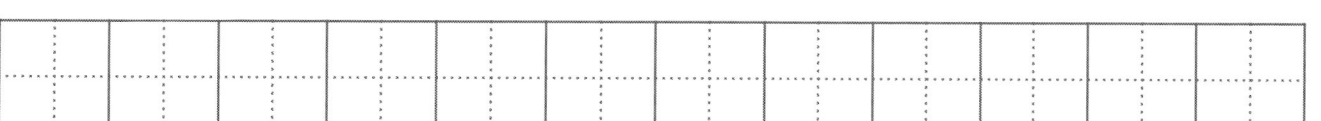
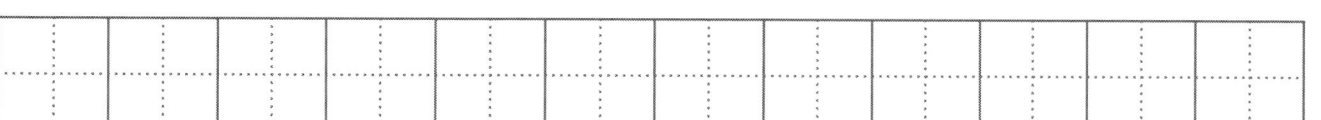

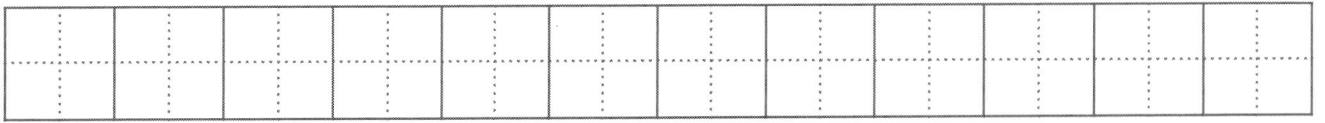
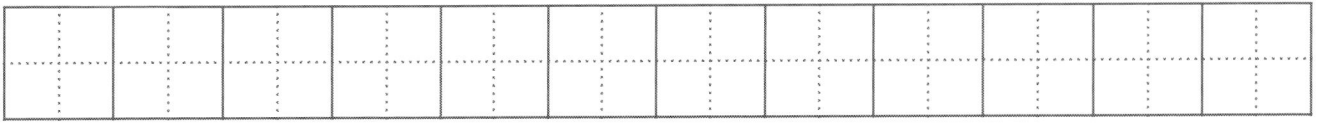
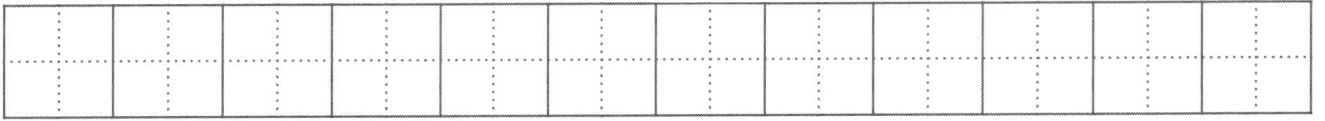
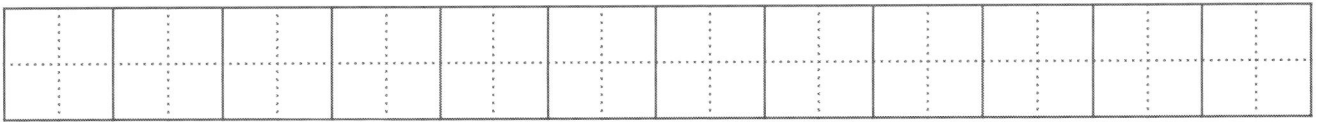
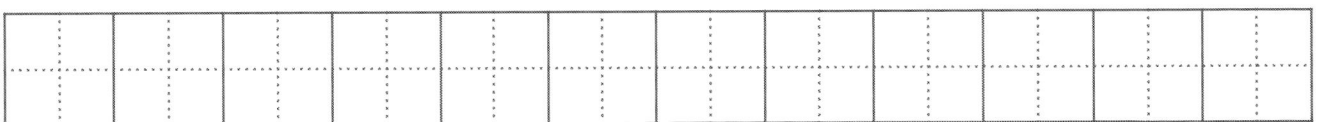
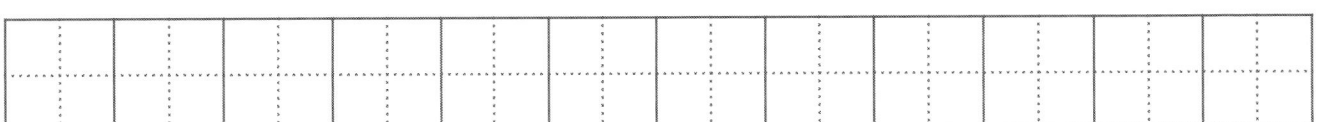
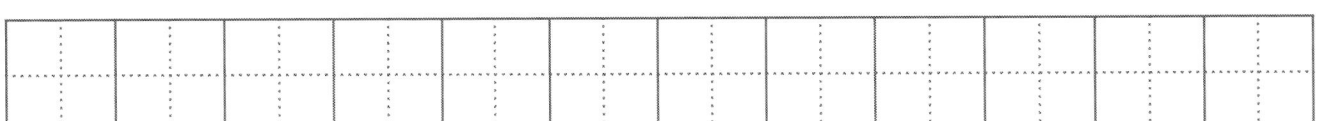
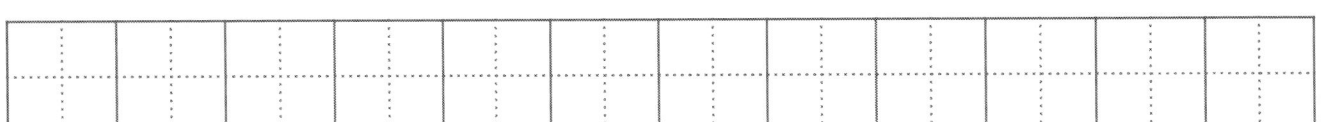
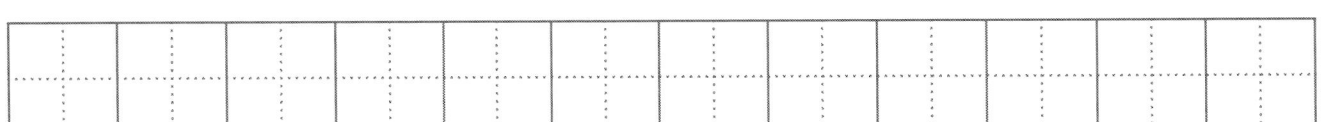
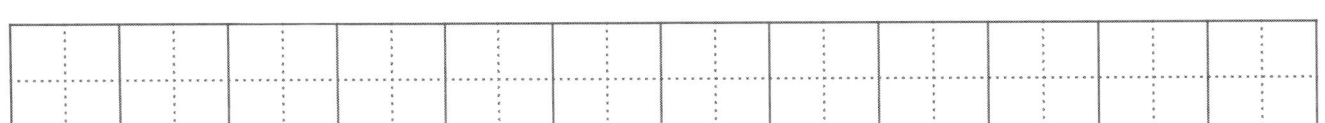
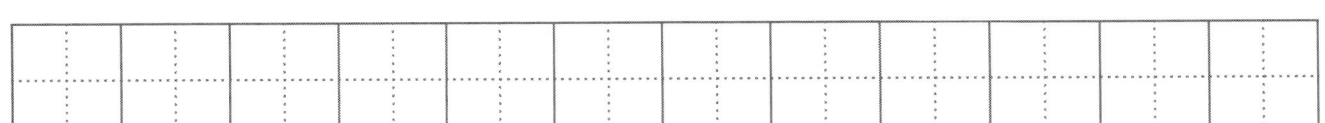
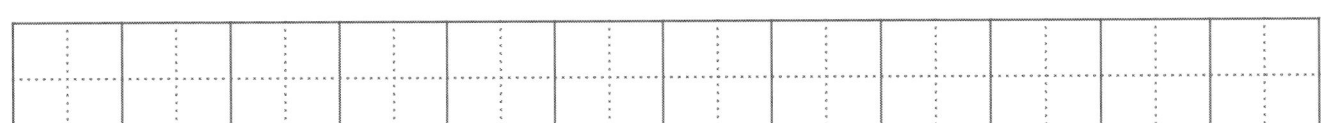

后 事 之 师

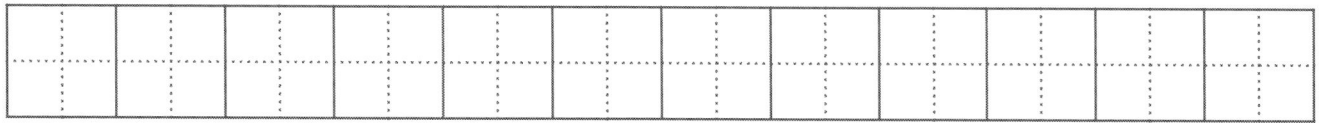
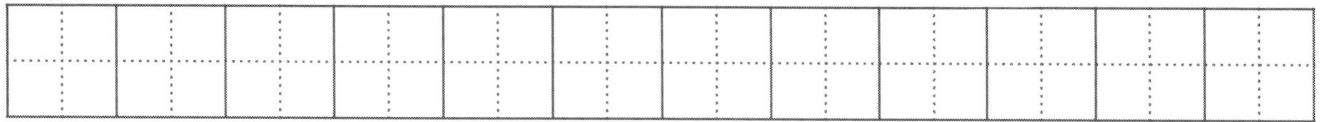
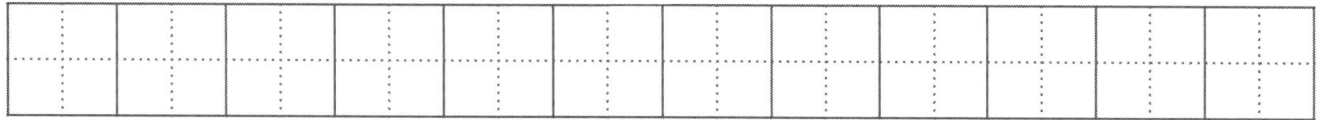
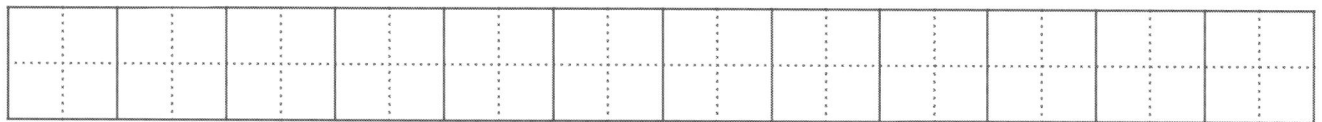

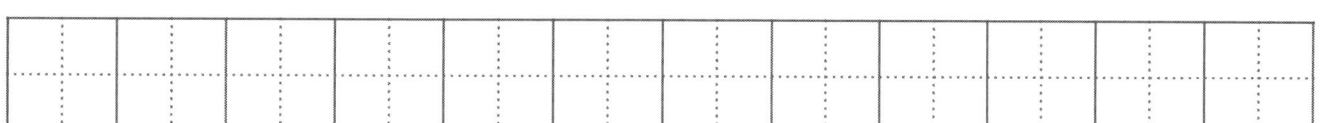
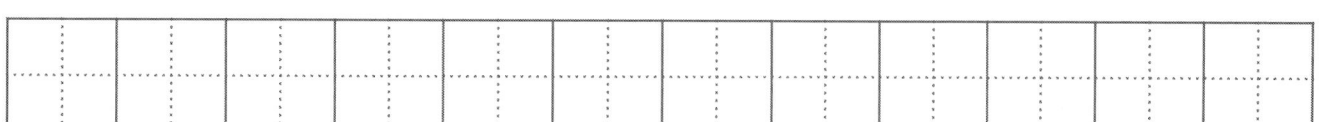
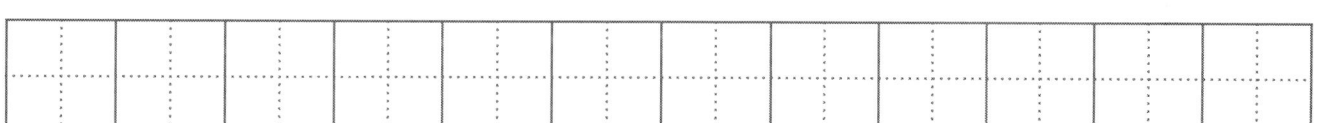
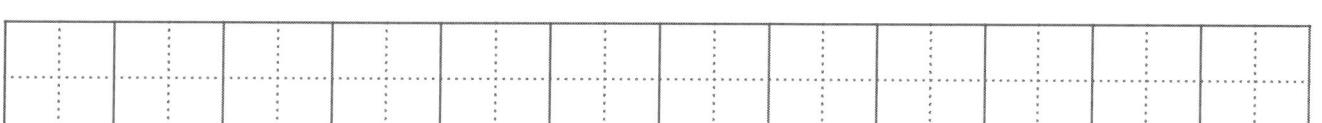
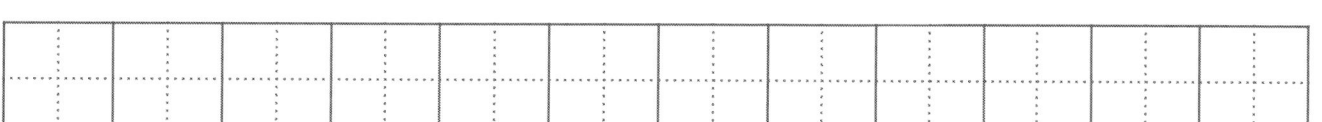
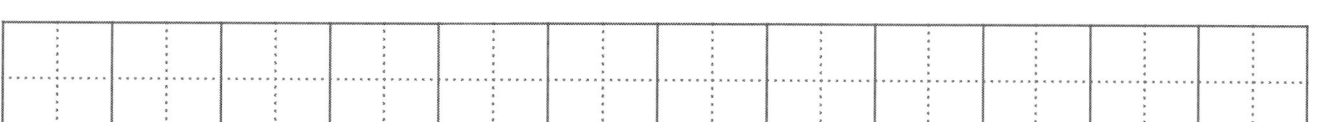
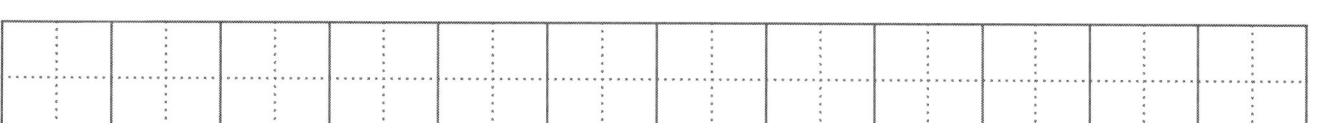

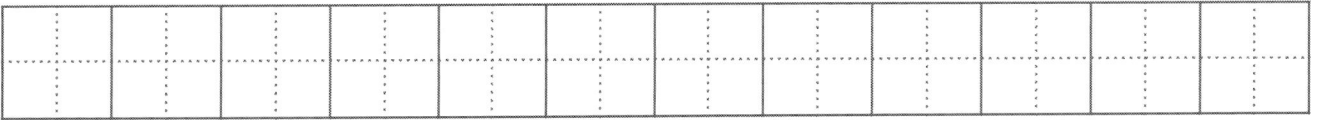
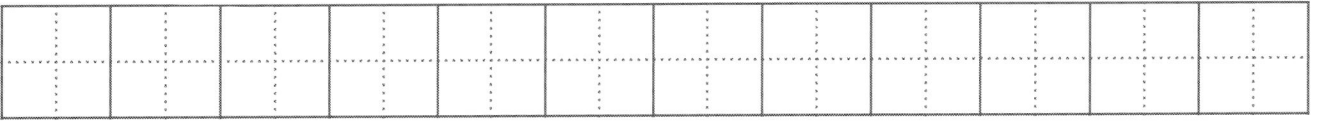
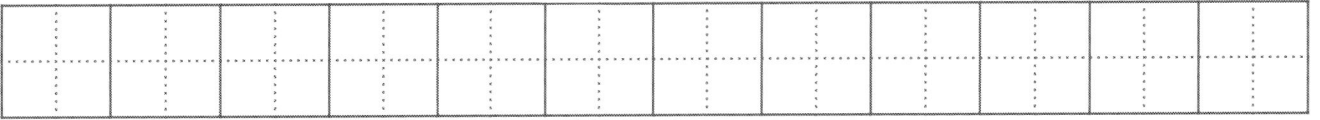
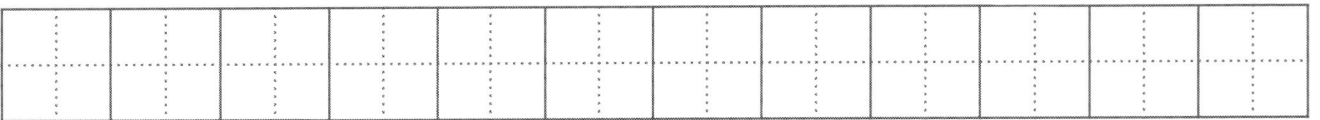
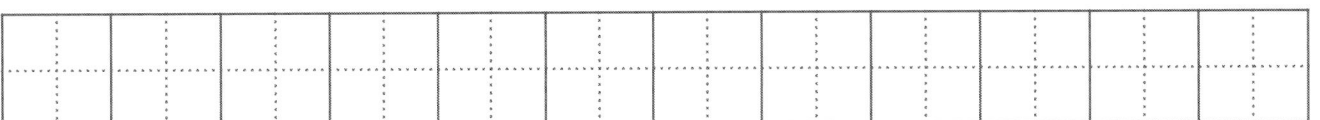
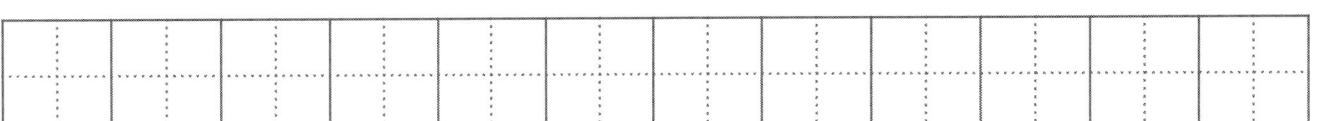
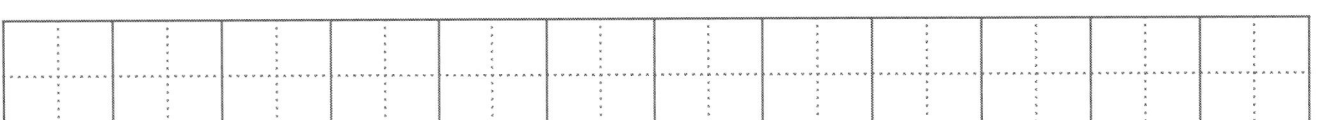
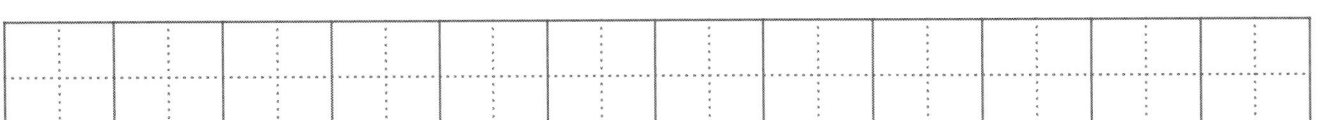
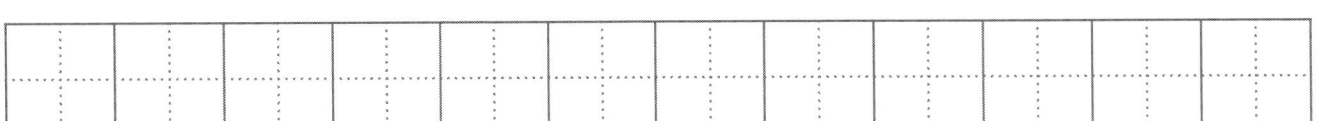
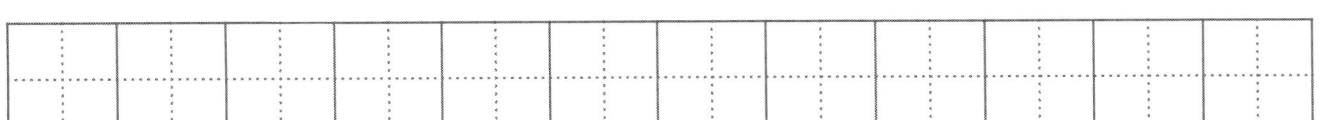
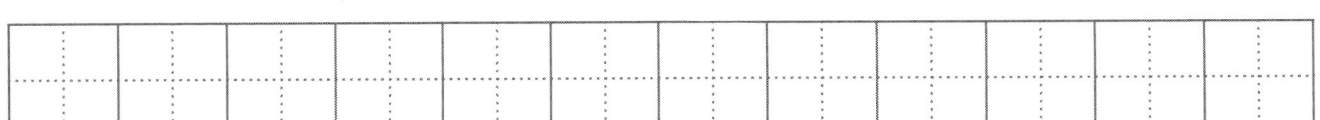
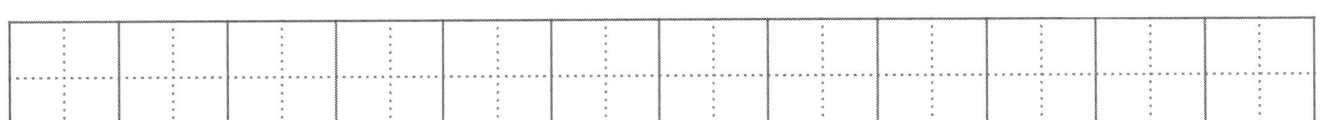

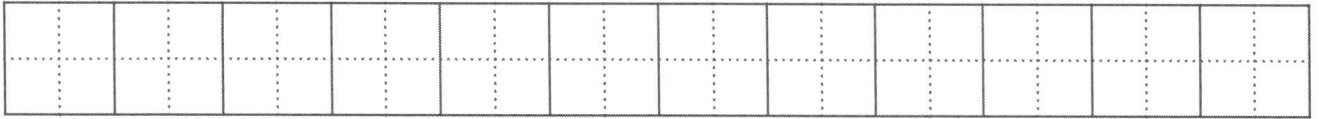
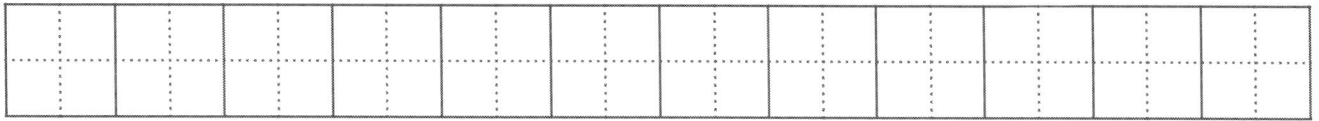
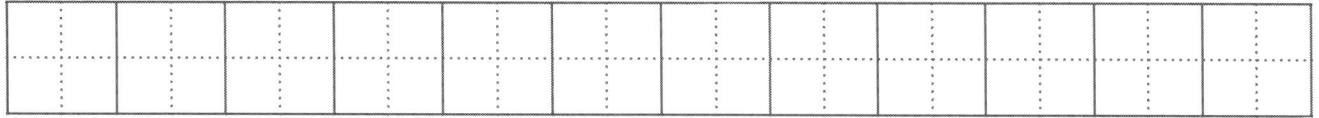

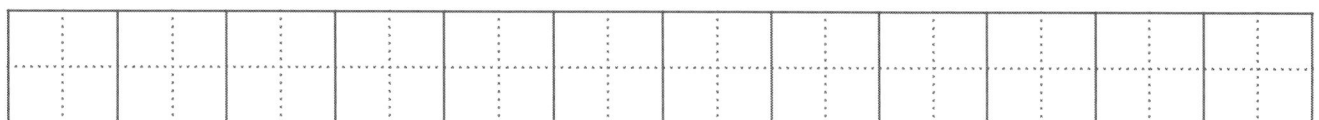

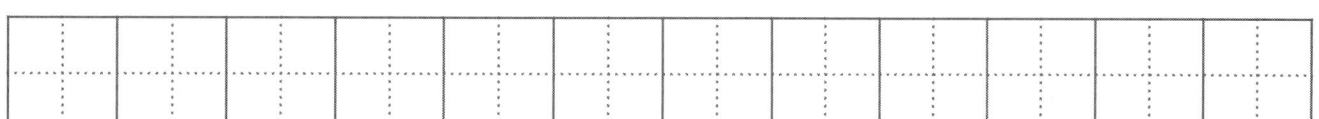
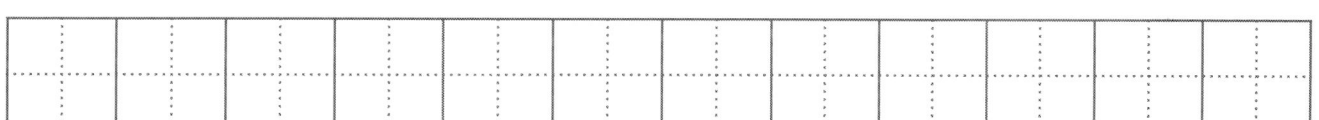
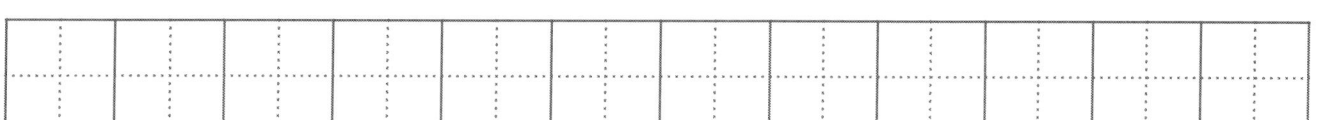
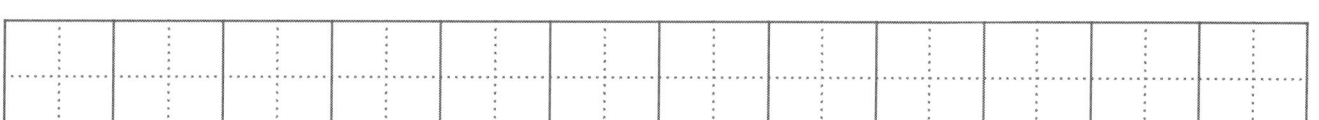
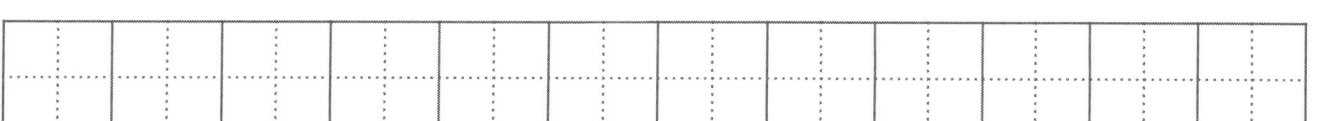
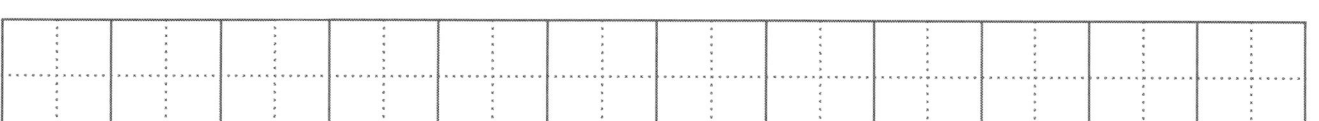

后事之师

海 阔 凭 鱼 跃 ， 天 高 任 鸟 飞 。

Boundless is the sea for fish to dive at will;
Unlimited is the sky for birds to fly at ease.

会当凌绝顶，一览众山小。

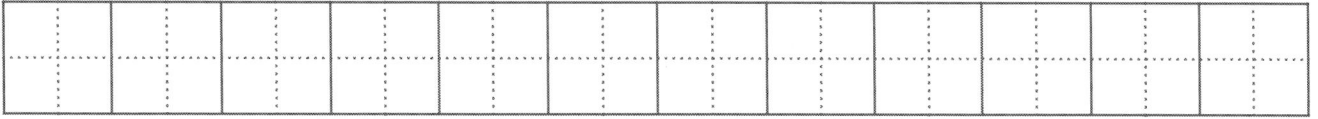

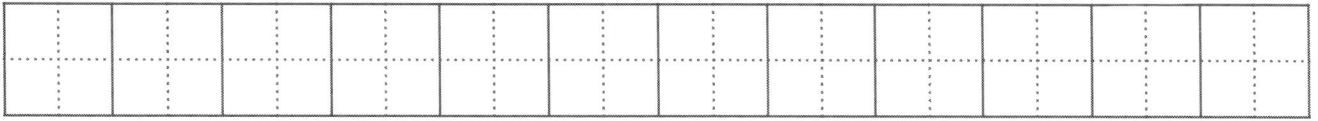

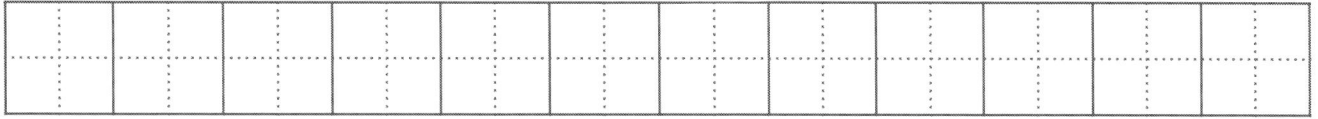

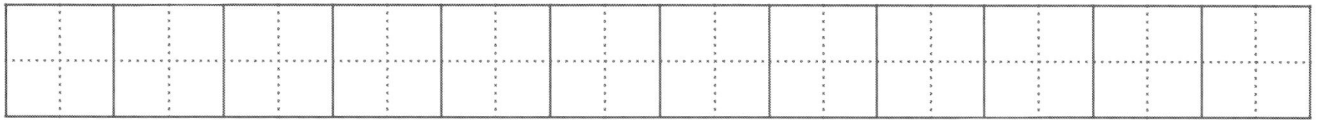

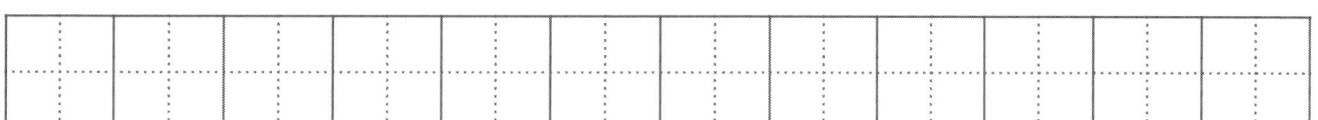

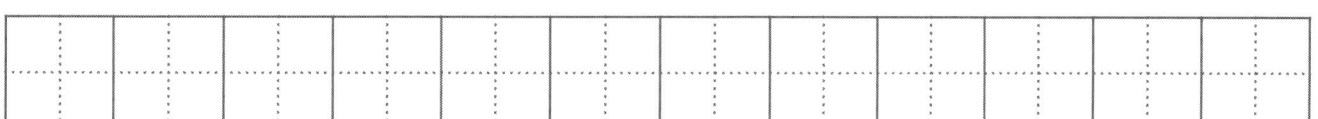

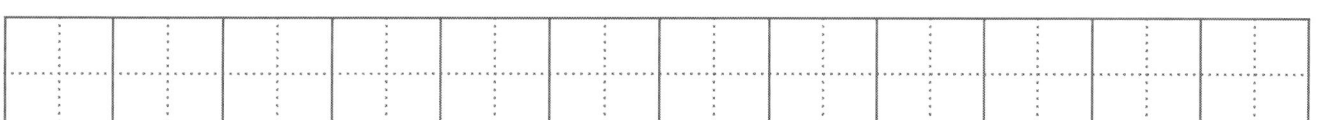

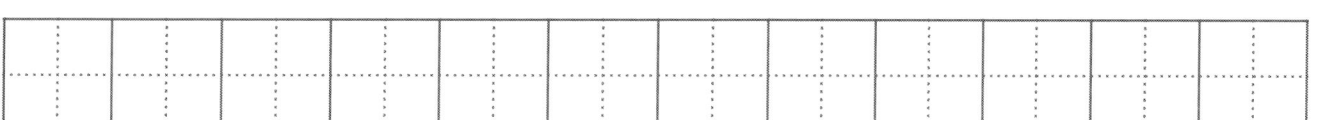

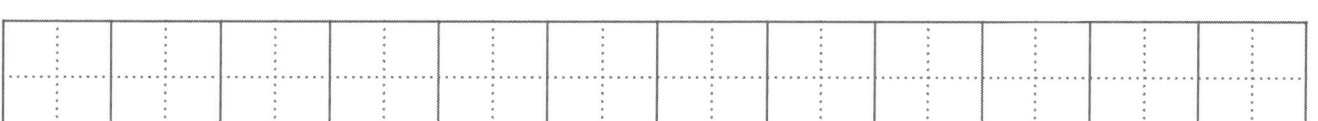

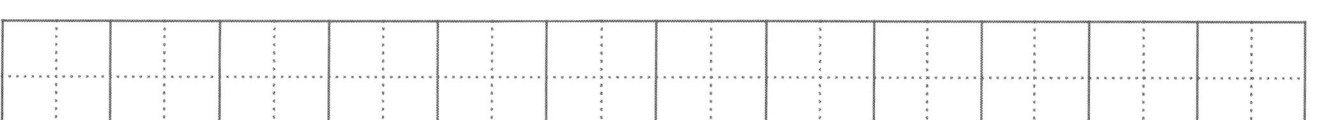

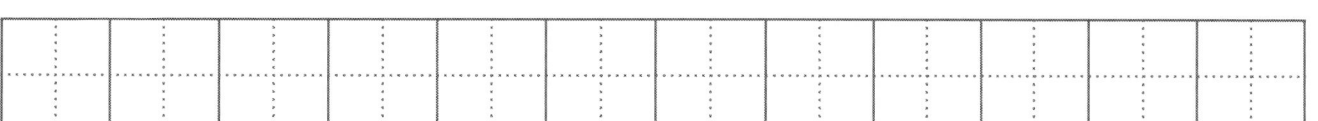

会当凌绝顶，一览众山小。

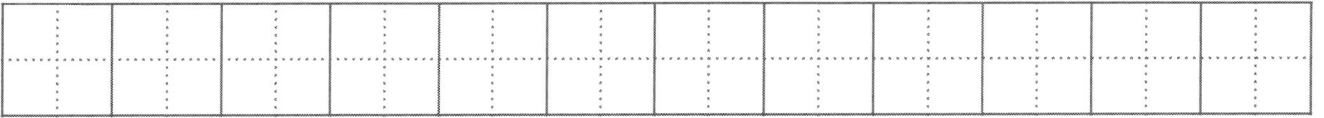
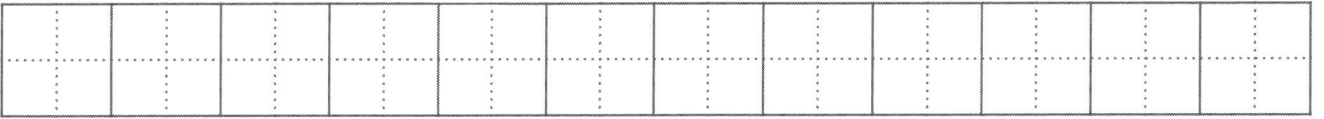
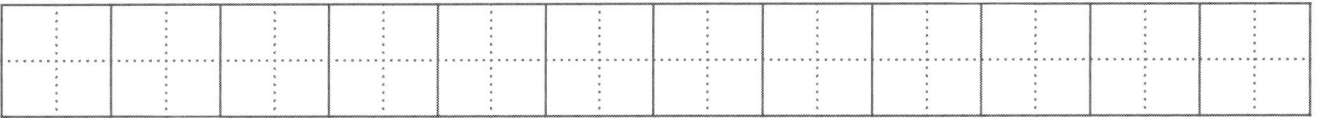
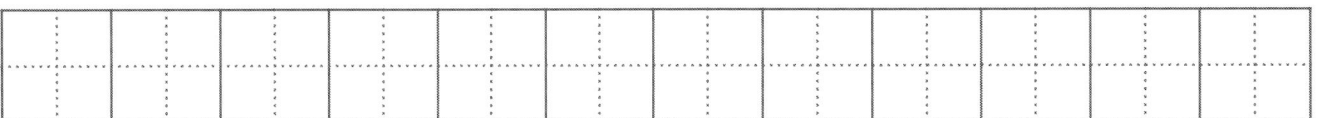
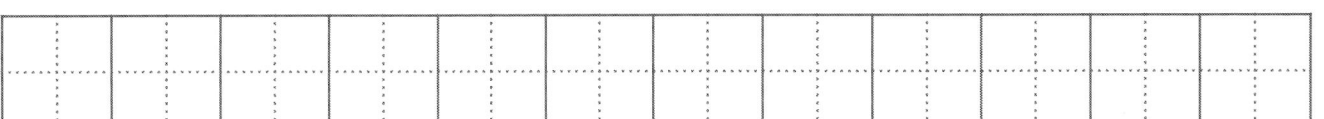
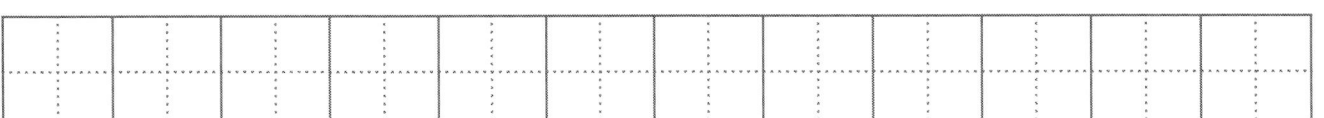
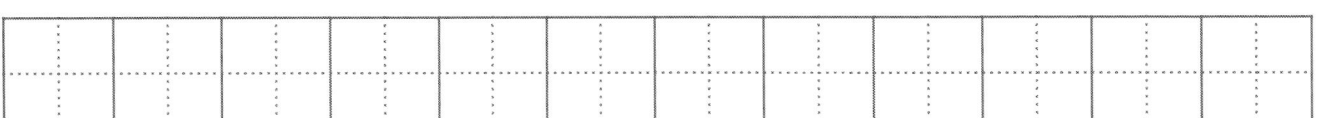
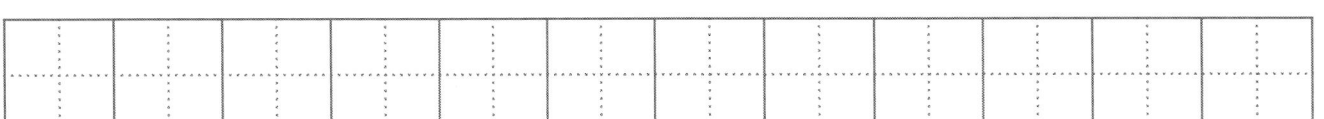
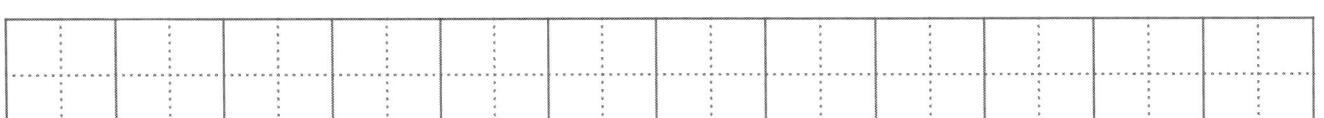
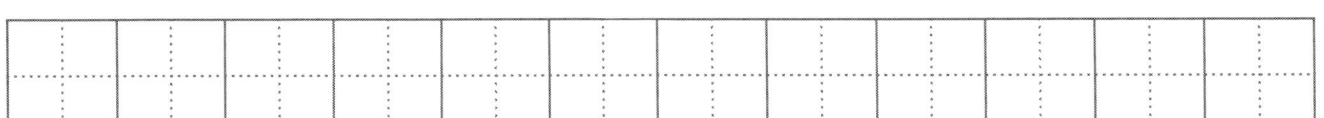
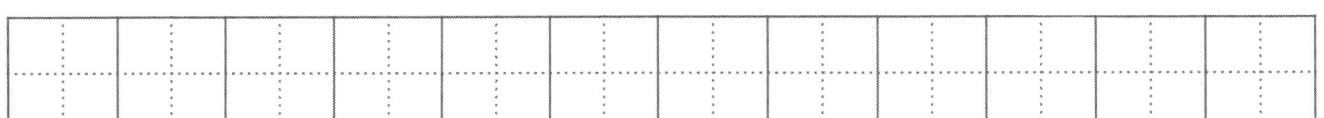

天高任鸟飞

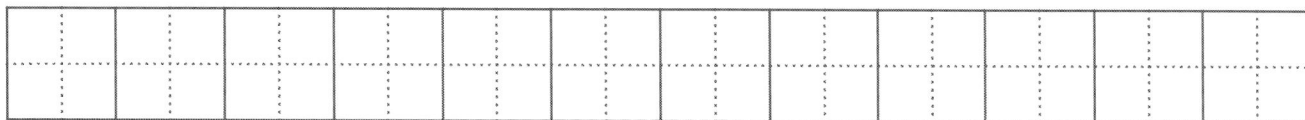
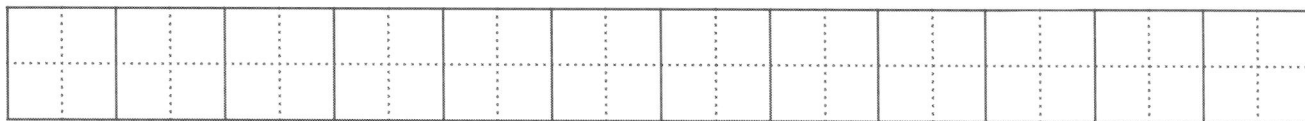
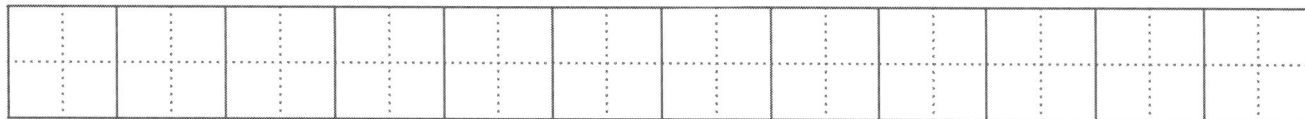
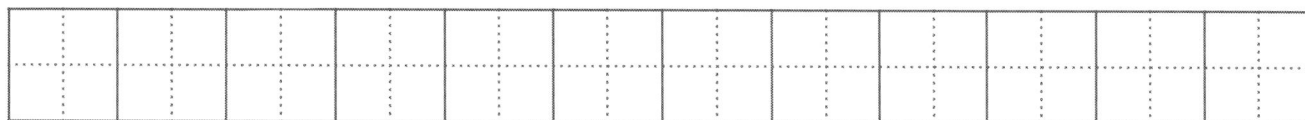
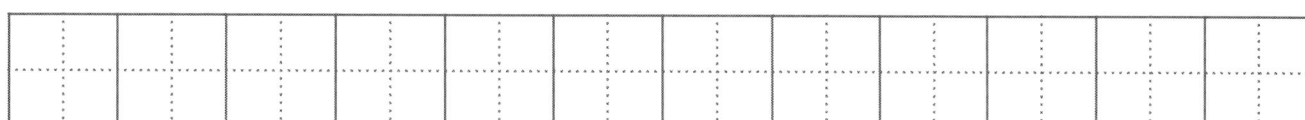
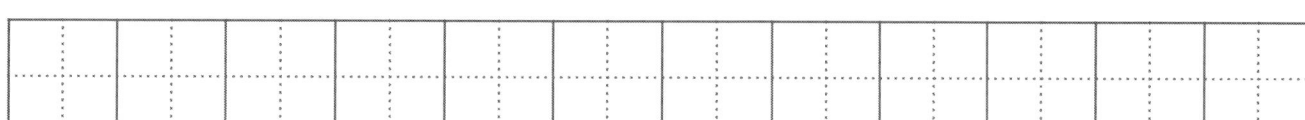
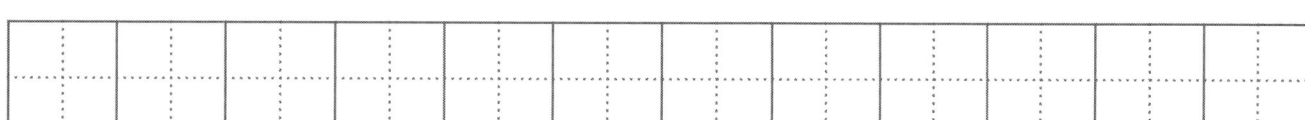
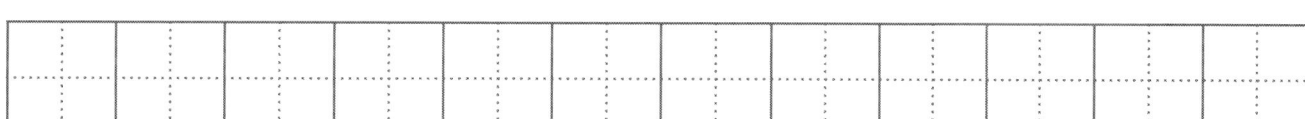
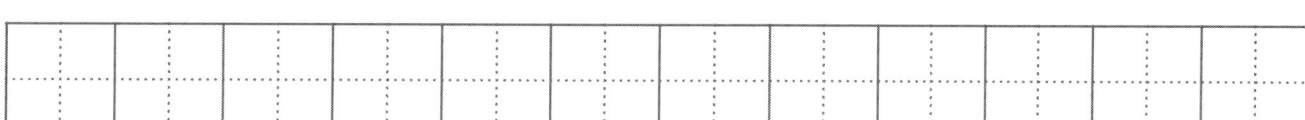
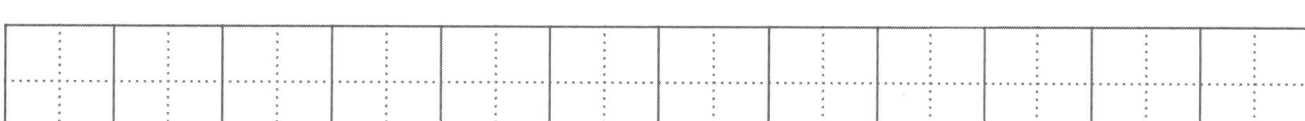
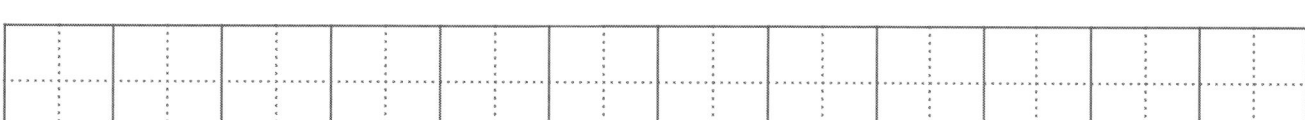
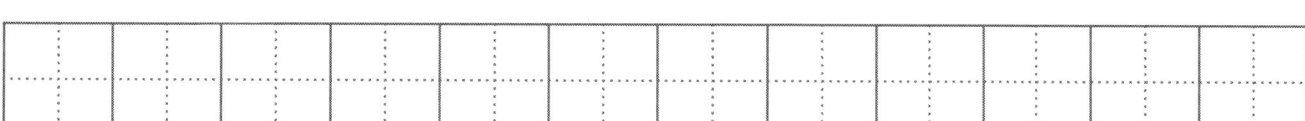

天高任鸟飞

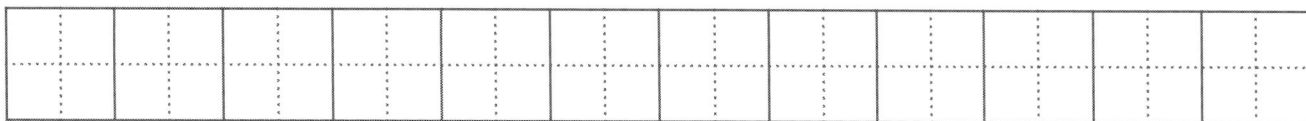
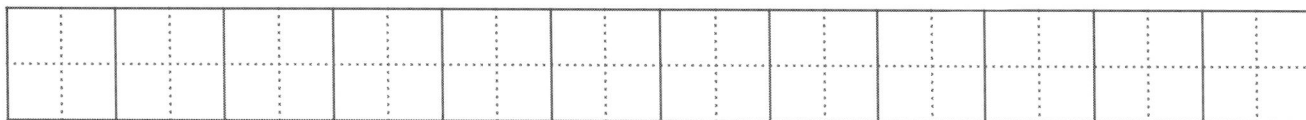
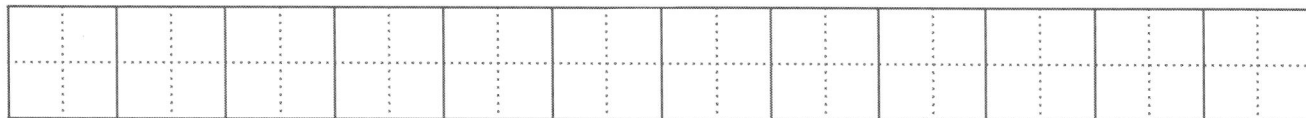
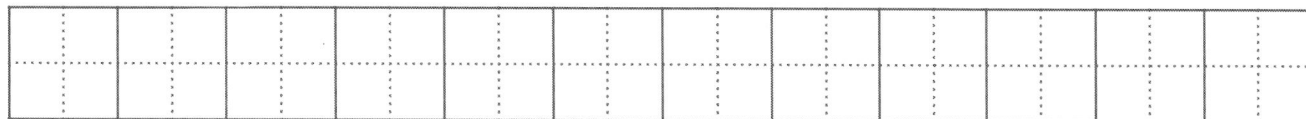
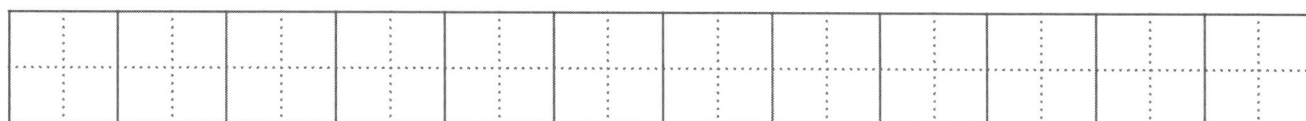
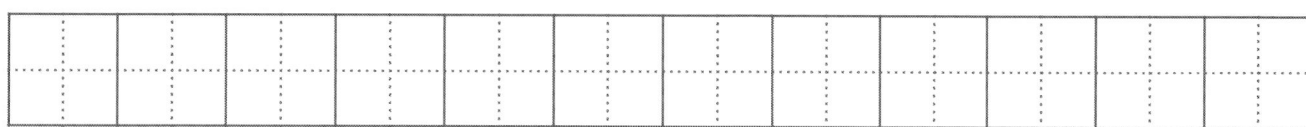
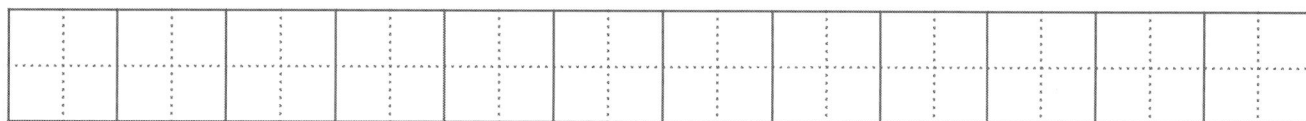
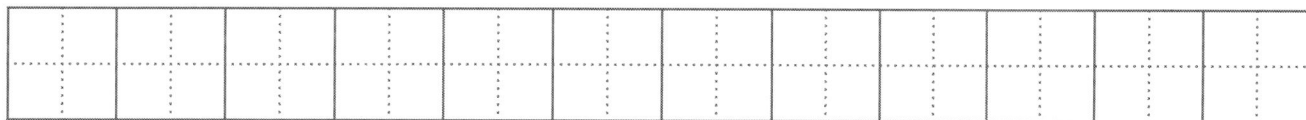
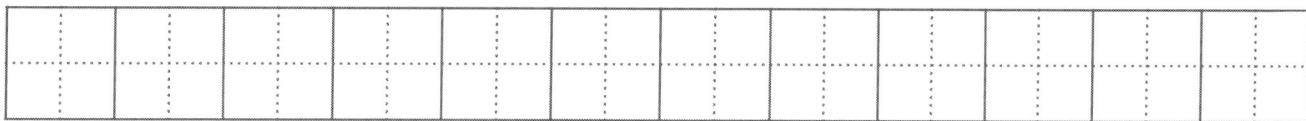
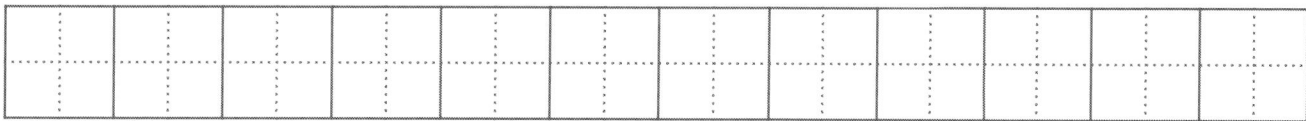
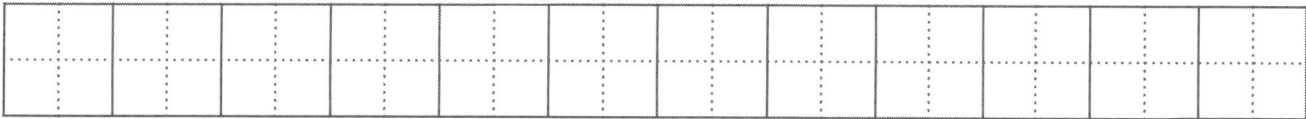
天高任鸟飞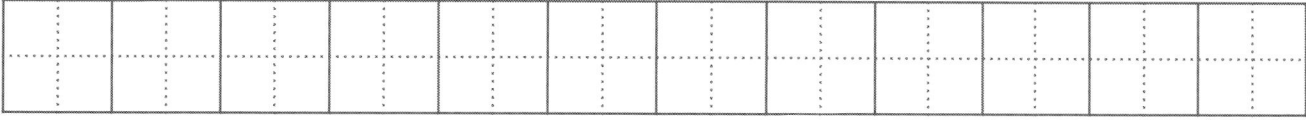

dàn	yuàn	rén	cháng	jiǔ		qiān	lǐ	gòng	chán	juān	
但	愿	人	长	久	，	千	里	共	婵	娟	。

May we all be blessed with longevity.
Though thousands of miles apart,
we still share the moon's beauty together.

生当作人杰，死亦为鬼雄。

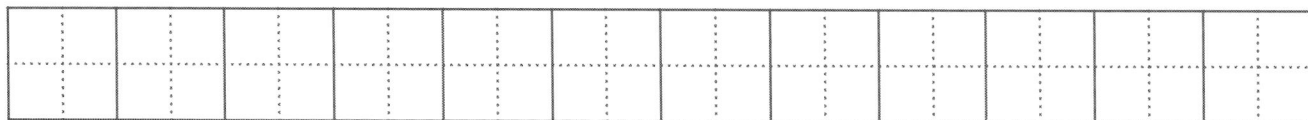

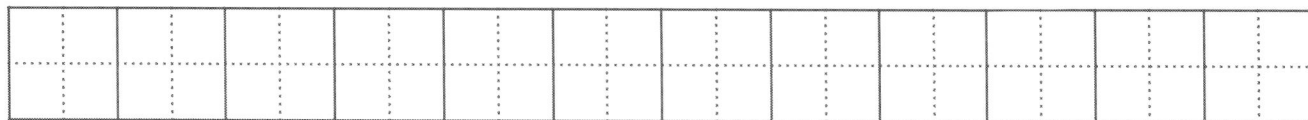

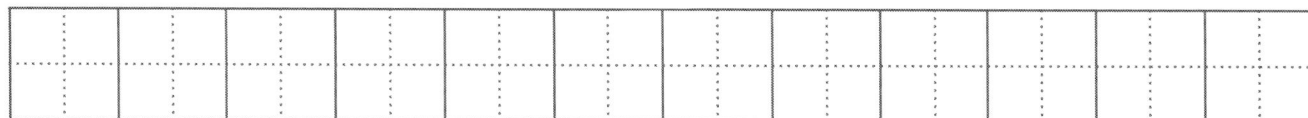

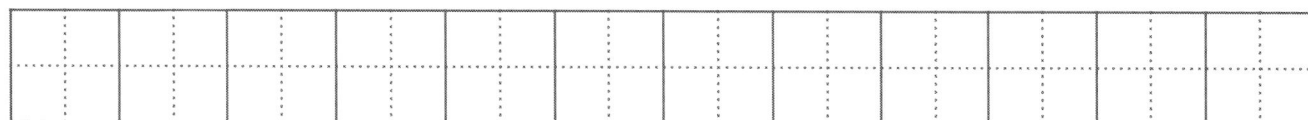

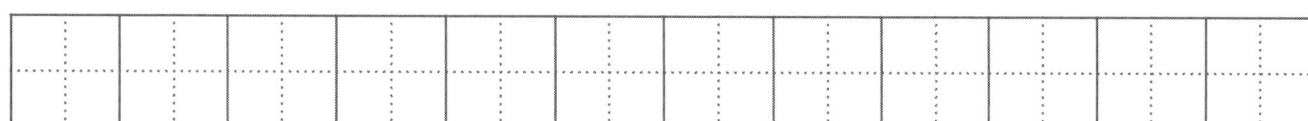

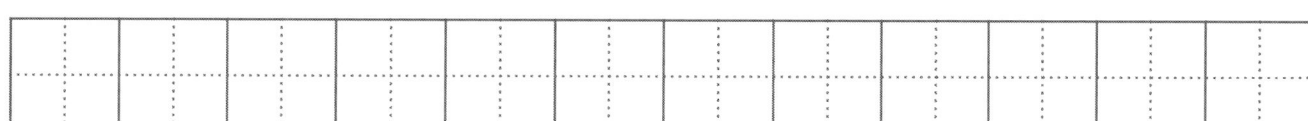

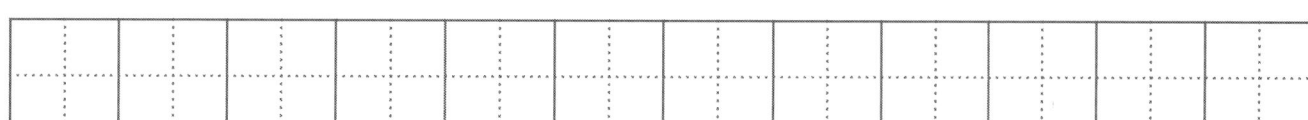

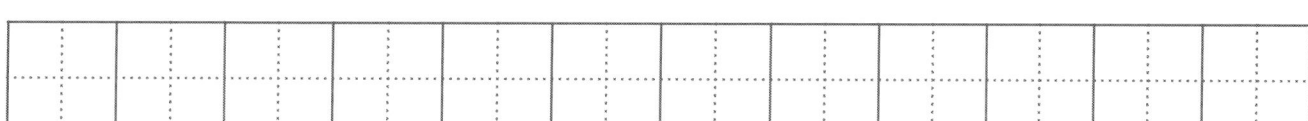

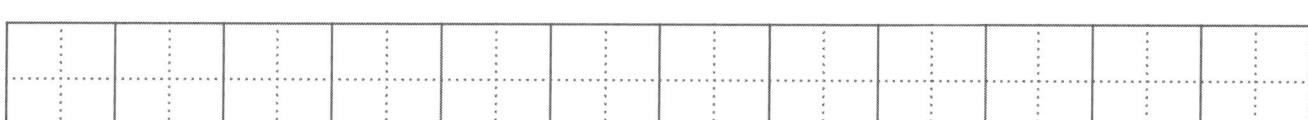

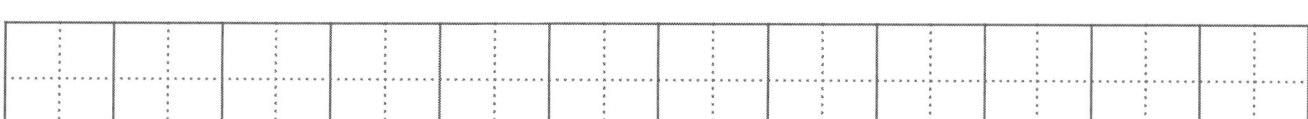

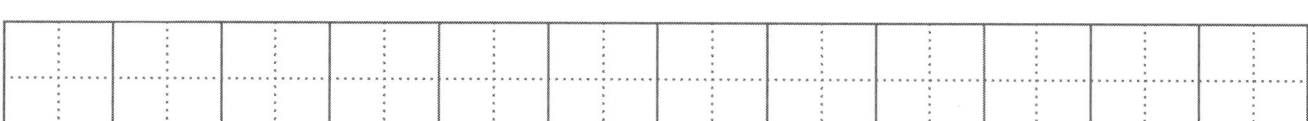

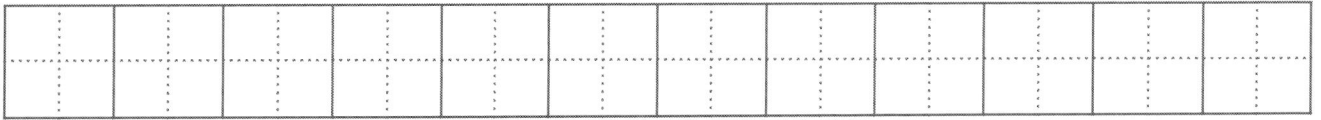
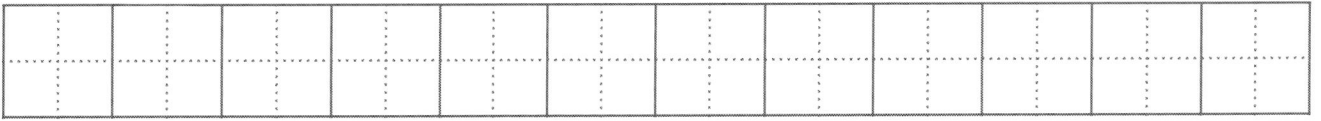
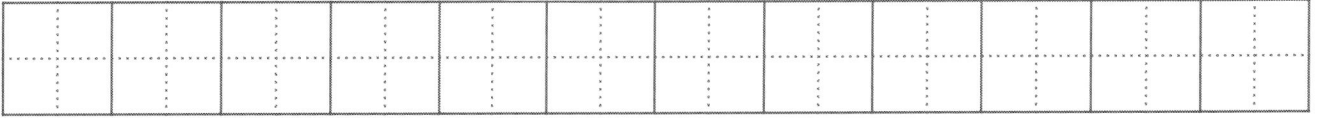
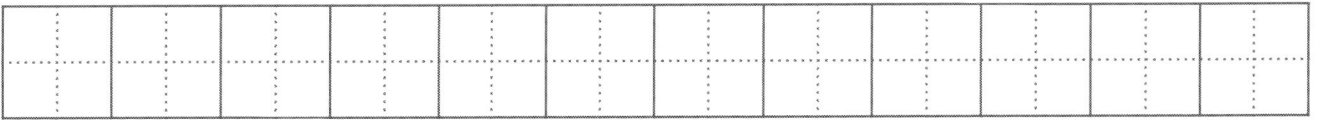
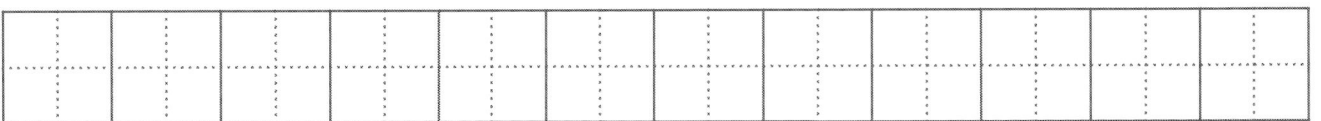
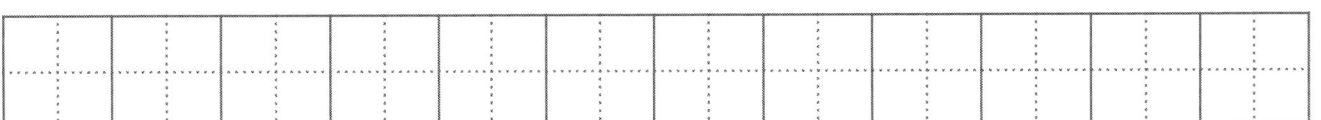
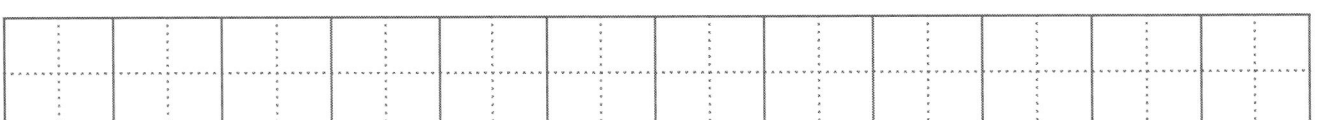
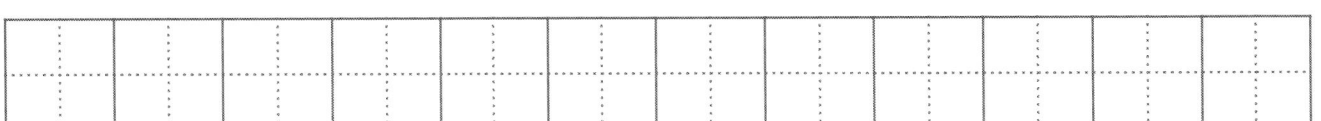
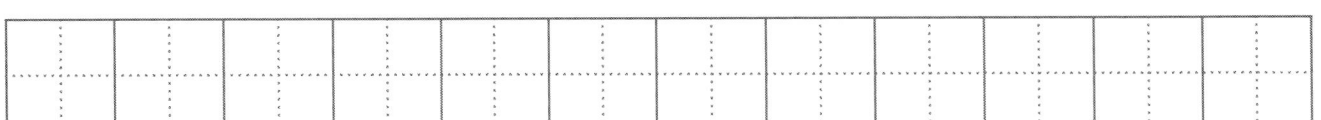
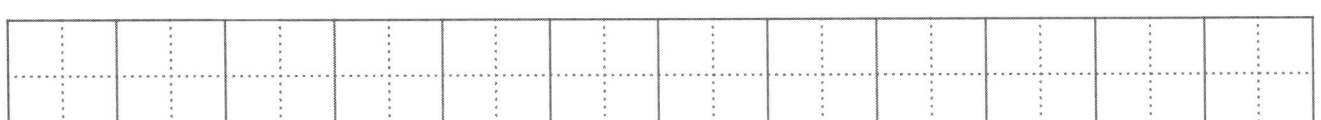
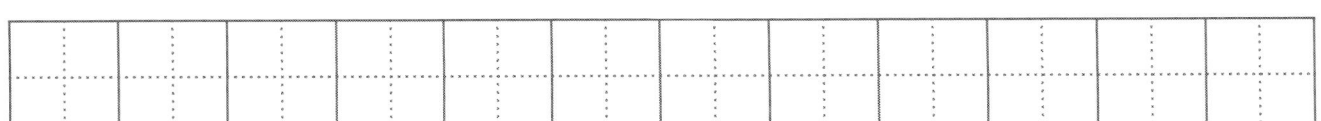
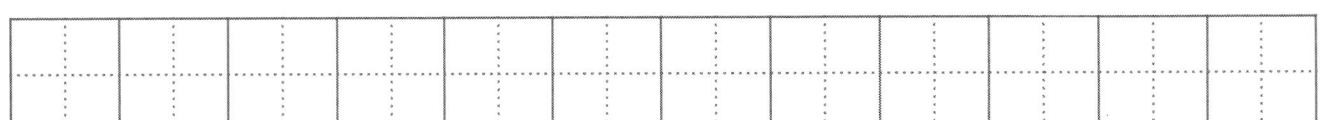

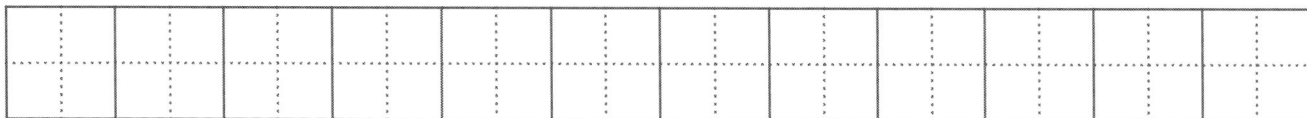
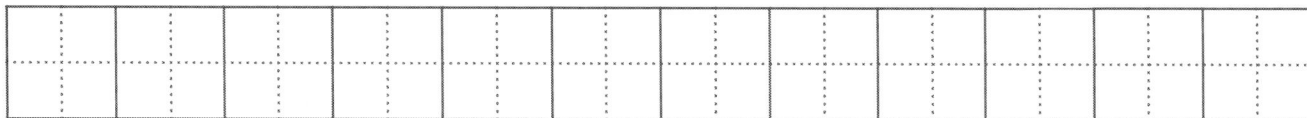
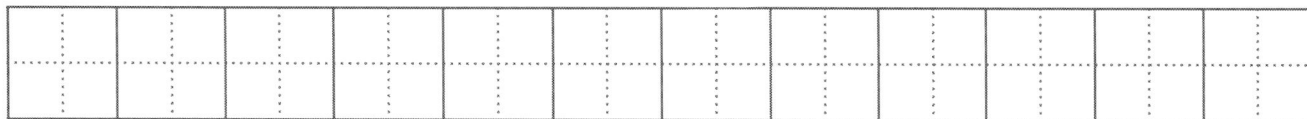

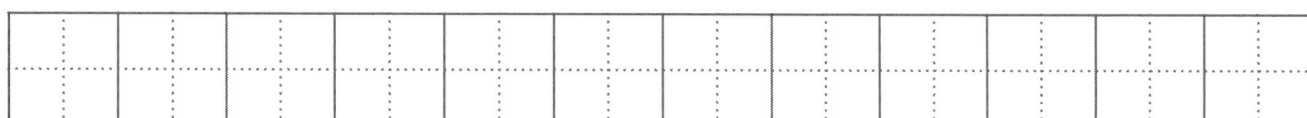
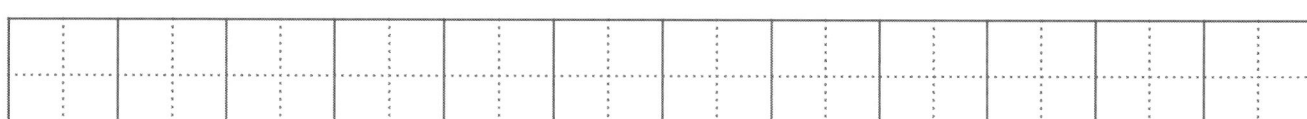
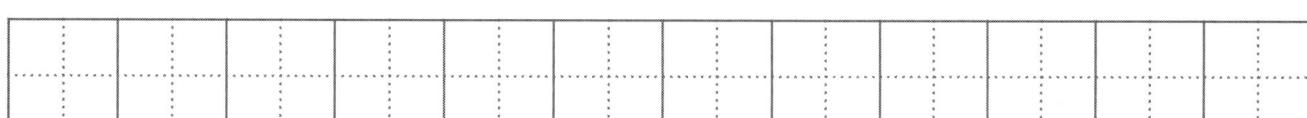
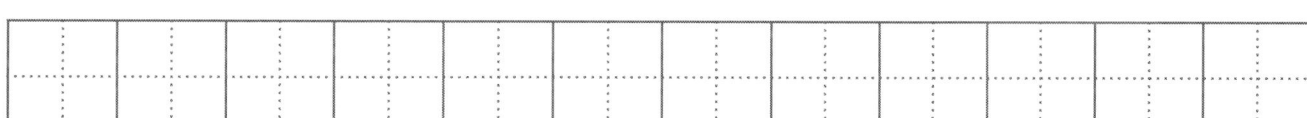
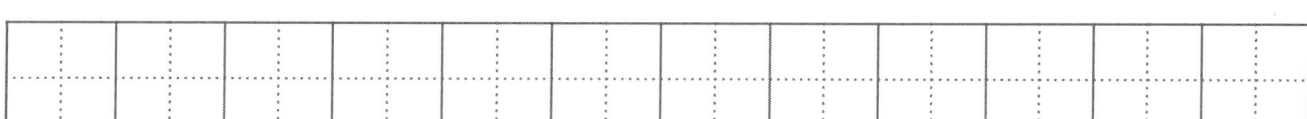
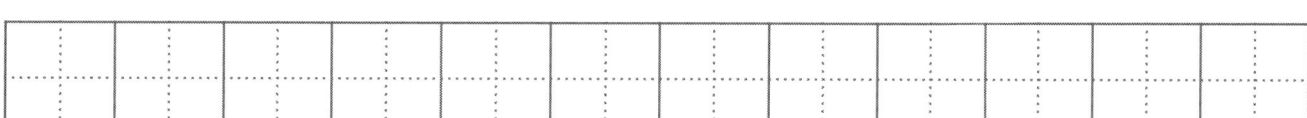
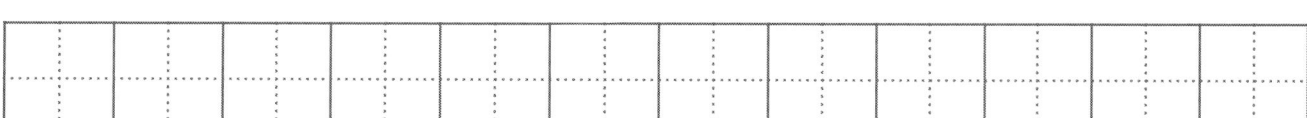

千里共婵娟

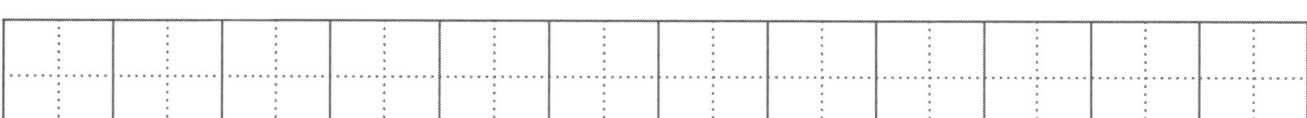

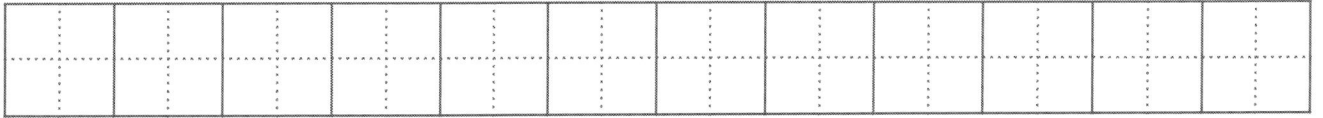
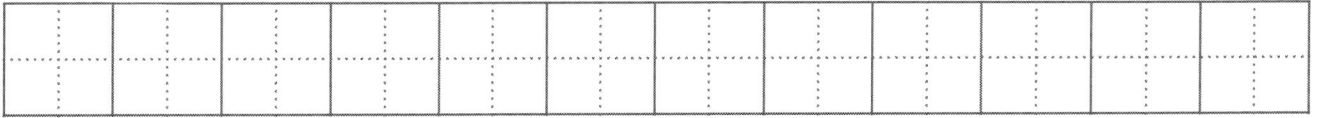
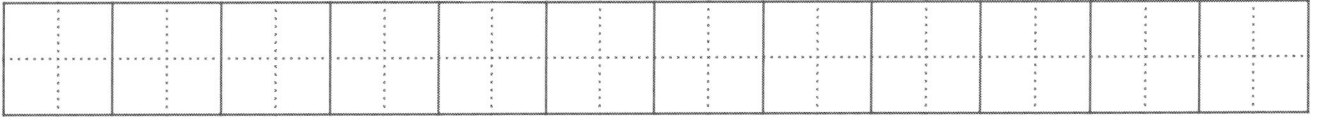
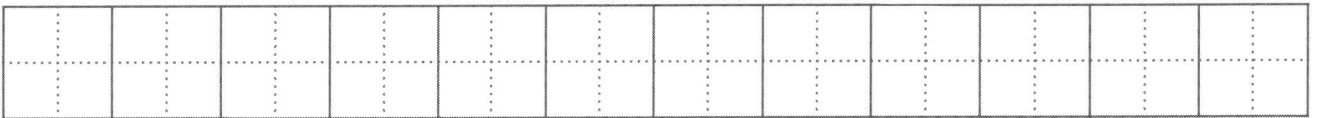
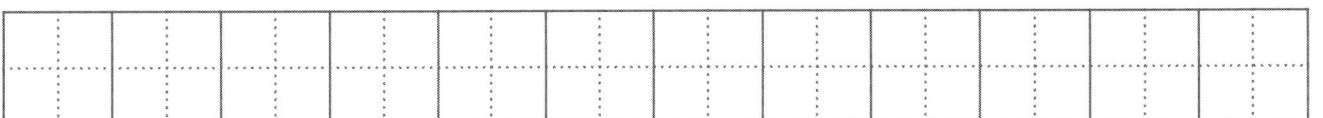
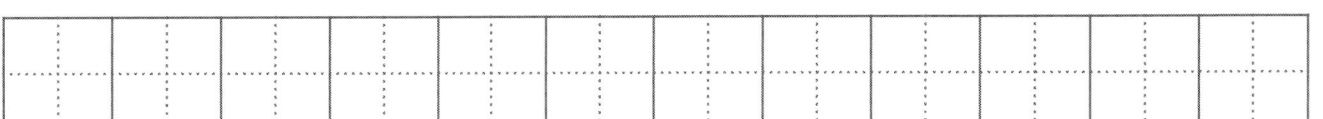
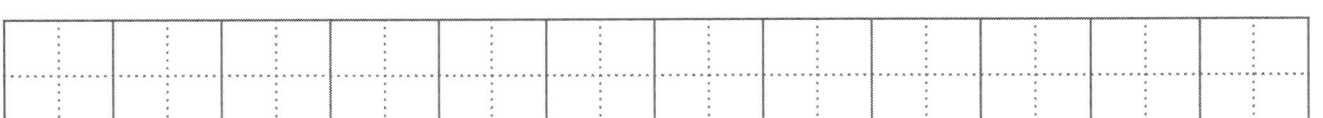
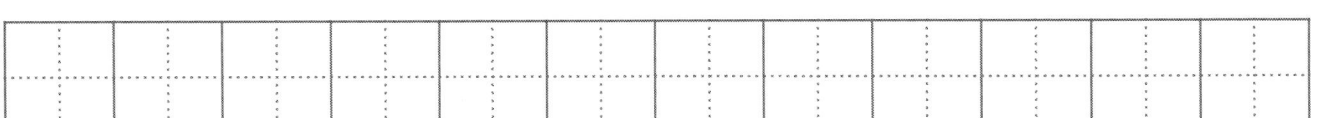
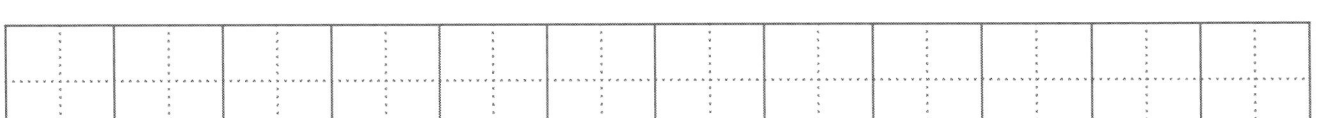
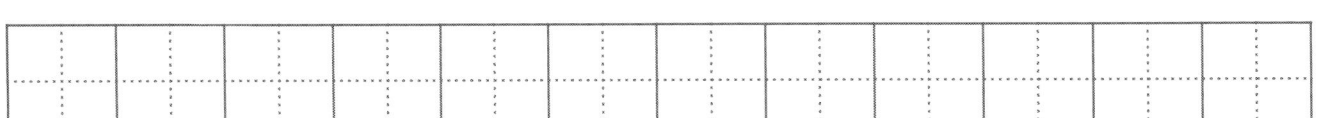
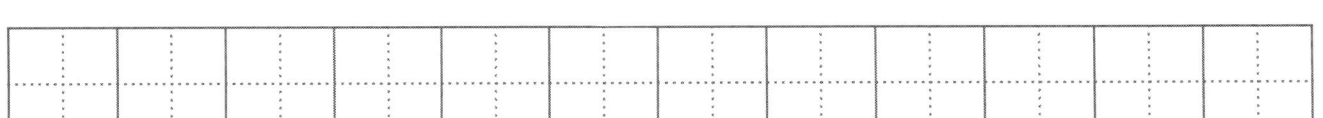
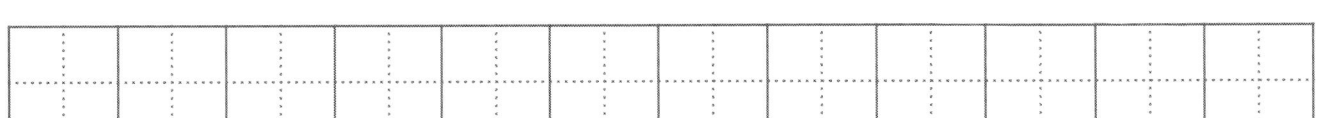

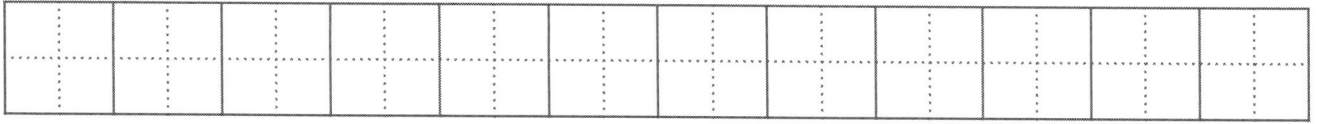
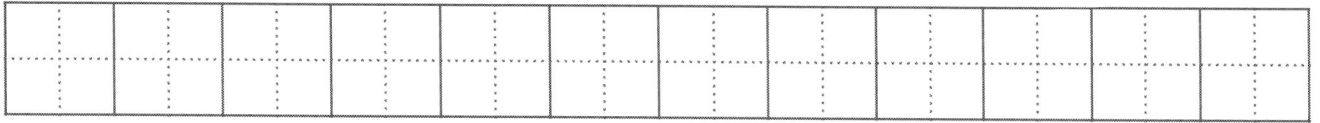
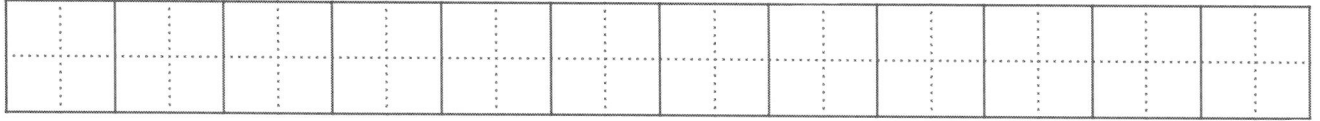
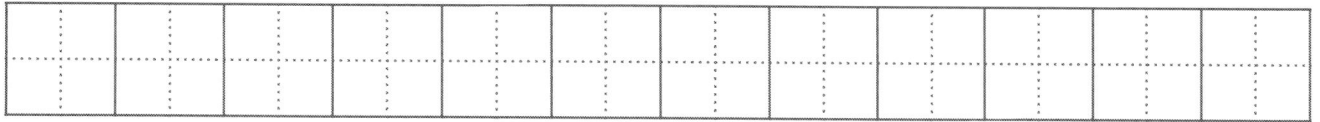
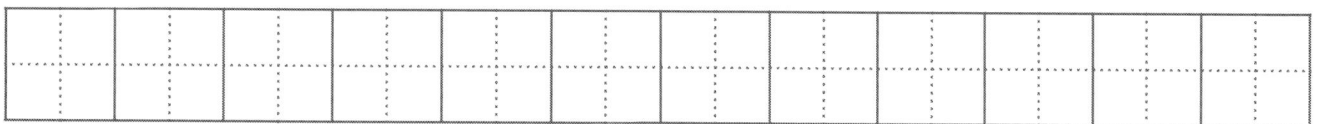
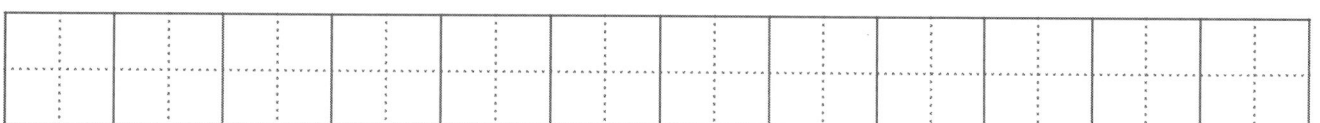
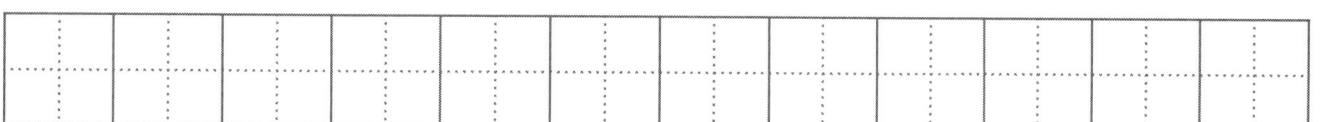
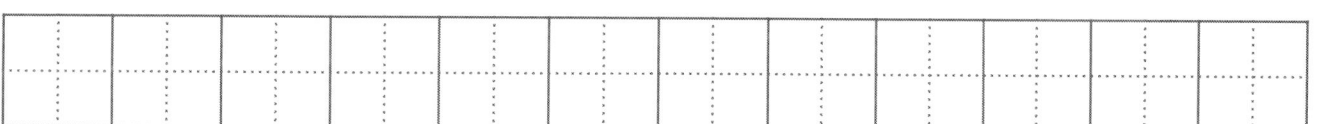
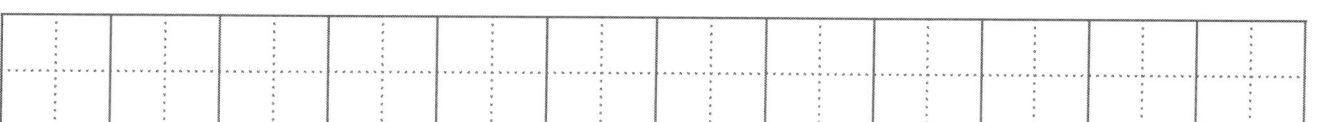
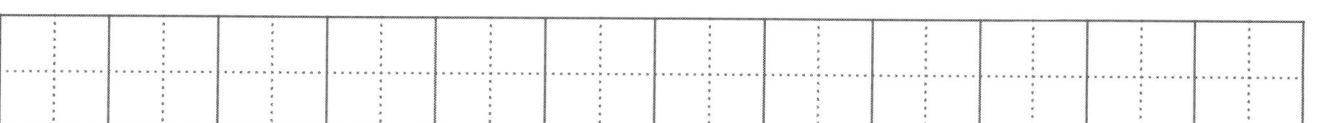
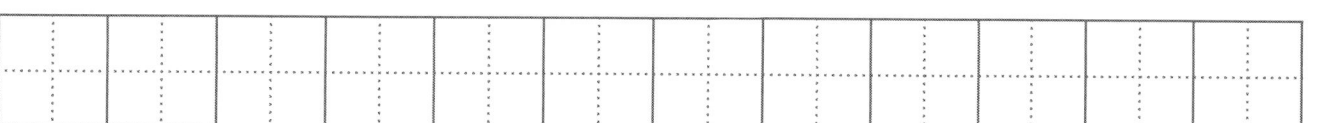
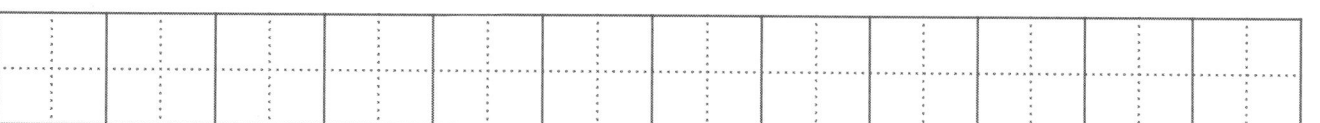

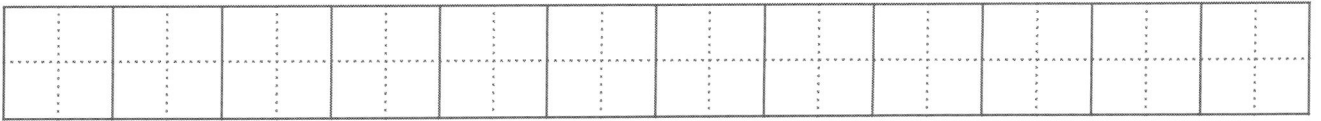
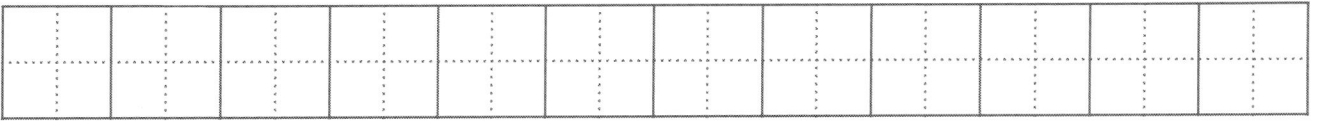
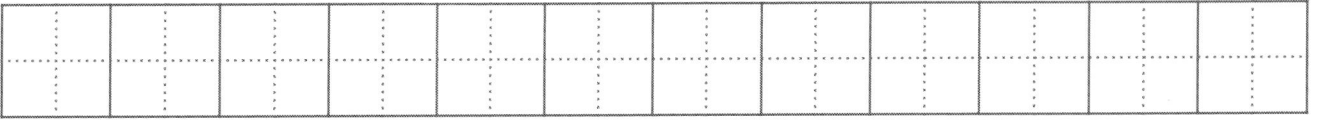
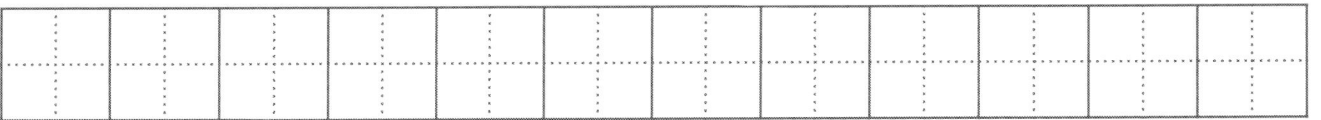
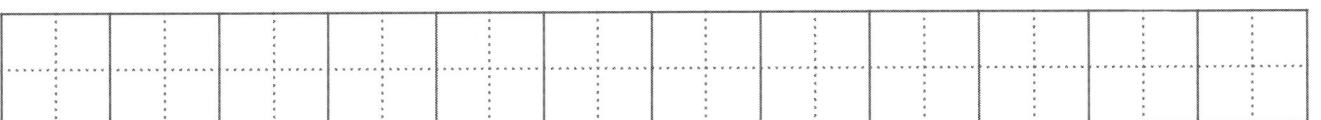
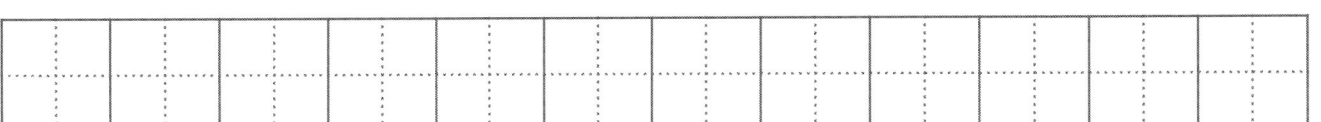
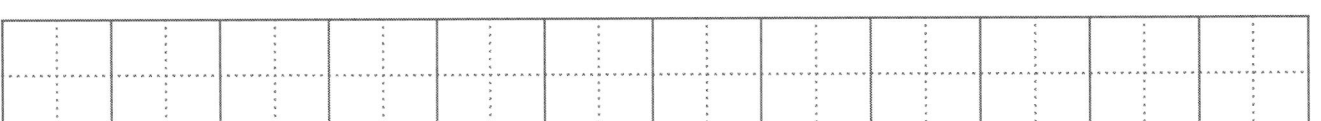
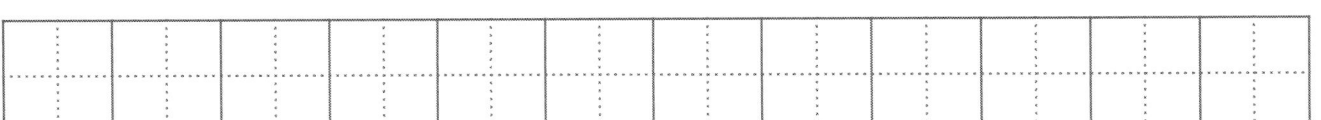
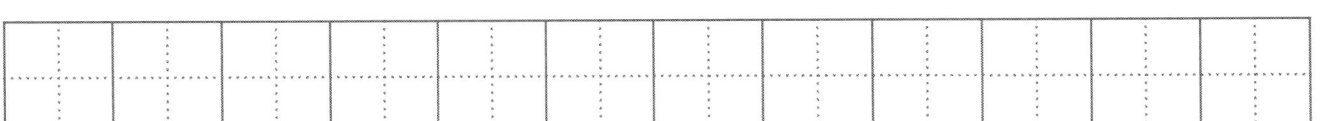
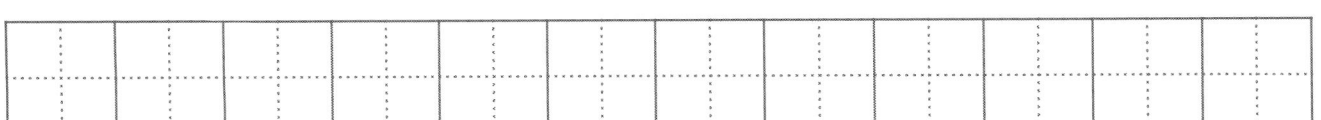
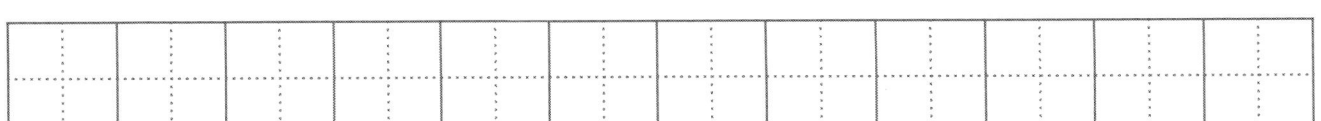
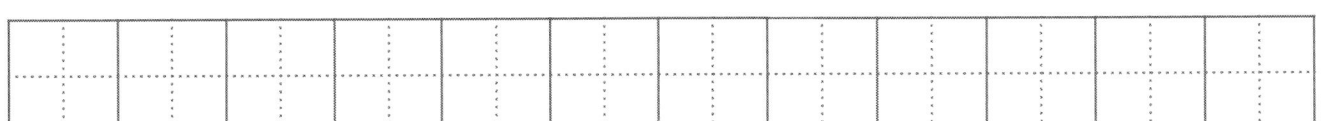

Made in United States
Troutdale, OR
11/26/2023

14966241R00069